# Prisoners of the Red Desert

# Prisoners of the Red Desert

The Adventures of the Crew of the *Tara*
During the First World War

**R.S. Gwatkin-Williams**

LEONAUR

*Prisoners of the Red Desert: the Adventures of the Crew of the Tara During the First World War*
by R.S. Gwatkin-Williams

Published by Leonaur Ltd

Material original to this edition and this editorial selection
copyright © 2008 Leonaur Ltd

ISBN: 978-1-84677-456-0 (hardcover)
ISBN: 978-1-84677-455-3 (softcover)

**http://www.leonaur.com**

**Publisher's Notes**

# Contents

Dedication
To M.13 and
the Duke of Westminster

I dedicate this book in
grateful acknowledgement that to
them, through Providence, my continued
existence and happiness in life is solely due.

# Introduction

The fortune of War has not brought out a more absorbing story than that told by Captain Gwatkin-Williams. It needs no introduction from myself, who had the honour to command the Light Armoured Car Brigade during the operations, but it gives me great pleasure to have the opportunity to congratulate the Author and all the officers and men whose courage and determination brought them through the severe hardships they suffered, and to thank all ranks serving with me in carrying out the orders of Lieut.-General Sir W. E. Peyton.

Grosvenor House
8th October, 1919

# Preface

I hold a philosophy which, briefly expressed, is this—that in all human affairs *that which happens is always for the best*. This is no fatalism, no blind belief in the inevitableness of predestined events; it is, on the contrary, a practical working faith in the providence which directs our ends.

The ways and methods of providence may not often be visible in their unfolding, but to those who know how to wait and to work, the final result is always sure. Man is no mere senseless tool—he is a workman—and circumstances; whether good or ill, are the tools with which he must work. And he who made the workman knows also how to direct the work, and to supply those tools which are necessary, so that they shall not fail the workman at his need. But, for his part, the workman must needs work according to the immutable laws of his trade, lest his tools be broken and his labour vain.

To those, fatalists and the like, who do not believe in a beneficent providence, but submit themselves to the blind gods of force and chance, I earnestly commend this book. It is true and a simple statement for plain men. It tells, so far as my present knowledge and ability permit, the adventures which befell me and the crew of the *Tara*. It shows how white men were reduced by suffering to the level of brute beasts; how these same men; trusting in providence; triumphed; how that same providence, inspiring with courage and skill the Duke of Westminster and his men, brought them in safety out of the Valley of the Shadow.

Blind fate, had they abandoned themselves to its coward doctrine, must inevitably have doomed them to a lingering death in the wastes of the Libyan Desert,

*R. S. G. W.*

# CHAPTER 1

# The Old North Channel

At the age of thirty-seven, with twenty-four years' sea service behind me. and a final three years' shore service in the Coast Guard, I, a Commander in the Royal Navy, found myself *on the shelf*, retired with a small pension. It seemed that in all probability I had finished with life upon the deep waters. Being of an energetic disposition, I at once began a search for work; and it was thus that two years later, August, 1914, found me at Oporto, where I was studying the Portuguese language and country, with a view to taking part in its future railway and dock development.

My first intimation that war was really imminent came to me through the British Vice-Consul, who told me that the Naval Reserves had been called out. Under an assumed name, a disguise I considered advisable, in view of the possibility of our being captured by the enemy, I at once took passage home in the first British vessel, the steamship *Hilary*; and while we were still upon the high seas war broke out. Running at our best speed, with ship darkened; we passed through the protective cordon of British armoured cruisers patrolling in St. George's-Channel, and arrived at Liverpool the next evening without incident. The day of the submarine was not yet!

It was a proud day for me, that on which I took command of my little railway steamer, for the *Hibernia* was owned by the London and North-Western Railway Company, and ran upon their Holyhead-Dublin service. All ships of the class had the same armament put on board—two extremely ancient six-pounder

13

Hotchkiss guns mounted forward, and a third one placed right aft. Their coal supply was also increased from the eighty tons normally carried in the bunkers in peace time to five hundred tons. This extra coal was carried in the holds, and the poor little overweighted vessels were pushed down another four feet in the water by it, and their speed reduced from twenty-one knots to seventeen. The railway company's officers and men were also retained, a good honest steady crowd of men; but they were also overweighted, like the ship, by having an equal number of scallywags, corner boys, and other riff-raff, picked up anywhere and anyhow, added to their number, our war complement being roughly a hundred. We had in addition some Naval pensioners—a signalman, a ship's corporal, and a couple of seamen gunners, and later on some hastily trained Scottish R.N.R. men.

I cannot be certain at this time of the exact date, but it was somewhere about the 20th August, 1914, that H.M.S. *Tara* (as the *Hibernia* had been renamed), painted a discreet but warlike grey, first ventured to sea as a warship. Our gun-trials ended, the last of the shore gang landed, the ship well clear of the land with her nose pointed for the open sea—we were free to open the sealed envelope which would determine our fate.

Alas for human hopes and the vain imaginings of men! Our orders were painfully short and clear, They were to the effect that we were to proceed to the North Channel (the narrow waters between Scotland and Ireland), and there patrol until further orders. When we required coal we were to go to Larne for it.

Our airy castles came crashing down all about us. Goodbye, Westminster Abbey now! The North Channel was about the furthest point from Germany we could imagine, nearly as far in actual mileage as Cape Finisterre. Reluctantly we turned the ship's head to the north-west and lumbered off at our best speed of seventeen knots.

It was there, in the old North Channel, that we were destined to spend our first year of the war, a humble but, I believe, useful servant of the State. A very happy year it was to me; it was one of no great excitement, but it was nevertheless full of emotion, of thrills, of hopes and of fears. In that first year we steamed 60,000 miles in the narrow waters; during the first few months we actually did thirteen days at sea out of every fortnight, and the fourteenth was spent coaling in harbour, either at Larne or Campbeltown. We never had a breakdown, and we faced out every kind of weather. In fact, I believe we held the record for both mileage covered and number of days at sea for the whole British Navy.

My personal duties at first were very light, for, according to the Admiralty instructions given us, the ship's old captain (Lieut. Tanner, R.N.R.) had sole control over the handling of the ship. My own work was really of an advisory nature. I was a *go between* the Company and the Admiralty, an interpreter of official orders, a link when working with other naval units. But on emergency Captain Tanner was bound to obey my orders on my giving them to him in writing. As may be imagined, this was a most unsatisfactory arrangement for both of us, and it was only our mutual personal good will which rendered its working at all possible, and the system of dual control was not repeated in any other ships subsequently commissioned. Gradually, however, my own sphere of activity became enlarged, as in course of time a quite respectable flotilla, including four destroyers, came into being and hinged upon the *Tara*. We were the only ship in these waters which had efficient wireless, the only one that could keep the sea on all occasions, and I was, moreover, the Senior Officer afloat in those waters. I posed as a demi-admiral and benevolent autocrat.

The days spread themselves out into weeks, the weeks into months, but winter or summer, the beauty of that wild North Channel gradually sank into me—I no longer wished to leave it. The great billowing clouds for ever drifting from the westward like some painted Armada in full sail, the mist, the sunshine, the storms lashing the great basalt columns of Fail-Head, the tumbling tide-ripped waters of that narrow strait—I know no more beautiful spot in the world—I grew to love them all; it was home to me. The ship was for ever busy with boarding work, and at night we scared many an unoffending tramp steamer by switching our search-light on to her at close quarters in the darkness; this done, we would vanish, zigzagging rapidly into the blackness of the night, lest a lurking U-boat had marked us.

We had been a full year in the North Channel, and were beginning to consider ourselves and the ship a permanent part of its scenery, when one day, during a short refit at Holyhead, we received new and unexpected orders. We were to proceed to Alexandria in Egypt.

I think most of us were delighted to escape the rigours of another English winter, and to vary the monotony of our life with what we looked upon as a pleasant yachting trip to sunny climes.

If we had but known!

Our crew was now a very different lot to the crowd of scallywags with which we had sailed a year before. We still had the old railway company servants, staid, respectful, dependable men, and some of the others we had first embarked were still on board. But a steady process of elimination of the unfit had been going on for twelve months, and now, though many were well advanced in years, some in the sixties and seventies, and though perhaps would not have been able to pass a very stiff medical examination, they were as a whole all men well up in their own line of work. A night alarm at any hour would find everything cleared away and all guns manned in less than three minutes. The men had learned to run and to move quickly.

# CHAPTER 2

# A Glimpse of the East

Thus, newly painted and refitted, with stores and provisions for three months, we left Holyhead in the late summer of 1915. Our voyage was a success in every way, and we arrived at Alexandria in October without incident.

At the time of our arrival Alexandria was one of the headquarters of the Gallipoli operations. The Naval Commander-in-Chief was then at Port Said, and from him we received telegraphic orders that as soon as ready for sea we were to form one of the North Egyptian Coast Patrol.

We also received at Alexandria two very important additions to our complement. The first was an interpreter, a Syrian Greek by birth, speaking Arabic, Turkish, and many other languages. His real name was Vasili Lanbrimidis, but he was always known to us as *Basil*. It was he who during our captivity proved himself to be the Admirable Crichton of the party.

The other addition, *Paddy*, was a four-footed one, whose special qualification was cheerfulness under all circumstances. Not of noble lineage was he. His mother, I think, was a fox terrier and his father a pug; but he was always fat, cheerful, and good tempered. Accustomed to fend for himself all his life, he had acquired one special characteristic—an undying hatred of black men. No overtures from them could ever induce him to make friends, they only evoked a special display of small teeth and high pitched snarls.

After completing with coal, we did our first cruise of eight days to the westward. It was a lonely patrol we were on, Rarely did we sight a vessel of any kind, and then it was only some small native dhow which we overhauled and boarded, or perhaps a Greek caique engaged in sponge fishing. Down to the south, when we sighted land, gleamed the golden plateau of the Libyan Desert, flat, treeless, sun-baked, terrible in its monotony and desolation, yet thrilling the imagination with its mystery and solitude.

We did not often approach the coast, for it was only half surveyed, with treacherous unknown reefs; the interior we knew was trackless, tenanted only by wandering Bedouin; but at intervals along the seaboard were small villages with Egyptian Coast Guard establishments, where landing in fine weather was possible.

Sollum, the western Egyptian frontier town, at the head of the gulf of the same name, was the only one with which we had any dealings. Colonel Snow, the officer in command there, was one of the most knightly and delightful hosts it has ever been my pleasure to meet. With a handful of British officers, he ruled the small garrison of a hundred or so coloured Egyptian troops and the festering little village at the foot of the cliffs.

From Sollum we could see the old Roman road which ran due south into the interior, that dim and fabled land where the Lotus Eaters had their legendary home. From somewhere there had come Cleopatra to move the fate of worlds. Down that old road came desert spoils—slaves, ivory, and wild beasts— passing upon their way to Borne. The shore is still littered with broken Roman tiles, and in the nullahs are rock-hewn Egyptian tombs. The convicts toiling in the sun, the modern criminals of Egypt, are a continuation of the age-long drama. Down to Sollum came the last of the Roman Legions, fighting a sturdy fight against the implacable barbarians who drove them to the sea. At Sollum they embarked in their triremes in some spot not far from where the *Tara* is lying at anchor now. For more than a thousand years no foot of white man has trodden that stern implacable hinterland, unmapped, unwatered, God-forsaken, inhabited only by those fierce sons of Esau, those dauntless fighters against authority, the wandering Bedouin. But yet another road passes through Sollum—it runs the whole width of Africa into Asia, from furthest

18

Morocco and Aghadir, to Mecca and Medina. It is the ancient pilgrim road that extends for the whole length of the North African coast. Down this road for ages have passed the countless Faithful, on their way to the Holy Cities, to the birth-place and place of burial of the Prophet of Islam. By faith alone is such a journey possible to the old men who trudge painfully along it. With one foot already in the grave, owning no possessions but a staff and a bundle of rags, they limp from well to well. Their only food is doles given to them by the faithful as they go. Their only drink is the semi-saline and viscous fluid from the ancient mud-holes. The journey may take anything from one to three years for its completion; but, upheld and sustained by unconquerable faith, they press blindly on, content if they may but lay their bones close to the sacred spot hallowed by their religion. What are we, that we can covertly sneer at such sublimity as this? For a man's life consisteth of more than the things which he eateth, or the raiment which he putteth on.

Before proceeding further with our story, it is necessary that I should give some account of the political events connected with it, and upon which the fates of all of us hinged in the late autumn of 1915.

At that time the British struggle for Gallipoli was in its death-throes; it was already doomed. In Egypt itself our position was also seriously threatened, for from the East loomed the menace of a Turkish descent upon the Suez Canal. Had such a crossing of the canal by Turkish forces been successfully accomplished, it was well known that this would be a signal for all Egypt to rise as one man and attack the European population. As Caliph of the Faithful, the Sultan of Turkey had the year before proclaimed a Holy War, and contrary to the impression which a perusal of English newspapers at the time tended to give, this Holy War was by no means the fiasco depicted.

In Egypt, sedition in the native army was rife—a great many of the Sudanese camel corps deserted to the enemy at the first trouble with the Senussi, taking their equipment with them. Of the civil population, the vast majority being converts to Islam, it may be safely said that their sympathies were inherently with the men of their own faith; the cry of "Egypt for the Egyptians" was in every mouth. The memory of Turkish cruelty and corruption was fast fading from the older men's minds; the younger generation knew it not. All alike looked upon the Turk as a possible saviour and deliverer, as one who would restore the ancient glories of Egypt.

But it was not from the east alone that the British power in Egypt was threatened; from the west also came ominous rumblings. There Germany had for long years cast covetous eyes on the North African littoral; subtly she had schemed to get a foothold in Tripoli and Cyrenaica; but the Italian war with Turkey in 1911-12 cut short these aspirations, and the desired possession fell as spoils to the victor.

But before the negotiations for them between Turkey and Italy were complete, England herself obtained from Turkey an extension of the Western Egyptian frontier, which carried it as far as Sollum, a town which it was known Germany was especially desirous of possessing.

This new Egyptian territory was inhabited by Bedouin, who, ever since Italy's war in Tripoli, had been busily engaged in frustrating that country's efforts to penetrate and colonise the interior. These Bedouin were both astute and treacherous opponents. Never accepting open combat if they could avoid it, they pursued a pitiless guerilla warfare from their inaccessible desert refuge; never once did they yield to the Italian yoke. Exploratory, scientific or trading expeditions which the Italians despatched to the interior., though received with apparent friendliness, were apt to be found at dawn with their throats slit. Punitive operations to avenge them were invariably unlucky. Led by native guides, easily procured for a sum of money, the troops marched forward into the waterless wilderness, buoyed up with the hope of surprising the Bedouin marauders, whose camp the guides had promised to locate. But, in the final result, the guides themselves had a habit of slipping away, leaving the exhausted soldiers hopelessly lost, half mad with thirst. It was the Italians themselves who were the surprised when their Arab enemies, all along forewarned of what was toward, fell unexpectedly upon them and slew them wholesale.

Massacre, mutilation and thousands of unhappy Italian prisoners, rotting somewhere in the unknown interior, was the only tangible result of the expenditure of much blood and treasure. The war in Tripoli was with good reason anything but popular in Italy, and the Italians found themselves once more back on the coast, closely beleaguered in the fortified ports.

It was in this country, in 1840. that the great Mohammedan religious sect of the Senussi was first established. Its original founder was an Algerian, Sid Muhammed Ben Ali es Senussi, who wandered, teaching as he went, through all North Africa; he also visited Mecca. It differed from most other Mohammedan sects in being far more rigorous. Not only must its followers eschew the juice of the grape, but also tobacco and even coffee. The devotee was allowed to wear no ornaments of gold or silver, and must have no dealings with Christian or Jew; in fact, even the killing of them was not an offence. In 1845, the Grand Senussi adopted the title of Khalifa, or successor of the Prophet, and as such he was regarded by his followers; his face was veiled, as that of a being too holy for mortal man to look upon. He died in 1857, and the succession devolved upon his son, and later on, upon other members of the family.

At its inception, the Senussi sect was purely religious and non-political; its followers were mainly earnest and sincere seekers after holiness, living a simple and ascetic life, devoting themselves to the worship of God. They came from all North Africa, from Asia Minor and Turkey, from the Isles of the Mediterranean, even from Arabia, bringing their gifts with them, and fanning into a flame the fast-cooling embers of Mohammedanism. But now the original and more or less pacific head of the sect was long since dead, and a warlike successor stood in his place. When the Italians brought war into Tripoli, Senussi-ism was the cement which, served to bind together the hitherto independent nomads of the desert; it made of them one compact band of warlike fanatics. The extirpation of Christianity, the driving of the Italians into the sea, now became the religion, the life governing motive of countless Bedouin tribesmen, who heretofore had been content with tending their flocks and preying upon one another.

Turkey, in this old colony of hers, still retained a number of officers busily engaged in fomenting trouble and organising the Senussi irregulars. Germany—though still officially at peace with Italy—had emissaries in the country, and between the two, and fed by liberal subsidies of gold, Senussi-land was aflame with ardour. England was awkwardly situated. On the one hand, she was the ally of Italy. On the other, she had always been and still was at peace with the Senussi. The Italians were vigorously blockading the coast of Cyrenaica, but Senussi-land was still open to the world through the Egyptian port of Sollum and the Western Egyptian frontier. It was necessary for Britain to compromise, and this she did by helping the Italian blockade to the extent that she prohibited the import of gold, arms, munitions and emissaries; but she bowed to the Senussi threat by permitting through Sollum the import of food (mainly rice from Egypt) into the country.

But in November, 1915, relations with the Senussi were becoming very strained. The Grand Senussi's granaries were approaching repletion, the winter rains were at hand, the time for the Turkish attack upon the Canal was ripe. The wealth and luxury of Egypt were for ever dangled before avaricious Senussi eyes by scheming agents; its inhabitants were coreligionists, whom it might be hoped would welcome them. And above all, the garrison of Sollum (purposely kept small in order not to excite apprehension), consisted only of a hundred black troops who would offer no serious resistance. The young Senussi bloods were fast getting out of control; unable to understand the methods of high policy which had hitherto restrained the Grand Senussi himself, they daily taunted the British garrison, as of old did the Philistines their Hebrew adversaries.

It was an anxious time for Colonel Snow and his tiny force; less than three miles away, looking down from heights six hundred and fifty feet above Sollum, were encamped many thousand cut-throat tribesmen, armed, moreover, with artillery and machine-guns, with whom sniping was becoming daily an ever more popular amusement.

To give Colonel Snow some measure of support, the *Tara*

had orders to call at Sollum daily; in the event of the place being rushed, she would embark the troops. At other times she patrolled along the coast further out to sea, boarding dhows in order to enforce the blockade.

We were now doing our second voyage in these waters, and the time was peculiarly dangerous, for a great Mohammedan festival was at hand and fanaticism might be expected to be at boiling point.

How much longer would the Grand Senussi withhold his hand? A straw might well tip the balance either way. With the Egyptian frontier open and unprotected from the west, he had but to loose his eager hordes, and it seemed as though they would fly forward like a denuding swarm of locusts—destroying, devouring, eating up the land as they went. Yes, of a truth, so evenly did one consideration weigh against another in that scheming brain, that the lightest straw in either scale might well decide the issue.

The *Tara*, in all probability, *was* that fateful straw, though, at the time, we did not, mercifully could not, know it.

# Chapter 3

# Eight Minutes

The morning of Friday, 5th November, dawned calm and bright, and it found the *Tara* nosing smoothly into a gentle swell, on her way to make her daily visit to Sollum.

There had been several S.O.S. calls a hundred miles or so to seaward of us on the preceding day, so we knew that at least one submarine was somewhere about. We were consequently very much on the alert, but I do not think one of us ever dreamed for a moment that a U-boat would visit this Godforsaken, out-of-the-way corner of the Mediterranean, where there was no shipping to attract him. We were really much more concerned for the safety of our good friends Colonel Snow and his little garrison.

At 10 a.m. it was getting hot, and most of the officers were congregated under the boat deck awning below the bridge, smoking or reading. No one dreamed of danger. In another hour we might hope to be exchanging greetings with our friends on shore, who always seemed so glad to see us. Observatory Point, which shuts in the town of Sollum, was already in sight, and some of us were idly gazing over the side to try to be first to see the sea-bottom, which in these crystal clear waters is often visible at depths of over ten fathoms (sixty feet). Its panorama of seaweed, sponges, and marine life was an endless source of fascinating interest to us somewhat jaded mariners.

And then the thing happened.

A hoarse shout, resonant with excitement and agitation,

electrified us; it was the man on mast-head look-out who had sighted something.

The actual report he made, the words he used, I did not clearly gather at the time; but their purport, the meaning of that sudden sharp yell, there was no mistaking. In all languages it is the same; it means only one thing—*danger!*

Overturning chairs and tables as we went we all with one accord sped to the ship's side, and there, looking to starboard in the direction indicated, we saw, and *knew* for what it was, the impending danger.

Probably very few of my companions (they being mercantile officers pure and simple) had ever before seen a running torpedo. But especially in a calm sea such as this a torpedo is of all things in the world the most unmistakable. There is nothing else in Nature which makes that hard white line on the surface of the water, nor which moves with such deadly incredible speed.

The white line, pointing direct at us like a finger-post, its nearer extremity not three hundred yards away, extending itself with the speed of an express train, eating through space like the lightning flash—we *all* saw it, and we all knew.

For a second my surprise was so great that I was speechless. I was fascinated, even as are birds and small animals by the baleful glare of a serpent; my tongue and my limbs were frozen, immovable.

Then, like a flash, my life's training asserted itself and I found I was gazing at my wrist-watch; it was 10.10 a.m. With this consciousness, paralysis fled, thought and speech returned to me.

Realising that it was a hundred chances to one that we should be hit, and, if hit, that we should certainly sink very quickly, I put my hands to my mouth and roared, "Away all boats!" Thus it was, that before the torpedo could strike home the men were already tumbling up from below.

At seven or eight knots the ship had barely commenced to turn when we were struck fair and square on the starboard side of the engine-room.

Contrary to popular belief, the detonation of a mine or torpedo makes no ear-splitting roar, unless they are on or near the surface of the water. A ship can be torpedoed in a fog a few cables away, without the next ship to her being aware of the fact. The sound is but a powerful muffled rolling crash and vibration. Simultaneously there arises in its vicinity a great black mountain which, after a momentary pause in mid-air, topples over and crashes tumultuously back upon the adjoining decks, generally bringing down with it, as it did in this instance, the wireless aerial, and smashing a good number of the boats.

After the thunder came the still small voice of lapping waters. Then all was quiet and peaceful as before. From the fore-deck little was visible to show that the ship had received her death-blow.

The master, Captain Tanner, was now upon the bridge, trying to stop the ship. Receiving no reply to his signals to the engine-room he put his ear to the voice pipe. No cry, no sound of struggle came to him along the tube; in their stead there echoed to him faintly the chug, chug of still turning engines, the gurgle, gurgle, swish and rush of many waters. Those who had been in the engine-room when the torpedo struck had all perished at their posts, overwhelmed in an instant by the in-rushing sea. No human hand would ever stop those engines now! But the sea itself, by invading the stoke-holds, quenching the fires and thus reducing the steam pressure, would in the end bring them to their last long rest.

As it was the ship still forged ahead at from four to five knots, rendering the safe launching of the boats a difficult matter. Nevertheless, after a sharp struggle, three of the boats cleared the ship in safety, taking with them the majority of the crew.

There then remained on board, besides myself, only the master, two wireless operators, the paymaster, and the guns' crews, with, perhaps, one or two others. Milward, the naval seaman gunner, had quietly collected his men without any orders, and they were now standing at their weapons, cartridge in the breech, eagerly on the look-out for the submarine to show herself.

The two wireless operators were meanwhile busily engaged in trying to get an S.O.S. signal through—but it was vain! With the smashed aerial and flooded engine-room nothing could be done. As I looked up I saw Tanner, the wireless boy, seventeen years old, rolling his steel chest of confidential books (which were too heavy for him to carry) down the ladder and over the ship's side. Mr. Dutton, the paymaster, at that moment came up from below, and reported that he had destroyed all the documents in the ship's safe; he stated that the water was already knee-deep where he had come from. Thus we waited.

At last the long-expected periscope, that ill-omened eye on a stalk, came into view, moving silently along abaft our beam; the white tell-tale feather of spray which accompanied it, helping to make it more visible. Crash went our little six-pounder, and at the third shot we got the range to a nicety and proceeded to plaster shell around the difficult target. But at the eighth shot the periscope dipped below the surface again and we saw it no more. Content that for the time at least the U-boat was blind, we had leisure to look about us once more.

The ship had now settled down deeply in the water by the stern, and she had that sluggish movement which told us she had not long to live. But, nevertheless, it was difficult to realise that there was any real danger in that calm sea.

Presumably it was some watertight bulk-head that gave at that moment, but of warning there was none. Suddenly, like a frightened up-rearing horse, the ship threw her bows high in the air, then sank stern first like a plummet.

The sea, hitherto so calm, now foamed and reared unexpectedly. It rushed at us like Niagara loosed, a terror-inspiring, murderous *maelstrom:* Upon its foaming crest it bore a myriad battering rams—rafts, spars, and jagged fragments of boats, which tore and hissed as though impatient to overwhelm us.

Now it was every man for himself, and the men left the guns with the water already above their knees, and scrambled and climbed as best they could up the reeling deck to gain some place of vantage from which they could spring overboard.

My own recollections are confused as to what I actually did then. I know that I did get overboard somehow from somewhere, just as the ship sank underneath me. And then the next tiring that I can remember clearly is being back on board again once more with the ship under water. The suction had done it, and I found myself struggling under the fo'c'sle awning, the daylight from the surface getting fainter and more distant every second.

I do not know if I am a religious man; I certainly hold to no orthodox belief, and my morals are my own. But there, in the rushing twilight, the thought came very clearly to me that in the depths of the sea *there* was God with me. If He could ever help me He could help me there, just as much as if I were safe upon dry land. And with that thought came the ability to reason clearly and to act quickly and sanely.

I realised that to struggle blindly would be fatal. If I were ever to free myself of that all-embracing awning I must do exactly the opposite to what instinct impelled. Instead of struggling to get up I must dive yet deeper and try to swim out by the side of the awning.

Fortunately for me I had neglected to put my lifebelt on, so diving was an easier matter than looked likely. A stroke or two and, almost before I realised it, I had succeeded.

As I got clear the daylight seemed so distant that, whirling and swishing round, as I was, it was difficult to know which was up and which was down—for I must have been twenty feet below the surface by then —but I groped blindly for the light. My ears were buzzing, my heart hammering, and a million bubbles racing past. Dark objects appeared and again vanished, striking me blows as they passed, which at the time I hardly felt.

Up, up, I went—bluer, brighter, and nearer came the surface. The pressure on my lungs got less.

Then, all at once, I found myself springing half out of the water, blinded by the dazzling glare of the full sunlight.

Hoarse shouts, cries and half-choked moans were borne to my ears as I took that first glorious breath. Near by and all around me men were struggling and fighting for life. And the sea, now a deep chocolate brown from oil and coal-dust, heaved and trembled tumultuously. It was the old ship saying her last good-bye, and every now and then the surface was broken when spars and other light objects shot out of the water, detached from the sunken hull now lying at the bottom fifty fathoms deep.

Somewhat exhausted by my struggle and immersion I seized hold of the first object handy to rest upon; it was a small raft, and it turned over as soon as I laid hold of it. Abandoning this, I swam to a smashed and overturned boat, and after a time succeeded in climbing on to her keel. From this point of vantage I looked around and recovered my breath, and discovered that I was little the worse for my adventure—an open gash on my nose, a bruised leg, my cap lost, and my wrist-watch stopped at 10.18.

How much of a life-time can pass in a very few minutes. Just eight minutes had passed since I first sighted the torpedo!

# CHAPTER 4

# The Hun Opens Aladdin's Cave

Looking round I was very pleased to see Captain Tanner close at hand. Having noticed a shark's fin some time before, he had just fished out Paddy, the ship's dog, who seemed very loath to abandon his sport in the water. To Paddy the torpedoing of the ship was a delightful and unexpected event which greatly added to his enjoyment of life.

By this time the three boats which had got away with the main body of the crew were approaching; the submarine had also come to the surface a couple of miles astern.

We began to busy ourselves with helping the injured and the more indifferent swimmers. One man, a stoker, called Mc-Nee, had acquired a broken arm, but far from making a fuss of his own injury, he had actually assisted and encouraged a non-swimmer, a young probationary officer of the name of Manning, in the water.

Many of the men were half dazed and badly bruised, and McKinven, a happy-natured and gallant Scot, was missing. Though quite unable to swim he had refused to leave his gun and take safety in the boats. And now his father, a grand old patriarch nearly seventy, who, in spite of his years, had signed on as one of our stokers, was left alive to mourn his son, and, if fate willed, to take the news of her widowhood to his daughter-in-law in a little town in Argyleshire. The dead body of Jackson, the ship's cook, floated close by.

Altogether, when we had time to reckon up, we found that

twelve officers and men had perished with the ship, most of them being those on duty in the engine-room. There remained in all ninety-two survivors.

Hardly had our boats picked us up when the submarine herself arrived among us. Her crew were all on deck, armed to the teeth; her two guns loaded and pointed at us. The *Tara's* men were obviously nervous at these precautions, anticipating that they might be fired upon and their boats sunk. But there was no need for alarm on that score; we received, instead, short sharp orders to get in tow, and twenty or thirty of us were taken aboard the U-boat.

I have no cause for complaint of our actual treatment on board the submarine, whose number I found before leaving to be the U 35. The Commander sent for me; he was a lean, rather mangy-looking man, but stamped on his features was a look of extraordinary alertness and efficiency, combined with an indefinable air of having controlled and subdued all human emotions.

As I learned at a later date, this was Von Arnauld de la Perrière, the most renowned of all the German underwater men. He alone was responsible for the sinking of more than a million tons of allied shipping.

Thinking that the submarine was going to tow us towards Sollum, and foreseeing the fate of the two Egyptian gunboats which I knew to be at anchor there, should Von Arnauld catch sight of them, I begged him not to trouble about towing us, assuring him that we could easily make land unaided.

A scornful smile spread over his thin face :

"Ach, no," he replied. "You vill zen escape to ze Englische port of Sollum; but I vill take you to a Sherman port."

We then noticed that we were heading to the north-west. As we neared the land, we recognised it as Port Bardia, a place of very ill repute.

It was there that some months previously Commander Holbrook, of Dardanelles submarine fame, had been wounded, He had gone in under a flag of truce with E 11 to what he believed to be Italian territory; but as he approached the shore a very heavy rifle fire was opened upon him. Since that date British

31

ships had been forbidden to visit the locality, and in the *Tara* we had only viewed it from a distance. There were rumours that a submarine had been seen near the entrance, but they were very vague, and nobody believed in them.

And here now was this U-boat making boldly for it, and acting as though he was well acquainted with this desolate coastline.

As we approached shore the German flag under which we had been torpedoed was hauled down and, in its place, the blood-red flag and white crescent of Turkey floated from the periscope.

As we got nearer still, an entrance opened in the cliffs like an Aladdin's cave, and, proceeding through this, we found ourselves in an enclosed stretch of water of about the same size and shape as Lulworth Cove, near Weymouth in Dorset.

From behind rocks and boulders, where they had been hiding, sprang large numbers of white-clad Arabs, who waved their rifles to us. Making use of one of our boats, Von Arnauld landed, and returning about twenty minutes later, informed me that he had made arrangements with the Turkish Commander-in-Chief on shore for our safe custody. I myself, however, he had decided, he would take back with him to Austria, where I could be better looked after.

Now, in reality this was a genuine kindness on Von Arnauld's part, though I could not know it at the time. He knew something of the kind of treatment we were likely to encounter on shore here as prisoners, though we did not. He could not take *all* of us back with him to endure our captivity in a civilised country, but he could take me, a being for whom he entertained a certain amount of compassion, as we were both regular officers in the service of our Governments.

But in the meantime my brain had been working. I knew that if once I were shipped to Austria my chances of escape were nil. But, landed here; on nominally Italian territory, and transferred to the Senussi, who were at peace with England, I believed that my exchange or ransoming would be a matter of but a few weeks at the outside. Therefore, I pleaded, and pleaded successfully, with Von Arnauld, to allow me to remain with the men.

# CHAPTER 5

# Foxes Have Holes

The disembarkation now began. Using our own boats we landed on the nearest rocks, and clambered as best we could to the gulley where we were being herded at the head of the cove. Most of the men were barefooted, and their feet were torn and lacerated on the jagged rocks as they toiled along carrying the wounded, their every movement dogged by the hawk-faced fanatic Senussi guards, who showered blows at every slip and with difficulty restrained their instinctive yearning to fire their rifles at us.

Before we left the submarine, most of our men received a cigarette or two, a drink of water and a biscuit from the U-boat's crew. I myself, the last to land, was actually given a hot meal under the lee of the conning-tower. How little I appreciated it then. What would I not have given for it later on!

The reason of our captivity was now beginning to be evident—*we knew too much.* This Port Bardia, which we were now at, was the explanation of that mysterious running of guns, munitions and warlike stores which no one had been able to prevent, and of which no one could explain the leakage. By running submarines to Port Bardia and employing them as cargo carriers and passenger boats, all the supplies and officers necessary for a campaign were being rapidly collected.

It was imperatively necessary, from the German point of view, that none of the *Tara's* people should again get in touch with civilisation, lest the existence of this secret submarine port of call be revealed and the hornet's nest be smoked out. We had accordingly been *sunken without a trace.*

The full significance of this fact did not, at the time, clearly present itself to me. Had it done so my courage might well have quailed at the hopelessness of our lot, at the certainty which it implied that we should not be allowed either to be ransomed or to be exchanged. As matters already were, they were quite bad enough.

The submarine, having disembarked her munitions and passengers, was now putting to sea again. And now we were left to think and to nurse our wounds; heap of misery that we were, surrounded by ragged banditti, in whose hungry eyes was written avarice and our death warrant.

The hour was now about 3 p.m., and the sun, in that close ravine, scorched our bare heads and blistered our skins. From the cork life-jackets which some of the men were wearing we tore strips of canvas to protect our heads, which, being donned, bore a faint resemblance to white Glengarry caps. No one was hungry at present, but the fierce heat and the salt water we had swallowed produced an overpowering thirst.

Nouri Bey, the Turkish Commander-in-Chief, and brother to the notorious Germanised Enver, did what he could for us, but it did not amount to much. Two miserable Bedouin tents were set apart for our use; but naturally they could not shelter more than a moiety of our officers and men. The rest frizzled in the sun's rays by day, and at night shivered on the bare rocks.

Some skins of water were carried down, but even now most of our proud British stomachs revolted at the stinking yellow fluid which oozed out of them. Presently a biscuit apiece was given to each man, and, as a special act of generosity, a goat was later on led down for us to eat. At our supplication an Arab killed it, by slowly sawing its throat with a blunt sword-bayonet until it eventually bled to death. Pity and disgust were in all our minds, and destroyed any desire for food; the dying animal's struggles were too horrible to witness, and the butcher's indifference to them even more so; it filled our hearts with a strange new terror to know that we were in the grasp of such pitiless men.

Before dark we buried Jackson; the ship's cook; whose body we had brought with us. He lies on the beach at Port Bardia, as deep as we could put him, a large cairn of stones above him, to prevent as far as possible his body being dragged out and eaten by the wild pariah dogs.

That night I, Captain Tanner, and Basil (the Interpreter) were invited to the General's tent, and so were spared some of the first rigours that befell our shipmates. Our host and gaoler, General Nouri Bey, is a dark-eyed gentle-looking man, somewhat slightly built, and with a straggling black beard; he is an ardent antiquarian and naturalist, and spoke much of the ancient ruins in the interior. These, he said, he would put the *Tara's* men to excavate, and hearing that I was fond of sketching he said he would provide me with materials to illustrate this work, only that I must give him half the pictures. In spite of the General's gentle and dreamy appearance, I was informed that he is a noted revolver shot; to this alone was probably due his immunity from the *accidents* which are so apt to befall those who have to deal with the Senussi!

Two other Turkish officers were also in the tent; Fevzi and Husni; I have their signatures before me as I write. They were both kind and compassionate. One of the two, who had but just arrived from Turkey in the submarine, supplied me with soap and cigarettes. They had both been prisoners of the Bulgarians in the last Balkan war, and their sympathy was obviously heart-felt and genuine.

The next day, a Saturday, we were made to move camp a couple of miles up the ravine, to a place where two water holes, a couple of wretched fig-trees, and a few yards of cultivated land were situated. How such a place could possibly maintain a family of human beings is a puzzle; but that it obviously did do so was manifest, though they must have existed always in a state of abject starvation and poverty.

Before we left the shore, the men were made to haul the two serviceable boats up out of sight of the sea, but the broken one was left where it lay on the beach. The Italians apparently much enjoyed stirring up the Senussi, and their patrol craft had a playful way of dropping a few shells among any camel trains visible from seaward. Only a few days previously thirty-five camels had been killed in this way in the vicinity. The savage Senussi, not having been educated to discriminate between the various European nations, regarded us all alike as accursed Christians, the destroyers of private property.

All day long camels and their drivers were toiling up the side of the steep ravine opposite, carrying loads of small-arm ammunition. The flies and the blinding sunshine, the bubbling, squeaking and groaning of the camels, were almost intolerable. The track was so steep in places and the loads so heavy, that three of the animals fell over the edge and were killed. Instantly the carcases were cut up by eager natives, a ravenous look in their faces as they bore off the disgusting looking joints of pink meat and sinew. We were quite unable to understand how any human being could eat camel-meat, though we ourselves were very hungry. For lack of cooking implements we were unable to cook the little that was given us, and our goat, after falling in the fire, was so tough and sinewy, that it was given to the guards. Our spirits were at a very low ebb.

The next morning, a Sunday, we were again moved. Before we left, however, we were given some scraps of paper and told we could write letters which would be delivered at the first opportunity. Delivered mine never was, nor was Nouri's promise carried out that the British authorities should be informed of the names of the survivors.

The journey was a terrible one for the men, most of them being barefooted; probably the distance was not more than seven or eight miles, but it might have been twenty, and there was a steep climb upwards of six hundred feet, along precipitous tracks. The desolation of the country beggared description. It was a plateau intersected by precipitous ravines running inland from the sea, and they had no trace of green in them. The rock was a kind of soft yellow sandstone, honey-combed and pitted by the wind; but exposure to the air and moisture hardened the residue until it was more rugged than a bed of larva, with the roughest and sharpest of edges.

Over this inferno our men dragged their lacerated feet, bearing the wounded with them. Poor William Thomas, an old Quartermaster, was the greatest sufferer. What must he not have endured from the double fracture of his leg, as, carried over the rough places in an improvised stretcher made from a boat's sail and oars, he was jolted this way and that, his exhausted bearers stumbling at every step. But, as always, not a sound escaped his lips, only the twitching of his face showed the agony which he bore so silently and heroically.

Our destination on this day was a place which we called the *Caves*, the site, we were told, of an old Roman farm.

The Caves was situated in a shallow valley-like depression of the plateau. The remains of a wall run round the edges of the valley, and on one side there were the ruins of a considerable building. On the opposite side were some very small caves, which I took to have been at one time rock-hewn sepulchres. They have only a small hole for an entrance, and the inside was like a miniature rabbit warren, with openings in which I suppose the dead have rested. They were indescribably filthy at the time of our arrival, having been used for centuries as a shelter by goats and other animals. Into these holes in the ground about half our officers and men were crowded; the remainder slept under the stars, chilled by the cold night wind in their scanty clothing,

We remained at the Caves a whole week, until the 15th November in fact, so that I had time to take stock of our surroundings. Captain Tanner, Basil and myself were still accommodated in the Commandant's tent; but my two Turkish friends, *ober Leutnants* Fevzi and Husni, left soon after our arrival, to my great regret. I knew, that in case of difficulties with the Senussi, they would have stood by us with their lives. With their departure went also much of that feeling of comparative safety which their presence had inspired. It was General Nouri Bey himself, agnostic though he was, who had quoted to me an injunction from the Koran, that "your prisoner is your brother," and I truly believe he tried to carry it out in our case. But, alas! a brother seems to need *so* little in that part of the world.

Dr. Béchie Fouad was our next Commandant, a dark, thick-set and immensely powerful individual physically. To look at him, he was not beautiful, but he had the kindest of hearts for us whom he made his guests. While we were there, a case of a dozen *Black and White* whisky arrived as a present from Nouri Bey to the officers, but none of it was ever seen outside his tent! Seated on the ground, we four played interminable games of cards, and drank alternate tumblers (vessels the size of a wine-glass) of sweet-brewed Arab tea and of neat whisky. This pastime was only varied by meals and by the playing of some cracked gramophone records, well choked with sand, a number of which had been captured from the Italians.

For all his kindliness, the doctor was ever a Job's comforter. His stories were nearly always hair-raising or harrowing. The doctor had been many years in Cyrenaica, and went right through the Italian-Turkish war in Tripoli, where he was wounded. He mentioned the names of one or two English friends of his, big game hunters after excitement, who fought on the Turkish side, and of them he had the kindliest recollections. Of the Italians he had a profound contempt and hatred, alleging that they were incredibly cruel.

But his tales of the ferocity of the Senussi themselves were by far the most blood-curdling. I do not know how far they erred from truth; possibly, like all our gaolers, he wished to impress us with the danger of trying to escape. But, from what I have heard from other sources, and especially from our own troops, I have no doubt that the major part of them were not exaggerated.

The doctor himself never attended the Senussi wounded in his professional position as surgeon without having at least two loaded revolvers on him; for, like any wild beast in pain, he found that Senussi patients were apt to turn and attempt to stab him.

By the tenets of the strict Senussi sect, smoking and wine are sternly prohibited, and their indulgence incurs a terrible pen-alty. A man smelling of tobacco is liable to a thousand lashes; a drunkard has his hand amputated. The penalty for a second of-fence is death. The doctor assured me, humane man that he un-doubtedly was, that he had been compelled to amputate several human hands for the offence of drinking. When he wished to demur, and stated that he was a Turkish subject, he was sternly informed that refusal on his part to carry out the operation would entail the loss of his own right hand. The grizzly trophy he had himself to deliver personally in a cloth to the Grand Senussi, to prove that the penalty had been duly paid, before justice was satisfied.

His stories of the sufferings of the Italian prisoners, dying by the score, festering in the far-off interior, and the nameless cruelties practised on them, I will not go into. We had a taste of them ourselves, though nothing we endured ever approached the horrors of which he told me,

## CHAPTER 6

# Life at the Caves

The doctor was especially trustful of me, which he certainly never was with his Senussi attendants, whom he strongly suspected would be led by their avarice and lust for gold into an attempt to slit his throat while he was asleep. Time and again he left me in entire charge of the camp for hours at a time, his money and his weapons confided to my care, with a request that I would not lose sight of them nor leave the tent, nor admit any native, until his return.

The Turkish methods of discipline seemed effective, if unusual from the European standpoint. One amusing instance came under my notice.

Two *askari* (soldiers) had been quarrelling, a very usual proceeding; but, unfortunately for them, the doctor caught them at it! With outstretched palm he soundly smacked both of their faces and knocked them down, the while they howled for mercy. With a parting threat that on any repetition of the offence he would have them both shot, he retired to his tent in a great state of rage. Reflection, however, evidently ameliorated his wrath, and he so far relented that an hour or two afterwards I saw him call them to him, kiss and embrace them both, and then invite them inside his abode, where they all had tea together!

While we were still at this camp of the Caves, several camel caravans arrived with clothes and stores for us—Nouri was evidently doing his best. With a few exceptions all the men were fitted out with cotton Arab shirts and drawers, a long thin woollen *burnous* or blanket (it was fourteen feet long and about four feet wide), and native slippers. We had in addition a tiny glass tumbler and a metal spoon apiece, besides a few pots and pans for cooking, and an enamelled iron basin for each score of officers of men to eat out of.

The food was a handful of rice and some flour daily, and an occasional ship's biscuit, and once a few cigarettes. Every now and then a small meat ration of goat was also given us.

Young Arab girls toiled up the slope with skins of water for us every day, but the supply was pitifully small. The filthy liquid we eagerly drank—scum, hairs and all—but it was much too precious to allow of any washing.

There had been no rain for eleven months, but. from the holes dug near the sea, water could apparently always be obtained in limited quantities. A small quantity of soap having arrived, and also a large consignment of goat-skin bags, we prevailed upon good Dr. Béchie Fouad to allow a small party of officers and men to visit the water holes under guard and bring back some of the precious liquid themselves.

They duly went—but on their return they were new beings, for they were coloured for all the world like a flock of canaries!

The reason for this strange metamorphosis was not far to seek. New skins are preserved by rubbing them with saffron and red pepper—and water, when first put into them, becomes, as a result, one of the most penetrating and permanent of dyes. We neither liked the colour nor the flavour of this new fluid, which somebody named canary sack; it had a weird taste. The doctor assured us it was *most* wholesome, which I believe it was; but I noticed that he always drank water from the older skins himself, in which procedure I imitated him.

The long walk and the steep ascent, carrying a heavy water skin, our party found to be so exhausting that they did not repeat it. We continued *sans* washing, and on the same small drinking allowance as before.

Whether one has leanings that way or not. one is forced to study something of natural history conditions in this country.

The first animals to force themselves on our notice were insects. The flies were legion. But someone (I think it was Mr. Morris, the Chief Steward) discovered that the flies disliked the smell of a certain blue-green shrub which grew abundantly near the Caves. A few twigs of this laid over the face and hands enabled one to obtain some measure of peace and rest.

The next disturbers of our rest were bugs, fleas, and lice. The Arabs, whom continuous attacks had made immune to the maddening bites, were always swarming with them, and now we ourselves were alive with them.

A third insect we saw something of was the scorpion. The poor old white horse, which had been kept hobbled near our tent ever since our arrival, was stung by one on the flank during the night. The poison raised a lump on him as big as an orange, which endured for several days, evidently causing the poor animal the most acute pain. He danced about excitedly and tried to get away, whenever even the most innocent little beetle came walking towards him.

The last insect which I shall mention was a peculiar kind of shiny fly, with a bite much more acute and sudden than that of our English horse-flies, whom in many of its habits it resembled. But it had this one great difference—that no amount of slapping appeared to affect it in the least, and it could not be squashed. To all intents and purposes it had a body made of two flat pieces of parchment joined together and without any *insides*. The only way to kill the insect was to seize it in the fingers (which it never tried to escape) and then to tear it in half.

Snakes there were in great abundance, and we killed a number of them; but the majority, I fancy, were non-poisonous. Of birds there were a number, including the English robin and thrush, and the Arabs sold the doctor some live quail and red-legged partridges, but I do not know how they snared them. Several times beautiful hawks and falcons, capped and belled, and of several species, were offered for sale to the doctor for a few pence, but he would have none of them.

It often struck me as curious that neither the doctor nor any other of the Turkish officers appeared to have much more affection for Germany than we ourselves entertained. They did not hesitate to express their disapproval and disgust at the murder of women and children by submarines. But their belief in the power of the submarine appeared to be unlimited. The rapid and entire disappearance of the British Navy from the sea, and with it of the British mercantile marine as well, was, in their opinion, but a matter of a few weeks.

I suppose, cut off as they were from the rest of the world, having themselves most of them travelled to the country as passengers in a U-boat, having also in most instances actually witnessed while on board her its destructive capacities, this opinion was natural. Moreover, they had seen the U-boat bring to them unmolested many hundreds of tons of warlike stores, and had come to regard her as a universal provider. The Senussi themselves undoubtedly believed at that time that the *Tara* was practically the last representative of the sea power of Britain, and her loss, besides the fact of our being their prisoners, had a tremendous effect in bringing them into the war. Both Turks and Senussi wished to be on the winning side.

During our stay an incident occurred, the meaning and significance of which I have never been quite able to fathom.

It was on Wednesday, November 10th, five days after the *Tara's* torpedoing, that the doctor informed me that an open British boat was approaching the coast, and he asked me for four volunteers, preferably those with brass buttons, to go down and meet the boat,

The four selected were then conducted to a place overlooking the sea; from thence, in the distance, they could just make out a steamer, with a boat pulling towards her. Our men were then told that they were no longer required, and, after being hospitably entertained by a sheikh, were marched back to the camp again.

Now, if this had been all, there would not have been much doubt that an attempt had been made by our gaolers to employ the four men as decoys and, by their aid, to try and induce some castaways to land; but that the latter, seeing a steamer near at hand, altered their minds about landing, pulled out to her and were taken on board.

But this is *not* all! In the *Daily Mail* of January 31st, 1916, there appeared an article, entitled *Prisoners of the Arabs—Tara Survivors in the Desert—Captain's Letters*. Part of this article read as follows:—"Captain Williams's relatives have received news that not long after the sinking of the *Tara,* a British officer who was in the vicinity landed a small force. A friendly native potentate came down to the sea-side and advised them to leave, else they would be exterminated by thousands of Arabs. The landing party *wirelessed* for orders, and were instructed to withdraw."

I think from this that it is probable that the *friendly native potentate* who warned off the boat was the same sheikh who entertained our men.

I am also of the opinion that the boat's crew were an organised search party, probably initiated by Colonel Snow at Sollum, who had, through native spies, already got news of the *Tara's* loss, and also information as to our being prisoners in the vicinity.

It was on the same day that we were visited at the camp by a Senussi sheikh of very great importance. We were informed that he was the uncle of the Grand Senussi, but I do not know if this was the same individual that figured in the boat incident.

Being so nearly related to the Successor of the Prophet, and therefore presumably a very holy man, one who would naturally carry out to the letter the strictest tenets of the Senussi sect, he was received with great reverence and ceremony.

The Turkish officers, and even Doctor Béchie Fouad, hastily concealed the remnants of the whisky, and buried their cigarette stumps in the sand. They then received him with much bowing and kissing of hands.

The holy man himself I did not personally find prepossessing, but I suppose I am too hardened a sinner for good influences to make themselves felt so readily. I saw before me a man of about fifty, with a full greyish beard and of exceptionally fine physique. By way of olive branches, he bore in one hand a new Mauser rifle and in the other an elephant-hide whip. Upon his features were stamped unmistakably and indelibly the imprint of a mind accustomed to wield unquestioned and despotic power. I also saw lined there the marks of lust, self-will, and craftiness. In other words, he was *Bluebeard* personified. Fixedly he regarded me at first with a sullen stare of dislike and calculation, the which, though fully aware of, I managed not to return, but bowed reverently. This appeared to gratify Bluebeard, and he thawed slightly and condescended to show me an ancient Papal gold coin which had been picked up recently in the neighbourhood; it was a beautiful and indubitably genuine antique, which I would have given a lot to possess, but the holy man was of the opinion that it was a forgery.

By way of pleasantry and no doubt to display his authority, he sat in the tent door and fired his rifle at any and sundry objects, quite indifferent to the safety of casual passers-by. Then presently, to the intense relief of all of us, he took himself off, laying out right and left with his sjambok in the most savage manner at any unfortunate Senussi who were not quick enough in their obeisances.

At his departure, I regret to state, his late converts fell from grace once more. The whisky was produced and smoking recommenced, and the Turkish officers, but lately so servile, were relieving their feelings by spitting and making wry faces, ere even the good man was fairly out of sight round the corner. Their personal opinions of him they voiced by such words as "savage" and "animal."

But truly the fates of us, his British prisoners, were in his hands. In his presence I had a chilled feeling at the heart, the emotions of a bird in the hands of a fowler who has snared him, and, lying in his hands, awaits open-eyed the fate that is in store.

Our life and our death to him were matters of personal indifference; high policy and personal advantage were the motives which, with him, would govern our future existence or disappearance.

# CHAPTER 7

# "Greater Love Hath No Man Than This"

Another visitor to us here was Jaffar Pasha (Jaffri was the name we knew him by), whom I believe was in the U 35 at the time she torpedoed us.

I am not clear whether he or Nouri Bey was Commander-in-Chief of the Turkish North African troops, but I think the former. He was a bluff old soldier, who had seen much service, and he had evidently come to see how we fared. We were all made to dress up in our new Arab clothes, the donning of which at first produced some hilarity; this accomplished, the General photographed us.

I am told that when the General was himself later on made a prisoner of the British at the Battle of Agadir (on February 27th, 1916) that this photograph was found on him, but I have never seen it. Even poor William Thomas, who was then near-ing his end, was dragged out and made to sit up in his stretcher, for inclusion in the group. A brutal act it appeared to me at the time, but I believe it was kindly meant, and the General said something about having our picture published in the papers, so that our friends would know.

Poor William Thomas was by this time in a terrible state; the entrance being too small, he could not be got into the cave, so all day long he lay in the sun, and at night endured the icy blasts. Mortification had set in in the fractured leg, but we had no palliatives nor medicine for him. A green tomato or two, a spoonful of rice, a ship's biscuit soaked in whisky, were all that we had to offer.

It was on Sunday, November 13th, that this hero and martyr passed away. A martyr he surely was, for he sacrificed his life to save that of another. When the ship was torpedoed he found that one of his pals was missing. Thomas at once went back and found his mess-mate, incredible though it may seem, fast asleep in his bunk. By the time they returned to the boats the last one was leaving, and in leaping into her Thomas's leg was crushed between the boat and the ship's side.

Just after dark, on the 18th, the Turkish doctor decided to amputate his foot, the boy medical student, who was the *Tara's* probationary surgeon, assisting. There were no anaesthetics and no proper medical instruments—a pair of blunt scissors and a sharp stone were used for the operation—and two of Thomas's messmates held his hands. He uttered no groan, but at 11.30 that night he passed away to the land where there is no weeping nor sorrow, and where the captives are free.

Before he died the Turks promised to send him to Sollum, and I think this thought cheered his last hours.

The question has often arisen in my mind, "Where is God's justice, that such a man should suffer for helping others?" I do not know all the answer, but I do know that most of us envied him his release at the time. We also wished that we could go whither he had gone and whither he undoubtedly wished to go; his old wife, to whom he was devotedly attached, had preceded him, for she had been killed in an accident some months before. Therefore, if there is an after, surely he is with her now, and it was the happiest and best that happened.

Of his physical pain we know nothing. I have suffered most physical pains—hunger, thirst, flogging, wounds, exhaustion—but they are *nothing* compared with mental pain. And Thomas, loved as he was by all of us, had a mind which was at peace after sixty-three years of struggle.

We buried him the next morning, Sunday, November 14th, a little way down the valley, in a shallow grave scooped with our hands and piled high with a cairn of stones.

This was the second burial we had during the week we had been prisoners, and my heart was beginning to be terribly afraid and lonely.

Gone was all the excitement and exaltation of the first day, the knowledge that we had acquitted ourselves like men.

What profit is it now, I asked myself, that we further play the man, that we are unselfish, helpful, forbearing with one another, if at the end we perish as do the beasts, pushed with our deeds all unknown into a hole into the ground?

I did not know the answer then, I thought only of the perils that beset us, of the years of terrible captivity which I foresaw before us. For a time I lost hope and faith, the tears streaming down my face were things I could no longer hide.

We were a funny lot of individuals, and many appeared puzzled and entirely unable to grasp the situation. The *Tara's* were not a select band of heroes as some have made out, but a very average lot of Britishers, good, bad, and indifferent. Up to the present I have confined myself to recording special acts of heroism or unselfishness; but there was already plenty of the brute beast nearing the surface and beginning to wear thin the veneer of civilization.

To start with, both officers and men were nearly all mercantile ratings, and in the merchant service, it was an understood tiring that when a ship was lost, from that date all pay ceased.

I had great difficulty in convincing even the officers that in the navy things were different, and that though the *Tara* was at the bottom of the sea, she was still in full commission until officially paid off, and that pay, discipline, and everything else, which would be in force in a sea-going ship, were still in existence.

The more brutal element in both officers and men was rapidly coming out. Offensive remarks were common. One officer frankly told me that I was responsible for their troubles, as I was always expecting to be torpedoed! I was so surprised at this statement that for a moment I had no answer ready; but it did occur to me that if precautions for our safety had been left in *that* officer's hands, no boats would ever have been kept turned out, provisioned and ready for lowering. We should have lost ninety per cent, of the crew, instead of the remarkably small ten per cent.

Another difficult factor for me was my invidious position in having a divided command with Captain Tanner. He and I always hit things off splendidly together; but if he happened to be absent, I was more than once told by the speaker that he was a servant of the London and North-Western Railway Company, that he had nothing to do with the navy, and didn't want to! A policy of grab became prevalent, a low scheming by some to get the better of others. People in England, who have had to deal with coupons and queues will know what I mean. And here with us, necessities were ten times greater, and therefore unscrupulousness by that much magnified.

The young and the unruly were eventually compelled by public opinion, which everywhere is the supreme arbiter, even amongst cannibals, to bend the knee. If this had not been so, I and the senior officers could not in the end have maintained discipline, for we had no real means for enforcing our orders. We were, in fact, a kind of republic, in which Captain Tanner and I were joint presidents.

But on this Sunday evening I called the men together, and addressed them from a rock adjoining the Cave mouth.

I tried to explain the situation to all so far as it was capable of explanation, and in the matter of discipline, I pointed out that although I had no service means for enforcing it, yet I was held responsible for it by the Senussi. That being the case, if anyone had to be punished, I would call upon the Senussi to do it, and this, as they all knew, might mean the loss of a hand or a good many hundred lashes.

On the conclusion of my address, the great majority showed their approval of my views by clapping their hands. The untameable ones muttered a little, but eventually slunk away, and we had very little difficulty with them thereafter.

Some of the men's previous views of the situation had been illuminating. One group, not unnaturally resenting their diet and general treatment as prisoners, were trying to devise some method whereby they could write through to *John Bull* to have the matter *shown up*. It apparently never occurred to any of them that the Grand Senussi, in his heathen ignorance, had never even heard of that enlightened weekly, and would probably one day sink into his grave without even having experienced its beneficent influence!

Béchie Fouad to the end continued in his *role* of a Job's comforter; from his lips we heard nothing but the misfortunes of the Allies. We heard from him of the sinking of the Egyptian gunboat at Sollum. The U 35 had opened fire, whereupon the Egyptian crew had promptly made themselves scarce, being hopelessly out ranged, and the gunboat shortly afterwards sank.

Another event that was to be of importance to us was the sinking of the Indian horse transport *Moorina* by the same ubiquitous U-boat; but of this incident I will speak later.

# CHAPTER 8

# Last Days at the Caves in Bondage to the Egyptian

Our stay at the Caves was now drawing to an end, though we knew it not. Lack of occupation and mental anxiety as to our future were our greatest troubles; but we had been promised that we should be sent to a beautiful oasis, where we would be well cared for, and that food and stores for our comfort would be sent to it from Alexandria.

We believed also that our friends at home would by now have been informed as to our safety, thus removing what was undoubtedly the most universal and deeply seated of all our worries.

That Sunday, November 14th, when we had buried Thomas, was the last night we were destined to sleep at the Caves. In the morning an individual, Osman Bey by name, arrived. He spoke fluent English, but was believed to speak neither Turkish nor Arabic, and was reputed to be a German.

By him I was blackmailed into giving my parole to attempt no escape. Pressure was brought to bear on me by the threat that if I refused to give my parole I would be separated from the others and sent to a distant place in the interior, where I would certainly die from the unhealthy climate. Whereas, if I gave the required bond, we would all be sent together to that earthly paradise, the oasis of palm trees and rivers of which we heard so much, but were destined never to see!

Reluctantly I gave my written parole, subject to seven days withdrawal, whereupon Osman Bey at once departed in haste.

I was the only one called upon to give my parole; none of the other officers being asked to do so; and I am rather at a loss to account for being the only one selected out of the ninety and two, for at the time I had no idea, no hope of escaping.

Osman Bey took our letters with him, and these were the first that were ever delivered in England, where they arrived on February 15th, just four months later.

That Sunday we had a kind of open-air service after sundown. The beauty of that eastern evening sky took our thoughts away back home, and we felt unutterably lonely and forsaken. In the day, while the sun glowered down upon us, I think it was a kind of shyness which kept us from expressing our feelings. But now, in the twilight and swift-falling darkness, we were not ashamed to say what we felt, to sing hymns, to pray even. Community of thought and purpose brought comfort to us.

I had written three or four letters home in this time, and all of them, and letters which I subsequently wrote, had a secret message on them telling of our pitiable plight. But I never breathed a word to anyone else of what I had done at the time, for I had an idea, probably erroneous, that its detection might lead to my instant execution.

Everyone has noticed that in writing telegrams; if the message be written with a sharp pencil, it is impressed upon the forms immediately below it; and it was with that idea in my head that I wrote a second letter with a sharp splinter over the first, hoping that someone would be clever enough to notice it.

Apparently it never *was* seen; and now, looking at three of those letters which I possess, I can see no trace remaining of this impressed writing. Probably the long period which has elapsed, and the dampness and pressure to which the letters have been exposed, erased it. But I had great hopes for my scheme at the time.

Our last morning at the Caves (Monday), dear old Béchie Fouad went off. I think he was sorry to leave us, and I had no idea at the time that he was going or good, but so it turned out.

In his place we found installed another individual, Achmed Mansoor by name, or Captain Achmed as we always called him. Short, plump, alert, with a well-trimmed pointed black beard and an unusually healthy glow on his sallow complexion, he was a very different individual to deal with, compared with the leisurely, gentlemanly Turks. As self-assertive as a cock sparrow, he gave one the impression that he had been specially designed by Providence for our annoyance in general and my own in particular. No longer did I and Captain Tanner share the hospitality of the tent as honoured guests whom misfortune had made prisoners. We were quickly told to go elsewhere, and from that date we shared in full the privations of the others.

This, though we did not appreciate it at that time, was a real blessing; for the physical misery we endured helped to dull the mental agony, a thing incalculably worse and harder to rise above.

Through Basil, who, in his position as Interpreter, we found also to be a truly remarkable prestidigitator and interceptor of the camp tittle-tattle, we were able to learn something of Captain Achmed's antecedents, which I have since amply corroborated. By birth he was an Egyptian, and a Christian of the ancient Coptic Church; he was also at one time an officer of the Egyptian Coast Guard. Unfortunately, however, he had also a bent for peculation, and being detected in tins he was dismissed the Government service. Upon war breaking out, he had turned himself into a Moslem, and joined the Turkish army to fight the British. And now he found himself selected as the most suitable person to be in charge of British prisoners.

Of course, we did not know all this at once, but we found it out a bit at a time, and his character and bearing towards us fitted in with this description in every way. He told us frankly that he hated us, and that he meant to get even with the. British. We soon came to attribute every trouble which befell us as being directly due to his malign influence.

He was, in fact, the *villain* of the piece, the *bad man* of the *movie* drama!

Achmed had been in the camp a very few moments when we received from him orders to prepare to march, presumably for the longed-for oasis. We had, however, been promised repeatedly that we would not be moved until all had been supplied with boots and clothing. Many men were still short of these, and I represented this fact to Captain Achmed. This was our first encounter, and I came off considerably the worse—our departure was but hastened thereby.

Now, though we did not know it at the time (in fact, I only found out eighteen months later), there was really a very good reason for hurrying us further from the sea.

H.M. Sloop *Jonquil,* Commander (now Admiral) G. P. Bevan, was cruising off Crete, when she intercepted a wireless signal from the British Admiral saying that the *Tara* had been torpedoed, and it was believed the crew had landed on the Tripoli coast. The *Jonquil* at once proceeded to Sollum, where Colonel Snow told them that he had news through his spies that some of the crew had been towed into Port Bardia by a submarine.

Acting upon this information, Commander Bevan took his ship into Port Bardia at daybreak the next day (Sunday, December 14th), and there he saw our broken ship's boat on the beach, just as we had left it.

He was on the point of anchoring and landing a boat to investigate, when a very heavy fusillade of rifle fire swept his ship. It was an awkward moment, for British orders at the time were very concise that no return fire at Senussi was to be permitted. A single screw ship in those narrow waters was very difficult to turn, and Commander Bevan was mighty glad to get out of the place again, which he eventually did after many narrow squeaks, but without any actual casualties.

On the *Jonquil's* return to Sollum the next day, Colonel Snow was already able to tell Commander Bevan that the *Tara's* had been marched further into the desert.

From the above it will be seen that Achmed had good reasons for hurrying us; also that the British spy system in those parts under Colonel Snow was surprisingly efficient. But from that day, when we marched into the interior, we were practically lost sight of by the civilised world until the date of our final rescue five months later.

But I am anticipating.

# CHAPTER 9

# We Reach the Dry Dock and Add to Our Number

Further argument with Captain Achmed being obviously not only useless but likely to lead us into further unpleasantness, I gave the orders, and the officers and men packed up their belongings for the journey.

We had very little in reality, but with many long days' marches ahead we found it a terrible load to carry. There was a hard reed mat between each two men, there were the iron cooking pots, and the enamelled wash basins from which we ate, besides our rice for the day, a flat baking-pan or two the size of a small bath, a spoon each, and a glass tea-cup—odds and ends saved from the ship—also our own and the Arab clothes and burnous with which we had been supplied. We had few cords and no poles with which we could carry these things, and we had to lug them along as best we could upon our backs or in our hands; the mats especially we found very awkward to handle, their large unwieldy expanse holding the wind, which was for ever blowing in our teeth.

The men were at this time organised into messes for the better cooking and distribution of food, each mess possessing one iron pot and one eating basin. The four seamen's messes had sixteen or seventeen members each, the petty officers thirteen, and the officers fourteen. Mustered now in our messes, with the officers leading, and the petty officers next, we started on our long pilgrimage to what we believed was an oasis only two or three days' journey distant.

Our white-clad procession, which at first had only been a few hundred yards long, rapidly lengthened itself, and the ordered start became a chaotic rabble.

Not one sailor in a hundred is a good walker; the flat decks of ships do not breed the athletes of the track, and muscular development is mainly confined to chest, neck, and arms. And now with us we had several individuals merging on the seventies, fine tough old *shell-backs,* but with a past innocent of pedestrianism. It was a sore trial for them, as carrying their share of the awkward utensils and clothes they staggered along.

That first day we were only made to march about fifteen miles, but a sad gruelling the men found it under the pitiless sun, the brown dust rising and choking us as we went. Achmed was ahead, seated on an ancient white horse, and smoking interminable cigarettes. On our flanks were scattered the twenty or thirty native guards, armed with every conceivable weapon, from the flint-lock with fixed bayonet of the Napoleonic wars to the latest and most up-to-date of magazine rifles. Ahead of all went the camels, eight in number, and later on others joined up with them; they carried our water in skins and petrol cans, and our rice, flour, and biscuit, their drivers invariably acting as guides to the convoy.

We crossed many dry nullahs and ravines, shimmering in the noonday heat, but from the first Achmed seemed unable to make up his mind which route to take, and we altered our course several times as we passed over the upland plain. But at length we reached a longer and deeper ravine, which we were told was our destination for the night. After what seemed an interminable interval some skins of water were brought to us; needless to say, we had long ago got over our early feelings of fastidiousness as to the colour, smell, and foreign substances in what we drank—anything which was wet was good enough, no matter how putrid or revolting.

This ravine in which we now were the men instantly christened the *Dry Dock,* and a most apt name it was. With steep precipitous sides, thirty or forty feet high by a hundred feet wide, it was of unknown length, but the end at which we were imprisoned ended in an upright cliff at right-angles to the sides, and was obviously the site of a waterfall in the rainy season, but now no drop of moisture helped to relieve its arid sterility.

Achmed improved the shining hour by collecting our money, watches, jewelry, and anything else we had of use or interest on our persons. His ostensible reason for this was the danger which their possession incurred to the owners from Senussi avarice.

However, our first impression of Achmed in the catering line was a favourable one. Four large and active billy-goats were led down and slaughtered by a native in the usual leisurely and horrifying manner, by slowly sawing through their windpipes with a blunt instrument, the struggling animal being held down by the horns, with its chin upon a rock. We watched the red stream of blood gush away and become instantly covered by myriads of flies.

Having cut up the still quivering bodies with sharp flints we then distributed them among us as evenly as was possible, and stewed half of it with our rice, reserving the remainder for the morning—for this was a previously unheard-of liberality of fresh meat.

Towards evening we saw a small party approaching on the far side of the ravine. It consisted of three Europeans, a coloured individual, and a Turkish officer.

We knew who they were; they were castaways from the horse transport *Moorina*, sunk by our old friend the U 35 a few days previously. The men raised a cheer and I went to meet them half-way across the gulley, forming a picture which whimsically suggested itself to my mind at the time as reminiscent of the meeting of Livingstone and Stanley in Central Africa.

That evening they shared our meal with us, and stated that they had been well treated, with the exception that not then being familiar with the friendly but acquisitive habits of the Senussi sect, they had had everything of value removed from their persons while they slept.

The party consisted of Lieut. T. S. Apcar, Lancer Regiment, Mr. Coalstead, Chief Officer of the *Moorina*, an engineer officer, and Joe, the black cook.

Apcar told me that the *Moorina* had been shelled at long range by the submarine, but that they managed to get everyone safely away in the boats; they then witnessed the dreadful spectacle of seeing the ship go to the bottom, taking with her some hundreds of beautiful horses, penned helpless in their stalls. Steering a southerly course, they eventually landed at Maressa, a spot a few miles from where we then were, being compelled by thirst and the sea-sickness of the terrified Indian horse attendants to land. Besides these four, there were some thirty other Indian natives in the boat, but they, being non-British, were kept apart from us and better treated. We never saw them at the time.

That night it rained, and our thoughts, as we crouched under an overhanging rock and watched the darkness stealing down around us, were uneasy and disquieting. The last of the light had shown us our fierce guards, squatting like expectant vultures around the edges of the ravine, their piercing eyes and Afghan features ever fixed upon us, with glances that bespoke only cupidity and fanaticism. We were only too well aware that, from their point of view, we were but cumbers of the ground, useless drones, who ate up the store of food they had gathered against a blockade; we were, moreover, infidel Christians, whom to kill their faith regarded as no crime, and we were also friends of their own old enemies the Italians, and carried upon our persons many articles which, to their poverty-stricken notions, were of great value. All that seemed to stand between us and them was the authority of an alien, an Egyptian; a man, moreover, who actually hated us, though for a different reason, as heartily as they did. If he were so foolish as to obstruct their will, they could very easily make away with him; the gold and valuables which he had taken from us would then become theirs.

I sat up with Apcar for a while, as, poor fellow, he was prostrated with ague. Presently the stars came out, and lying upon my back I gazed up at them; there is a curious optical illusion in this land of shimmer and mirage, begotten by the atmosphere at night. If one lies very quiet, the stars appear to swing backwards and forwards, as if they were the luminous bobs of pendulums.

Thus gazing, I fell into a reverie; memories of a British Army,

58

which once essayed to retreat through the mountains of Afghanistan, flooded my consciousness. Their enemies were even as ours were. Here, in this wild spot, nobody was answerable for our lives; the ruler of the land, the Grand Senussi, was in all probability already at war with Britain. Were we to meet with a similar fate to that of that other British Army, pent in this dark ravine, at the mercy of foes who know not the meaning of the word? It appeared probable. Of our death in this secret place, the world would know nothing, and while we lived we remained as a festering thorn in our enemies' side.

Again I looked at the stars. That night they seemed to be beating a familiar half-forgotten tune with their pendulous waving movements. The refrain came surging back, far away an organ was pealing, the air was tremulous, and in that rugged silent glen I seemed to hear a Psalm of Praise to One, who is "a very present help in trouble." And the stars were watching over us— the same stars that watch over our loved ones at home, who as yet knew nothing of our danger ... "And the same God over all ..." Ah, yes. Just that, and I had nearly forgotten it. Comforted and strengthened I fell asleep.

When I awoke at earliest dawn the camp was already astir. There was consternation, for thieves had been among us in the dark; many of our goods and chattels, and above all the goat's flesh we had saved from the previous day, had disappeared.

Achmed appeared highly amused at this *contretemps*. He himself had slept comfortably at the block-house near by, where he had also dined sumptuously and lost nothing.

By 4 a.m. we were ordered to march, although Apcar was so ill that he was scarcely able to move.

All day we plodded on over that khaki-coloured plain, every now and then descending into a ravine, to clamber once more up the opposite side; this greatly tried the exhausted and over-burdened sailors, who began bit by bit to discard many of the little things they had brought with them, and which would have been of inestimable use afterwards.

At dusk we arrived at a spot which Basil told us was called the Mosque of the Senussi. Mosque I saw no sign of, but there were five or six wretched mortar-less flat-roofed buildings, about the size of a cow house, with occasional stones knocked out to serve as windows. Here we were herded into a filthy open court-yard, with stone walls around it, in which there was barely standing room for our wretched ninety-five, dropping with hunger, thirst and exhaustion. We implored Achmed to allow us to lie in the open instead of penning us into this loathsome cage, and after a time he allowed us to move to an open field near at hand. The field was surrounded by a thorn-hedge, and under the lee of this we spent the night upon the bare ground. The night winds were already very cold, the ground as hard as rock, and we huddled together to obtain what warmth we, could. Many had already developed dysentery, but as yet our young probationer had not made up his mind what the complaint was. In any case, it would have made no difference. Sick or well, we were all treated alike. The sick had to march the same as the others, to carry their burdens, and there were no medicines, bandages, medical comforts, change of foul or wet clothes, or any of the other decencies of civilisation procurable.

We were already beginning to approach the condition of the brute beast, without having the latter's initial advantage in having been bred to it. We crouched on the soil, and lay half naked in the open like cattle. Our faces were un-shaved and unwashed, our hair unkempt, and our bodies swarming with vermin. We tore our food with our fingers and ate it ravenously as wolves. The necessities of nature even had to be done in public, for no prisoner was ever allowed to move outside a narrow rifle-guarded circle.

The next morning we enjoyed the almost unheard-of luxury of a wash. There was a good well at this spot, filled by infiltration, and not one of the *bir* or bottle-shaped cisterns so universal in the desert, which depend upon the rainfall, which is so cleverly collected from a large rocky area and made to drain into them.

There were still two or three small pieces of soap among the party, but anyone possessing such a treasure jealously guarded the secret of its existence, and only one's special *Baggie* or chum was ever allowed to see or to handle it. But the soap question brought into being all our native cunning. The owner of soap would strenuously deny his possession of it, nay, even its very existence. His every movement was watched by eager eyes, and should he draw apart, their owners developed a habit of following him, to see if peradventure they could not see and borrow this pearl of price. It was only in the secrecy of darkest night that the happy possessor was wont to steal out and try to remove what has been defined as his *matter-in the wrong place*. And we all had plenty of dirt by now on our poor blistered bodies.

But I speak with feeling, for I myself then possessed a fragment of soap, which was about the size of a small slate pencil.

This neighbourhood was evidently fertile, according to the lights of the country we were in. There were fields with sweet red pepper (capsicums) growing in them, and a native brought round a basket of eggs to offer for sale to us wretches. But his attempted barter was fruitless, among the whole ninety-five we could not produce a single coin; Achmed had seen to that. Those were the last eggs we were to see for many months.

Some of us drew water from the well. Near by a small black Arab boy was snaring birds. In this dry and thirsty land the process is simple; a few horse-hair loops arranged around a puddle of water, and the poor feathered victims coming to it to drink draw the nooses round their own necks.

As the expected camel caravan with our provisions and water did not arrive until noon, we were allowed to rest awhile; but at 3 p.m. we recommenced our trek once more, Achmed evidently having every intention of making up for lost time!

This was the first, but by no means the last, of many night-mare marches. The Arabs, who were presumably guiding the party, lost their way; again and again we altered direction, each time being assured that we were just on the point of reaching our destination. Our eyes eagerly scanned the vast rolling plain ahead of us, looking for the palm trees and houses of the promised oasis. But the immense red-brown sea of desert remained featureless as before, its monotony unbroken by a single rock or tree. Occasionally we would catch glimpses of our camel-train, moving like brown ants in the distance, just visible through the khaki hell of dust which we raised, twisted and distorted by the shimmering mirage. The horizon receded as we advanced. Sometimes a mound would be sighted, which our guides stated marked a well. Parched throats would bind the harder, as the eager pilgrims pressed forward—but it was always the same! Choked with stones and the dust of ages, the wells were dry and waterless.

On, on again, ever onward, old men and young, we fainted and sweated, with bleeding feet stubbed and tormented by that terrible sea of loose stones, scarce able to put one foot before the other, bent and trembling, but still holding on, still held up by the belief in the lying stories that were told us for our encouragement.

This first day's journey was only five and a half hours, from 3 to 8.30 p.m. At about the latter hour, in the starlight, we were halted; we had arrived somewhere.

Some natives were sent ahead; it was necessary to warn people of our advent, lest we be fired upon in the dark. Presently the messenger returned, and dragging ourselves to our feet with as much effort as a prostrate horse, we filtered in to some sort of a village, passing a cemetery of cairn-like graves on the outskirts.

There was a large tent with a thorn barrier round it, inside which burned a bright and cheerful fire, which looked inviting. The officers and petty officers were crowded into the tent, the remainder of the wretched crew huddling in hollows and excavations of the ground, the remnant of some ancient work, probably Roman cisterns.

That night our rice and water arrived too late to cook before we fell asleep exhausted, too worn out to bother about food, though we had eaten nothing since mid-day. My last recollections were of the fleas which invaded my person in unusual numbers from the rugs of the old tent, rugs on which I rested my head, and in which were wrapped a wonderful armoury of antique firearms and weapons, So ended our first day in Purgatory.

# CHAPTER 10

# A Pilgrimage and Some Tears

The next morning we arose at early dawn, and with a very short water supply we consumed our rice breakfast, and were on the march by 8 a.m.

Our journey to-day was a little easier, being in two stages, the first taking us to Ras-el-Leucca (Cape Luc), where we were once more able to view, and sigh over, the sea, although at a considerable distance.

On the dim horizon we were able to perceive a steamer; and when we had gazed for some time, we saw also a long low-lying object in its vicinity. It may have been a reef, but Achmed and the Arabs exultantly claimed that it was a submarine that was attacking the vessel.

They must have been ten miles distant at the time, and although I have unusually good eyesight for a European I could not be certain of anything at that distance. None of our guards had glasses, but from what I have seen of Arabs, their own unaided eyesight is as keen as that of a European with the best lenses, and the haze and shimmer of the atmosphere appear to deceive them very little. I have no doubt they were able to tell whether the object was a submarine or not; at the same time, they loved to harrow our feelings, and lying in the East is a birthright of all. So, unconsciously and irresistibly do they always substitute falsehoods for facts, that even when it is to their own advantage, they are quite incapable of telling the truth!

But the sight of the sea, of the unconscious ship in peril and our own powerlessness to help or warn her, were poignant reminders of our unhappy lot. We longed to shout, to scream, but we squatted there silently in the dust and gazed—we could do nothing!

Presently Achmed took himself off to one of the rough stone flat-roofed hovels in the neighbourhood, where, reclining on a long divan in the shade, we watched him feed heartily and smoke innumerable cigarettes, whose aroma was borne by the wind to our tobacco-starved senses. Turning away, we cooked our rice, and sizzled on the rocks in the sun.

There was that about Achmed which is so well expressed in the words of the old ditty: "It ain't so much the words 'e sez, it's the nasty way 'e sez it!" He had a way of so obviously enjoying our miseries, of flaunting his own comforts. Was the night cold and the ground hard? Then Achmed would lie in a comfortable camp-bed in full sight of us, with half-a-dozen luxurious rugs over him. Were we hungry? The Egyptian would call in his friends, kill a goat and make a special feast for the occasion, taking care to be on the windward side, so that we could smell every savoury odour. Were we footsore? Fainting from thirst? We saw his plump figure lolling on a white horse, armed with a capacious water-bottle, obviously enjoying the sunset and his cigarette !

Achmed, it was your turn then. The mills of God grind slowly. The sighing of the prisoners was as music in your ears. But now you are in a land where you can no longer trouble the desolate or the afflicted. Your well-tended carcase is becoming part of the dust of the felon's grave in which you lie. For the mills of God grind small!

The sun was getting low when we recommenced our march. To our great surprise we crossed a road, the first we had ever seen in this country. Through Basil we inquired of a camel-man what the meaning of it might be. He replied that it was the road leading to Sollum, and had been constructed by order of the Sultan of Turkey, On further inquiry we elicited the astonishing news that Sollum was only one day's journey distant; and all this time we had fondly imagined that it was nearly a week's journey!

When I speak of a road in this country, you must not picture a smooth, ballasted and macadamised track such, for example, as an English highway.

This road required no construction, it was but the bare desert, with the larger rocks removed from it, and the larger bushes, when there were any, uprooted.

But such as it was, it permitted of wheeled traffic, though we had never seen or heard of anything on wheels. The camel caravans never used it, as they preferred the bushier parts, where the camels could browse as they marched.

But we conjectured it might be used by artillery, of which we knew there was some in the country; and, anyway, it appeared to be a definite track, leading from somewhere to somewhere else.

It made a mark across the infinite, a something one could gauge and measure things by, where all else appeared feature-less and void. It played an important part in my future plans to escape, and—but again I am anticipating.

Our progress was very slow that afternoon, and we probably only covered eight miles in a westerly direction, the weak, sick, and sore-footed trailing our column out to over a mile in length. It was about 8 p.m. that we rested for the night, as usual on the bare ground. Our water supply had been very limited lately, and we had had no goat flesh or other meat for some days. Many of our company were seri-ously ill; one officer was so bad that he was eventually placed upon a camel, but repeatedly fell off in a state of insensibility.

That night he appeared to be dying, but quite resigned to his fate. I reasoned with him and tried to comfort what seemed to be his last hours on earth, and I promised to break the news for him when I myself was free.

He did not die. He was one of the happy crowd who at a future date saw the green meadows smile once more in dear old England. But to this day I cannot look at his last message, written in the corner of my diary for safe keeping, and which he wished sent to his daughter, without the tears coming into my eyes. It was: "Your daddy died on such and such a date. Inform———"

I have never seen the lady. There was no need ever to deliver that message, and I do not suppose her father ever informed her of it. But should this ever meet her eyes let it tell her that a father's love reaches beyond death, and that, whatever faults he had as mortal man, he at least was not afraid to die.

Just those few words, written with a stub of pencil, in the corner of an old red-covered account book which I had commandeered from the paymaster to keep as a diary, a log, of', the *Tara's* doings.

What a mine of human history, of sufferings, of events are held in the tattered pages of that little red book! All in eight pages, five inches by three; but my writing is small, and I knew not for how many years it might have to last. It held also the names of our dead, and a list of the possessions we had had to give up. I wrote it up daily, and the pencil with which I wrote it was Princess Mary's Christmas gift to the fleet for the first year of the war—a rifle cartridge pencil-case, with a royal *M* and crown stamped upon it.

I wonder if any other of these gifts have had such adventures as mine? Time and again it was taken away from me, under the impression that it was a live cartridge. But it was always returned when found only to be a pencil.

Besides my little red diary, which I always kept on my person, and was of the briefest possible description, I also wrote up a second diary, composed of loose sheets of foolscap, some of which was given into my charge to distribute as necessary for letter-writing. These sheets I kept folded up in a piece of rag in the corner of my tent, and in them I expanded beyond what was possible in the red book.

I have but to look at them now, to glance at those almost illegible pencilled lines, and the desert has closed around me once more.

# CHAPTER 11

# Medicine, Music and a Madman

That night none of us slept, the cold was too bitter. In the morning when we moved on we only covered six miles to a locality known as Sachla; though how a place can be named, when it is only a, bare flat plain with nothing in sight, I am puzzled to explain.

In the distance were three or four tents, but no permanent building that I could discern. We lay and suffered throughout the heat of the day, as neither food nor water were forthcoming until sundown, and thirst kept us mute and lethargic.

Captain Achmed took himself off in the direction of the tents, and we did not see him again until after dark, when he appeared with well-distended paunch, having apparently much enjoyed himself. However, with him a goat appeared on the scene, and we were able to enjoy stewed goat and rice for our combined breakfast, dinner, and supper; so for once the Captain was welcome.

Our young probationary surgeon scored over us all on this occasion. A deputation from the distant tents called upon him, and stated that there was a mysterious illness there which they wished him to investigate.

Assuming his best bedside manner he departed; with Basil to interpret, and remained away all day. Upon his return we offered him his share of the goat stew, but to our astonishment he declined it.

The cause of his diminished appetite gradually leaked out. He had been called to see the wife of a local sheikh. At first there was some difficulty, as they wanted him to diagnose her

67

symptoms without even seeing her. But even his slight knowledge of professional etiquette revolted against such unheard-of procedure! Here was a dilemma. How could a fair and virtuous Mohammedan dame be exposed to, the sacrilegious gaze of a stranger and infidel?

But with good will every problem has its solution. Mrs. Grundy was satisfied; propriety was not outraged. The lady eventually appeared clothed even as Mother Eve before the fall, but her modesty was in no way affronted thereby—for her *face* was veiled.

The doctor examined the mysterious complaint; it was situated on that part of the lady's anatomy which in small boys is associated with corporal punishment. There, plain to see, was a large painful swelling; in other words, she had a boil!

Having assured all the anxious relatives that the lady's malady was not mortal, the doctor, having nothing else to offer, prescribed a wash. Such a heroic remedy, being almost unheard of, created a great sensation. Obviously overwhelmed by the medical skill and acumen of their visitor, the natives then regaled him and Basil with a (to them) sumptuous repast and sent them back rejoicing, to reject scornfully our humble meal.

It was about this time that we learned to make the Arab tea. Senussi-ism forbids the drinking of coffee, but apparently tea was overlooked by the prohibitionists, and it is, as with us, a great feature of social occasions.

Any kind of tea suffices, but it is made in the same way as Eastern coffee, by being brought to the boil and then allowed to simmer, with the sugar in it. It is tremendously strong and sweet, and a *dope* of the first magnitude. We dearly loved it on the rare occasions on which we were able to obtain any. After the first brew it is watered down and a sprinkling of the wild desert mint thrown in—a quite excellent addition.

In the last few days we had more than once passed over tracts of land which had been recently cultivated, though we saw no growing crops. The Arab plough-share is but a stick as thick as a broom-handle and about a foot long, on the end of which is a nib of iron. It merely scratches the ground to the depth of an inch or so, and large bushes are left growing all over the field untouched by it.

That night (Friday, November 19th), we completed the second week of our captivity. There were terrible cold fogs at night by then, and as we lay shivering upon the ground, we were soon soaked to the skin by the mist and dew. However weary, by midnight we were all afoot once more, pacing up and down to try and keep some vestige of circulation in our cramped limbs.

Each night before dark we built up little zarebas of shrubs and thorns to make some sort of shelter against the wind, and then crouched under the lee of them, nestling together for shelter, and hoping for the best; but in an hour or two the wind would change and search us out behind our frail shelter, and the temperature fall to near the freezing point, and all alike were drenched with dew and mist. We were glad to move our position on the hard stones and try again.

The next morning it was discovered that one of our number was missing, a coal-trimmer, Thomas Owen by name. This youth had been strange in his manner for some time past, and his misery had apparently unhinged his mind. He had escaped in the night without having made any preparation, or having the least idea where he was going.

Our minds filled with fears for his safety should he fall into the hands of wandering Senussi, whose atrocities had been eternally dinned into our ears by our gaolers, I at once informed Achmed. All was fury and excitement, and messengers were sent flying in all directions.

The sergeant then collected the callow youths who had slept so soundly on night sentry duty, and soundly thrashed them with a formidable stick.

Such is human nature, that their piercing yells filled us with unholy satisfaction, their exquisite gambols gave us a greater pleasure than ever did circus the truant schoolboy. It was with an effort that we refrained from applause.

But what appealed to us in this instance was that it affected our sense of poetic justice. Night after night our attempts at sleep had been murdered by these self-same guards. Never did Thomas Cat, holding high carnival upon the roof-top, loose such anguished refrain as the chant—high, piercing and nasal—with which these sons of perdition had riven the firmament. Their caterwauling was intended to keep themselves from sleeping; in that attempt it failed—but it effectually checkmated all our own efforts at slumber.

With many a chortle and sideways grin, we began our march, chastened only by the thought that somewhere on that lone rolling plain poor mad Thomas Owen would, ere two suns had set; lay himself down to die; to linger, mayhap, yet a day or two more, while yet a drop of moisture remained in his blood, and then—choked, dried up—perish from thirst, the ravens perched on his body, scarce waiting until the last movement had ceased before beginning their meal.

# CHAPTER 12

# Thirst

"He laughs best who laughs last." Never was proverb more speedily and fully justified.

We had packed up, and were already upon the march, but Achmed lingered behind; something seemed to interest him! We observed that he was poking about with a stick in the ashes of a fire. He called me back to him. Wondering what on earth could be the matter, I returned and saluted. He had a peculiar expression on his face. It was composed of many emotions—satisfied malice, bitter sarcasm, contemptuous anger, but above all, it was of triumph.

He held up a sticky blackened object for my inspection. This conveyed nothing to my mind, and I looked enquiringly at him.

"You see what ees this?" he remarked. "It ees rice. You Ingleesh-men waste ze food when many man in this country starve? Zen I weel show you dam Ingleeshman what ees the value of food."

There was justice in his remark.

For a moment I was silent, not knowing what excuse to offer. Then I moved off to rejoin the column, now nearly out of sight, remarking that I would make enquiries.

In my own mind I knew quite well what had happened. Up to the present we had had sufficient food on the whole, though our bellies sadly missed the liberal meat diet three times a day to which our life at sea had accustomed us. We knew there was a long day's march ahead of us, and some foolish improvident sailor had tried to burn the fragments of his morning meal, instead of carrying it with him the livelong day. I enquired stringently into the matter among the men, but everyone was equally emphatic that it was some other mess which had been the culprit. Their own mess had eaten or removed every fragment.

Adam-like, we tried to attribute the offence to the defaulted Thomas Owen. Achmed smiled scornfully, examined his carbine and said nothing.

We had been afoot since 6 a.m., but the escape had delayed our start, and it was 10 a.m. before the camels, returning from their night's pasturage, were driven in. With a tremendous squealing, groaning and bubbling, the kneeling animals were loaded; then, amid a torrent of oaths and resounding thwacks, they rose clumsily to their feet. As they moved off, their long sinuous necks and vicious eyes bore quite an uncanny resemblance to a covey of monstrous serpents.

As I stood there, facing Achmed, in a very few moments the loaded animals were swallowed up in the red-brown monotony of the Desert Sea, where all things are coloured alike. The nasal, wailing chant of the drivers still came trailing over the silent wastes long after the caravan itself had passed out of sight. The men had followed after, their loads upon their backs, and presently they, too, were lost in the dust cloud, against which momentarily now and then a white figure stood silhouetted for an instant, then vanished once more.

The sun climbed to his zenith, and the heavens flamed, as I followed after. The salty earth glowed like a furnace, and, as did the Israelites of old, we moved with pillars of cloud, a fog of choking dust around and before us. It was the only shadow.

On, on, it seemed for ever, towards the eternally-receding horizon. No bush, no rock, broke by its outline the smooth rim of that appalling infinite circle. Like unto us must the spirits of the damned move through Hades.

And Achmed? Indolently lolling upon his dejected steed, he looked complacently from his God-like eminence upon the toiling throng. With just such indifference had his Egyptian ancestors looked down upon their Hebrew slaves withering beneath the lash, when Pharoah built the Pyramids.

What was it to him that the hated English suffered? Was it not just retribution, that men of the race who had ignominiously dismissed him from their service should now lie in the hollow of his hand? Then let them suffer!

Men began to drop. First one, then two or three together. The Arab guards, despite many undoubted good qualities, are never very notable for their gentleness.

And to-day, sore from their morning's thrashing, they were vindictive above the normal. Dead or alive, they intended to get their prisoners to their destination.

A kick—the steel muzzle of a rifle rammed into the ribs of a fainting man—and the exquisite pain can generally be relied upon to restore consciousness. With dazed eyes, the victim struggles to his feet and stumbles on.

With parched throat and swollen tongue, with dead sensation-less feet and blinded eyes, they stumble forward over the pitiless stones. Their trembling hands still clutch convulsively at the ropes which bind the packs to their shoulders, while the sweat pours from grimed and furrowed brows.

On, on towards the west, where the sun sinking low, gazes level, blood-red, into their mad, unseeing eyes. But at last the sun is gone. It drops out of sight, and the Egyptian, dismounting from his horse, calls a halt. We have been eight hours on the march without food or water.

The camels came up, knelt and were unloaded. The slaves approached to draw their evening rations and water, and they saw that Achmed was there. In his hand he held an Italian carbine, to which was permanently fixed a bayonet, which shut up as does the blade of a knife.

The bayonet was in the fighting position, and a clip of cartridges was in the carbine. He stood between the prisoners and the stores, and sneering contemptuously, waved us back.

There was no food for them that night! The English dogs should learn their lesson! But they were given about a claret glass full of water each.

A line of sentries was posted between us and Heaven, and through the gaps we could look in and see a banquet, where

Achmed and his satellites ate and drank, and presently rolled themselves up to sleep. We might not even eat, as Lazarus was permitted to do, of the crumbs which fell from Dives' table. But we might look on.

We spent the night mostly on foot, our frail bush shelters vain against the chill winds and reeking dew. And at the first red rays of the rising sun we struggled into our packs once more and blindly marched. Marched, and with a terrible fear of losing the camels, those camels who bore a load of life-giving water. Blows and threats now availed our tormentors no more. We were past noticing them. But at the thought of the camels and their load, our laggards—the old men and the very young ones—pressed on in a very fury of dull despair.

The more that our lives become a misery to us, the more do we wish to cling to the wretched remnant that remains. In the day of happiness it is easy to face death. But in pain and suffering we fight for life.

Achmed's wrath had by now nearly spent, itself; reason slowly resumed her sway. Realising that however pleasant the spectacle we presented might be to him, we should inevitably all drop and die in our tracks, instead of arriving at our destination, he at length relented.

At last, an hour before sunset, we were given water. It was almost the first liquid that had passed our lips for thirty-six hours, and during that time we had covered over forty miles; moreover, we had eaten nothing.

Glorious, God-sent, priceless water. At home, neither dog nor thirsty horse would have more than sniffed it. They would have turned away in disgust at that thick yellow salty fluid, ill-smelling, covered with a frothy scum, drawn from a heated, dirt-grimed goat-skin.

But now. Oh, God! How beautiful it is! How eagerly we line up to take our turn. How we bless the grinning black who ladles out to each their portioned wine-glassful. How we snatch the rusted tin from his hand, and lave the precious drops round our parched tongues and gloat in their wetness.

# CHAPTER 13

# El Zebla, and the Perils of Cleanliness

And that night we had *more* water, and *food*—entrancing pearly rice. Did ever food have such flavour before? Did ever gourmet taste anything so subtle, so appetising, so pleasing, both during and after eating? Surely not.

We were happy. Probably that was the first really happy moment since we had been prisoners. Past anxieties, hunger, thirst, all were forgotten for the moment. We were content, the world seemed good. We actually sang songs.

Thus passed the evening of the third Sunday of our captivity, Sunday, November 21st, 1915. Our hearts were filled with gratitude, and we lifted up our voices in praise to the Maker of all good things.

Truly were some stiff-necked Britishers learning a lesson. Surely but slowly it sank in. We could never be the same men, never again think in quite the same old ways. We had learned something of what the real value of food was, never more would we take it all for granted. Whenever and wherever we ate, though our lips might form no words, yet our hearts would unconsciously give thanks to the Giver of our daily bread.

At this time there was another officer, second in command to Achmed, with whom we had a good deal to do. He was a Senussi, Mahomet Zoué by name, and a fine-looking specimen, standing six feet in height. He wore what I understand was the Senussi officers' uniform, a gorgeous affair of bright blue, with multitudinous embroideries. He had joined with us at the time of our departure from the Dry Dock, and it was by reason of him that I first began to modify my views as to the savagery and untameable-ness of the Senussi. He and Achmed shared the old white Arab horse between them, riding it in turn, and alternately walking.

Rough and hearty in his ways, I never knew him to do an act of cruelty. He was humane and generous, and did much to modify the harshness of Achmed's regime. During our terrible food-less two days' march, he had more than once taken pity on the fallen. We had among our party three men suffering from rupture, and poor Mr. Cox, the boiler-maker, endured agonies from stricture; these had lost all the surgical aids and appliances which used to help them. Mahomet Effendi (as we called Mahomet Zoué) himself got off his horse, and placing Cox upon it, tramped beside him. He performed many other kind acts, giving drink to some from his water-bottle, and it was at his solicitation that Achmed eventually relented, and permitted us food and drink.

The next morning, still very weak and exhausted from our two days' gruelling and famine, we moved on again shortly after, day-break, and with the exception of a short rest at mid-day, continued steadily on the tramp until 7 p.m., long after dark.

Hunger had long ere this made us look round to see if we could not find any substitute for the food which we did not get. We found one. This part, of the desert was literally white with the shells of countless millions of snails. Indifferent as to whether they were wholesome or not, so long as they served to fill the cavity in our gnawing vitals, some of us experimented with them. Tentatively they placed them round the edges of the fire, and having thus roasted them, ate some. The result being sufficiently satisfactory, many others overcame their disgust and did likewise.

It was thus that we first gathered a small additional supply of food. I have no doubt it saved many lives.

The country never varied except to get more stony. This part of Libya is known as the Red Desert; dull maroon in colour, flat as the sea, it rolls endlessly into the distance, where there is often an appearance of low hills. These hills, however, have a rainbow-like habit of disappearing when you reach them. They are probably only a few feet in height, and the ascent is so gradual that it is imperceptible. The stones are strange and fantastic in shape, much of the rock being formed of ancient coral reefs, pitted and perforated into the appearance of honey-comb; others are soapy in texture, varying in colour from the deepest black to a vivid red. In the lower lying parts, sand and clay have been washed down by the winter rains, and here grow dead-coloured shrubs and camel grass.

The more bare the country the greater became the number of animals apparently frequenting it; or was it, perhaps, only that they were more easily visible? Paddy, who ever since we had been on shore had been in Paradise, was now having the time of his life. His little round body had got more shape about it, his short legs had become stronger and sturdier. No fears for the future clouded *his* bright and happy existence. *His* home was here with us his friends, and he did his best with bright and never-failing good spirits to cheer us and instil some of his own faith in Providence into our brooding minds. Why do not *we* look at it as he does, as a picnic, and make the best of everything? With red and dripping tongue he pants excitedly in the wake of some indolent hare, which scarcely deigns to look round at him.

Anon, he thrills at his near proximity to an unoffending lark, which, frozen, motionless, is pretending to be a stone, until at his nearer approach, with a flick of tail, and a shimmer of wings, she flies nonchalantly away.

Never tiring, always gay and debonair, when all else failed, our little doggie friend sometimes remembered his special canine duties. He flew into passions of simulated rage, and barked in fury at our Arab escort. Even Achmed was subjected to this affront! The guards themselves, good fellows that they were at heart, laughed good-humouredly, and made friendly overtures to him. But in vain! Paddy would have no dealings with coloured gentry!

He never hurt anyone, and no one hurts him. With such an example, to be an *infidel dog*, had lost, even for the Arabs, its meaning and reproach.

We had a trying time of it that day before we rested for the night some hours after dark, having been afoot for thirteen hours. We were given a little flour in addition to our rice that evening, and with it we made *damper* in the ashes, and went to sleep less hungry than usual.

Our camp was in the vicinity of the wells of El Zebla, which were about a mile distant, and we remained there for forty-eight hours to rest and recruit, as Achmed for once was satisfied with the distance which his driving had forced us to cover in the last few days. The wells furnished us with an abundant supply of sweet fresh water, by far the best we had had as yet, and we were able to indulge in a wash, the third since landing;

It was about time, for by now our persons were indescribably verminous, and although washing did not kill the lice, it temporarily checked their ardour, and also, by making them more visible, rendered their capture and execution more feasible.

Washing, however, was not without its difficulties, for there is no greater stickler for the proprieties in the whole world than your *wild man* of the desert. Many Britishers whom I have met seem to labour under the delusion that because a Moslem has the courage to betake to himself more than one partner of his joys and sorrows he must therefore be lacking in all sense of morality and decency. They associate the East, not only with spices, but with everything that is spicy.

Now, as a matter of fact, the exact contrary is the ease. Morality in the East is of a far sterner, if perhaps less spiritual type, than it is with us, and the burden of the proprieties is at times overwhelming. I have never yet seen an Arab wash, except for the formal sprinkling of his fingers before eating with them. But Arabs have told me that if ever such a catastrophe occurred as to render a wash imperative they would do it in the privacy of their tents.

A sailor-man is used to living in public. On board ship he must necessarily bathe often in company with his fellows, and, in any case, he had here no tent in which he could conceal the fact of his ablutions, even if he had so desired.

Perhaps some of our men *were* a little *décolleté* on this great occasion at El Zebla: it evidently appeared so to the Arabs.

Showers of stones descended upon the offenders; they had to run for their lives naked as our first parents, barefooted across the thorny, stony plain, their yells and prayers of entreaty unheeded. This sounds as though it were meant to be funny; but I can assure any and everyone that when you yourself are the target of sharp flints, hurled violently by lusty arms at your naked cuticle, the situation by no means strikes you as ludicrous! It is one of the most painful experiences which it has ever been my lot to suffer, and it is but avoiding Scylla to be wrecked on Charybdis, when, if in nimbly leaping to dodge one stone, you find you have landed barefooted upon half-a-dozen others.

Thereafter we restricted our ablutions to one limb at a time, with a comrade standing handy, your boots in his hand. Only by such means could safety in flight be assured.

It was while we were at El Zebla that we saw what was apparently a searchlight playing against the clouds up to the northward of us, in the direction in which we knew the sea to be. We learned subsequently that on the night before our arrival we had been within an hour or two's march of the Italian lines at Tobruk. Had we but known it then, I think we would have tried to overpower our guards and make a rush for it. But the fact was hidden from us.

Hares were very numerous in this neighbourhood, and we also came across tortoises and hedgehogs. Of birds we saw a vulture or two, and ravens, besides hawks, robins, and numerous larks and wagtails. There were two kinds of lizards, one a very ugly fellow, and there were many snakes. There were plenty of butterflies, the commonest being *A. cardui,* popularly known in England as the *Painted Lady.*

# CHAPTER 14

# The Military Situation and the Promised Land

It was while we were at El Zebla (November 22nd) that we were first informed by Achmed that the Senussi were at war with England. As a matter of fact, it was not until the following day (as I subsequently ascertained) that Sollum itself was actually attacked. This attack was made by a force of about, seven thousand Senussi, who for some time, together with some ancient 1871 Krupp guns, had been looking down from the heights commanding the little frontier port. The British garrison had by that time been slightly reinforced, and a squadron of twelve naval armoured cars had been rushed up from Egypt, with a complement of about a hundred ratings in all; these cars were distributed all along the coast at El Dabaa (Railbeard), Mersa Matruh, Sidi Barrani (the word *barrani* means frontier, and it was the ancient Egyptian frontier town previous to 1911), and Sollum. The attack on Sollum took place in a dense sandstorm, and the garrison had to evacuate the place at half-an-hour's notice, but accomplished this successfully, and embarked and took passage in the gunboat *Rasheed* for Matruh.

There had been some fighting between Barrani and Matruh for a week previous to this date, and Barrani itself was evacuated on the same day that Sollum was, and it was observed to be in flames from the *Rasheed* as she passed along the coast.

All the British frontier garrisons were thus withdrawn to Matruh, which place was entrenched and generally put into a state of defence, the defence being assisted by British trawlers and a French submarine; these latter, presumably, more to keep the ubiquitous U 85 quiet than anything else, and to prevent him from shelling the place at long range at his leisure.

The British had thus been forced back roughly a hundred and twenty miles, or eighty miles inside the old Egyptian frontier, and the enemy was within a hundred and seventy miles of Alexandria.

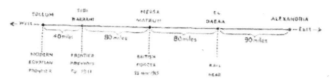

The above very rough linear map will give an approximate idea of the situation. To the north was the sea, to the south the desert, and the line of advance or retreat for both sides was more or less tied to the coast, along which ran the Khedivial road from El Dabaa to Sollum, and near to which also were situated the wells.

Almost up to the moment of actual fighting the Grand Senussi had simulated friendship. He had dined with the British officers and shown great interest in the armoured cars. The first real sign of actual trouble was the cutting of the telegraph wires between Matruh and Dabaa, and the placing of obstructions in the road, also attempts to wreck the cars and steal military stores. But now, at last, the old fox had shown his hand, his hordes were advancing, and it indeed looked as though, at that time, they would eat up the land of Egypt, even as did Pharaoh's plague of locusts.

Three days after the evacuation of Sollum, on November 26th, the Sudanese Camel Corps deserted and went over to the Senussi; we prisoners actually saw some of them as they passed through our camp, and one camel in particular we were told was Colonel Snow's. The sight of it did not help to hearten us.

But the garrison at Matruh from the first held firm. Based as they were to a great extent upon sea power and sea transport, they had the advantage of the enemy, who was compelled to toil painfully with all his stores the hundred and fifty miles of coast road from Sollum, and exposed to constant bombardment from seaward if he kept to the road.

The Senussi, who had been all aflame at their first rapid advance, began rapidly to cool down after their check at Matruh. On November 29th, heavy rains began on the coast, making such a quagmire of the desert as to render transport for the time being almost impossible.

Had the submarines really been capable of accomplishing all that the Senussi had been led to believe such a state of affairs could not have continued. But as it was, our artillery was too powerful for the antiquated Turkish weapons opposed to them, and the British sloops bombarded systematically the ravines along the coast, where the Senussi were wont to take shelter. On December 13th the *Clematis* knocked out the Turkish 4·7-inch gun.

This was too much for the Bedouin, and for the time being they became half-hearted. The brother of the Grand Senussi himself visited Matruh and confessed as much, and by December 19th, the British had reports that the Senussi were *fed up*, and that large bodies of them were moving to the west. This was no doubt greatly expedited by continuous bombardments of the coast by the *Clematis* on December 15th, 16th, and 17th, and by our batteries; also by an Italian gunboat on the 19th.

The Turks had, however, managed to salve and recover on December 18th the guns of the Egyptian gunboat sunk by the TJ 35 at Sollum, and had also got some of our smashed and abandoned motor-cars running.

On December 12th there was fought a battle on a small scale just west of Matruh, and at it occurred an incident which recalls the deadly sunken lane at Waterloo; in this case the British were the sufferers.

A squadron of British yeomanry were being fired at from a wadi, which, like most of these valleys is invisible at a short distance. The yeomanry charged, and charged home, and it was only at the last moment that the terrible fact was discovered that there was a precipitous drop of fifty feet over the edge. Men and horses fell mangled into that terrible chasm, and those who in falling escaped instant death, were at once terribly mutilated as they lay wounded and helpless by the pitiless savages who awaited them. The wadi was eventually cleared of these Senussi by our men in what developed into a kind of cave fight among the hiding-places of the ravine.

That gallant gentleman, Colonel Snow, also lost his life on the same day. He was speaking to a Senussi personally known to him, when he was treacherously shot from behind.

Such incidents, and there were many more, filled our troops with a great hatred of the enemy. The Senussi themselves never gave quarter, and our forces were in the end reluctantly driven to the same stern methods when dealing with Senussi irregulars. More untameable than tigers, the only *good* Senussi were dead ones!

Thus, at the end of 1915, no decisive action had been fought, with the exception of the Battle of Christmas Day (of which I will speak later), and both parties were inclined to settle down for the winter, the British at Matruh, which was now well fortified, the Turco-Senussi forces at Barrani.

But of these things, nothing did we prisoners know definitely at the time. Wild rumours came to us from passing caravans, elaborate lies were invented for our edification by our gaolers, in which British successes were never told to us, but British checks and reverses were magnified a hundredfold.

We were, as it were, a man living in an underground cellar, to whom sounds of the outer world distorted by echoes, faintly reached. But to my readers this little chronology of actual events up to the end of 1915, will help to make more clear the problems, and explain the contradictory webs of evidence with which we were surrounded. We were always seeking for a key to the riddle, but, as prisoners, we never found one. It was no more possible for us to reason intelligently, as to what was actually happening in the outside world, than it would have been for the man in the cellar.

It was about 4 p.m. on November 24th that we left El Zebla and started on the final stage of our journey to the *Promised Land*. We were still told that it was only two days' journey (the same distance as it was upon the day on which we left the Caves), but we no longer credited such fables. By reiteration they had ceased to stimulate and inspire us.

Before leaving we had two days' flour served out to us, with which we were told to make bread for the march, for our water supply would not permit of its use for boiling rice on the way.

This night march was one of the most dreadful ones in all our mournful catalogue. The stones were pitiless, and in the dark we stumbled and fell blindly; it was a super-nightmare. The sick, the feeble and the lame (and more than half of us came under one or other of these categories by now) soon began to trail behind. Terrified of losing touch with the rest, fearing to lose sight of the camels with their precious loads of water, dreading to die deserted in slow agony in the wilderness, they cried to their companions to help them. Their companions, for their part, had all they could do themselves to keep up at the killing pace at which we were moving. Even Achmed was sweating with fear, lest he himself should be lost, and he kept taunting and threatening us with all manner of brutality. He freely offered to flog all and every straggler, and urged on the guards to employ yet more freely those restoratives which they were always so ready to use—blows with the butts and pokes with the muzzles of their rifles—upon the bodies of their helpless, almost insensible victims.

After a while I could stand this no longer, and losing patience, in a fury of indignation I informed Achmed that we were all doing our best. I told him that, being sailors, the men were not accustomed to marching, that it was impossible for them to go any quicker, and that, in fact, it was not their fault. He caught me up at these last words: "No, it ees *not* their fault: it ees *my* fault," he said. "It ees to them too kind that I am! Presently we shall lose sight of the camels; then shall we all perish from thirst."

I could do no more. When the moon rose at about 11 p.m. things got a little better; we could at least see something of the stones that hurt us.

Long before daybreak the next day we were packed and ready to move off. But Achmed had an indolent mood on; the camels did not come in until later, and it was 8 a.m. before we actually marched. Most of the men had by now already eaten their two days' bread ration, and went hungry all day; but to our pleased surprise, when we camped for the night, we were given a ration of rice, and water to cook it with. We noticed that since leaving El Zebla we had been marching almost direct south; before, that date it had always been in a westerly direction that we headed.

Again that day we crossed a road, similar in all respects to the one we had seen the day we left Ras el Leucca, and again our enquiries elicited the same astonishing reply, that it was the Sollum road. As far as we could judge the road ran east and west the whole breadth of the country.

We had had no meat for a week now, and only half rations of rice or flour, whichever we preferred to take up. There had been no biscuit for a long time, and the tea and sugar were infinitesimal.

Friday, November 26th, was the last day's march that the majority of us were ever to do in the desert, though we knew it not as we shivered for two hours before daybreak, waiting for Achmed to arise and give the word of command.

Each mile we went the country became more flat, barren and pebble-strewn, a vast red marine cemetery of fossil shells and coral. Just before noon we arrived at a bir, marked by the usual tent-shaped mound of soil excavated from it, and to our pleased surprise found that it contained water.

A couple of miles further on was a second bir, which also contained water. A villainous-looking old Negro apparently dwelt there, and he had a fine tent, a buxom wife and a numerous family; they, accompanied by an old hag or two, came out to greet us, as though they had been long expecting us, and I noticed the old man had hanging from his shoulders a magnificent Crusader's sword, which I found on subsequent investigation was stamped with a cross and orb, and engraved with a coat-of-arms, part of which was a boar's head, and a motto in Latin.

We were just wondering how any person could reside here, year in and year out, in such a herb-less hell of stones, when the blow fell.

Basil, who had been talking to Achmed, at that moment came

up; he had a puzzled look on his face, and stated that this bir was called Bir Hakkim Abbyat, which is Arabic for the *White Doctor*, and so named from the light colour of the well-mound. The other bir we had just left was the *Red Doctor*. And this—this awful and accursed spot he had just been told was our destination.

We had arrived at the *Promised Land!*

## CHAPTER 15

# Bir Hakkim Abbyat, the White Doctor

The news stunned me, it stunned all of us !

Sitting in the dirt, our heads between our hands, worn out, unhappy, verminous, ragged and forsaken wretches that we felt ourselves to be, we gave ourselves up to despair and grief.

A few weeks here and we felt sure that if insanity did not first come to numb the despair with which our souls were filled, then we should surely die of broken hearts, of homesickness, of unimaginable longing. No way in which we looked could we discern a ray of hope; all was blank unfathomable darkness, release by kindly death was the only escape.

Presently we raised ourselves from the torpor into which we had fallen, and looked around.

To the east there was a blank plain, with stones and yet more stones. To the south it was the same, with a very few wretched, stunted and wind-swept bushes. The west was like the south, but with a few more bushes, and to the north, the way we had come from the Red Doctor, there was an almost imperceptible ridge, perhaps in places ten feet high, at the highest point of which some stones had been piled up a few inches, making a cairn or beacon. The edges of this ridge were slightly terraced; in the primeval past it had unquestionably been a sea-beach, and the fossil shells and coral lying about so abundantly everywhere, had once known the waves lapping over them, where now all was a dried and wind scoured desolation. The white glaze of salt in the shallow depressions still presented to the eye the effect of shimmering water.

The well-mound itself was a good sized one, perhaps twenty feet high, shaped like the sector of an orange, and beside it was a similar but smaller mound, much decayed. Where the ends of the two, mounds joined company the entrance to the bir was situated. Another bir was close by, but this was partly filled with rubbish and was dry.

On the upper southern face of the large mound were two or three crumbling un-mortared sepulchres, which may have belonged to any age or faith. Twenty or thirty yards away was a small rough stone blockhouse, slightly larger than a pig-sty, and by it Achmed pitched his tent, and told us to "make ourselves at home!"

The palm trees, where were they? We found *one* some days later, an unhappy derelict, struggling for existence, growing in the shelter of an ancient lime-kiln. There were two or three of these tiny tower-shaped kilns, though who could ever have required lime in a wilderness where there were no houses, and where there were no signs of houses ever having existed, has ever been a marvel to me. But lime-kilns they undoubtedly were, and, sheltered in their dark recesses, struggled the unhappy palm, which could never have existed in the full blast of the eternal sand-laden wind, which for ever blew bitingly across the plain.

Perhaps there had been houses once, for the ground was littered with broken red pottery, some of a refined terracotta type. The houses may have been pulled down to build the graves; there were half-a-dozen of these situated a few score yards to the south-east, and round about lay loose bones and mummified skeletons of donkeys, camels and the like.

Where were the tents which we had been promised? They were there all right, but as there were no ropes nor poles for them, it was explained to us that they could not be erected. But the poles and ropes would surely arrive to-morrow.

So we made ourselves at home as we were bid; and explored this charming winter health resort. Never was more salubrious spot, The winds tore with the force of a gale from every point of the compass in succession, bearing with them mementoes of torn-up shrubs, sand and small stones. Our eyes smarted and our skins tingled.

Towards dusk we collected the larger stones, and built ourselves low walls. Under the lee of these we lay, thankful for the worn ragged fragments of tents which we spread over us and with which, by huddling together, we contrived to cover the majority of our bodies.

Have any of my readers ever noticed a flock of sparrows, or other small birds, going to roost at night? Half-a-dozen snuggle up together, and presently a drowsy chirping bespeaks approaching slumber. Suddenly there is a flutter and shrill angry squeaks and quarrelling is heard. A late comer has arrived on the scene, and he wants to take the warm inside billet. The outside birds get all the cold and discomfort, hence the quarrelling and fighting; no bird wants to be on the outside. So it was with us; the outside sleepers could not get under those old tent flaps. It was a prime cause for disputation.

Perhaps I cannot do better than now describe some of the people by whom we were surrounded.

Captain Achmed Mansoor, the Egyptian, was still in command, with Mahomet Zoué as assistant. These two dwelt apart, in the bell tent by the blockhouse.

Our guards were at this time about twenty in number, and before we had been long at the wells these were joined by their wives and families, who, like their lords and masters, were of all types, colours and descriptions, from a fairness of skin approaching that of the Southern European, to the shiny blackness of the most ebon Negro. Their features likewise also varied through the Aryan, Semitic and Negro types, but the Aryan strain strongly predominated. With the use of a razor and a little soap and water, I believe many of the Senussi could have passed for rather dark, aquiline and decidedly aristocratic-looking Englishmen. Others, on the contrary, might from their appearance be excusably mistaken for golliwogs.

Some were so quaint looking, that the men soon gave them nicknames.

*Sparrow legs* we all knew; he was a being of diminutive height, with thin calf-less legs wrapped tightly round in khaki puttees, and he hopped merrily around all day in the sunshine, for all the world like a cockney sparrow.

*Charlie Chaplin* was another, and he combined devoutness of life with zeal for military exercises, and sometimes I fancy got the two a little mixed. He would unexpectedly drop from a proud demonstration of. the goose step and complicated juggling with his rifle into devout meditation, generally ending in prostration and loud cries upon Allah.

Yet a third was *Filfil Bill,* a name by which he was only known to the officers. He was the fiercest, most piratical-looking of all the ruffians, with ragged clothes, bloodshot eyes, and a thin white burnous made apparently entirely of darns; at one time the mere sight of him in a lonely place would have made my blood run cold. But he had an endearing quality; it was his possession of a hoard of *filfil,* the Arabic word for sweet red pepper.

Filfil Bill had a large family, whom it was necessary for him to provide for; hence he came to us secretly by night and exchanged some of his red pepper for an equal quantity of our rice. The taste and bite which the pepper imparted to our food more than compensated us for the small quantity of rice which we had to give him in exchange, so both parties benefited; but it was necessary to keep the transaction very secret, for should it have been discovered that we were so bartering our rations, they would have been most certainly yet further reduced.

But the individual with whom we had most to deal, and the one who exercised the greatest influence upon our lives at Bir Hakkim, was the holy man, a priest in charge of the wells, whom we soon got to know as *Holy Joe.* I believe his real name was Osman.

This individual was an Ethiopian, a tall, fine-looking Negro, but with twisted, shrivelled legs and a straggly, greyish beard; I adjudged him to have been about sixty years of age. Apparently he did well by his water tolls, and was always well dressed as compared with the ragged soldiery. He had quite a palatial new tent and a plump, pleasant wife, who, judging by his family, all as regularly graded in height as the rungs of a ladder, evidently made an annual event of adding to their number. He also had dependent on him a couple of hags, one reputed to be over a hundred years old—but whether the old crones were earlier wives, or merely near relatives of his own, I know not. He possessed two donkeys, a few goats, and his own stock of barley and rice, a yellow pariah dog or two, and a sjambok (elephant-hide whip). Being a holy man appeared to give him much temporal as well as spiritual authority, the which, whip in hand, he applied freely to all and sundry. Unlike the others, it was not supposed to be dignified for him to tell lies, and I never knew him deliberately tell a falsehood.

As priest he repaired three times a day to the summit of the well-mound, and from there called the faithful to prayer. Before dawn, at sunset and about, 9 p.m., his nasal and extremely powerful voice would sound forth, making invocation to Allah and rendering hopes of further sleep of no avail. Wherever in the desert a Mohammedan force camps they form a *mosque*, facing towards Mecca. These mosques were a pitfall to our unwary selves, for they were simply single stones arranged on the ground, even as a child arranges the old bricks in a rubbish heap at home; we had no suspicion that they enclosed holy ground. Blundering unthinkingly across these spaces we were the recipients of many cuffs and sticks and stones, until we learned their meaning.

At Bir Hakkim there was a simple arrangement such as this for worship, and here the faithful gathered for worship at Holy Joe's summons. I have heard much of Mohammedan devoutness, and was rather surprised to find the number of worshippers was generally confined to two or three; the rest slept on, and the women, of course, never attended. This mosque was situated hard by the block-house, whence the smoking Achmed, squatting on his mat, looked on with supercilious and undisguised contempt. Renegade Christian that he was, he believed in neither God nor man.

Of the bir itself, the rock-hewn cistern or well, which fixed the location of our camp at the White Doctor, I will give a description, as it was similar to, and made on the same principle, as thousands of others throughout the length and breadth of North Africa.

In Roman times there is no doubt whatever this country supported a, large agricultural population. The corn was planted in the autumn before the rain fell, and if this latter was sufficient the grain came to maturity as an abundant harvest in early summer. For the rest of the year it was fallow. Even in modern times before the war very good barley was exported, principally for brewing purposes.

To support these resident agriculturists for the rainless nine months in the year, and also to keep alive the camels, flocks and herds, some system of water storage was necessary, and this was done in an extremely efficient and economical way by the bir.

There are large tracts of non-porous limestone rock in the country on the surface. Stretches of these are selected with a very slight slope, as at the White Doctor. On this slope an area is enclosed by two low water-walls, a foot or eighteen inches high, meeting at the lowest point of the slope; and where they meet the bir is dug. They are generally in pairs. The entrance is a small square hole in the rock just large enough for a man to enter, and once inside it opens out bottle-wise into a chamber the shape of a flask of burgundy, about eighteen feet in diameter, and ten or twelve feet deep. This limestone chamber, though quite soft to excavate, becomes very hard when exposed to the air, and makes a solid rock-hewn cemented cistern. The soil excavated is thrown up oh the lower side of the well, and forms the well-mounds, which are by far the most conspicuous object of the landscape. I have had as many as twenty in sight at one time together.

On the very least rainfall the water running down the rocky slope, hemmed in by the water-walls, collects in the bir at the lower extremity. A single night's good rain will fill one, and there it will remain sweet, cool and fresh for years, the evaporation through the small opening at the top being practically nil.

When we arrived at the White Doctor there had been no rain for eleven months, innumerable caravans had been watered from the well, but there was a depth of water of at least nine feet remaining. Most of the wells I believe to be of Roman or even more ancient origin. Our well had no markings on it, but the Red Doctor, a couple of miles distant, had some Roman lettering which I never saw, but was told about.

# CHAPTER 16

# Rain and the Black Hole

It had taken us eleven days of actual marching to get from our position at the Dry Dock, near Maressa, to our camp at Bir Hakkim, and I had kept a pretty good record of the directions we took and the distances we covered daily. Being a sailor I could always tell the direction when sun or stars were visible, and by the same luminaries I knew also for how many hours we had been marching. Luckily, I was also a pedestrian, and all my life had been accustomed to reckon the number of miles per hour I was moving at. At the end of each day I recorded these courses and distances carefully in my diary, and now had a very good general idea as to where Bir Hakkim, the White Doctor, was actually situated, and also what the lie of the land generally was. We appeared to have moved round three sides of an oblong; this may have been done for the purpose of confusing us, as it certainly was not the route usually taken by natives; but I can hardly credit that our gaolers would ever have taken so much trouble for such a puny purpose; it was too energetic an idea altogether for the easygoing Turkish or Arab intellect thus to expend needlessly so much effort.

I think the real reason why they went the longer route was probably only because they wished to keep along the line of the wells. With the meagre transport available, they would never have been able to keep our party of poor walkers supplied with water for the period required if they had taken us direct; we should almost certainly have died of thirst on the way, and they did not care to take the risk. Achmed was quite nervous enough as it was, and though he hated us so, yet he had a good idea of the retribution that was likely to befall him at the hands of the British Government had we perished in that way, if he himself should subsequently fall into their hands.

After the first few days we cheered up a little, and set to work to do what was possible to better our lot. Our rice ration, which had been ruthlessly cut down at the time of Thomas' escape, was again increased slightly at our urgent, solicitation. We also heard that Thomas himself had been recaptured, and was not dead after all as we had feared. In the course of a few days the missing ropes and poles of some of the tents began to arrive, a little bit at a time, and we did what we could to erect the tattered rotten old fabrics into some kind of a shelter; for the rainy season was at hand and it was necessary to bestir ourselves.

The first rain fell on the afternoon of November 28th, but providentially it did not amount to much, as at that time only the officers had been provided with a tent, and that of the most ragged threadbare description. As it was, this little rainfall almost led to a catastrophe, a *Black Hole of Calcutta* on a small scale.

Achmed had been watching the gathering clouds for some days, and held numerous consultations with Holy Joe, the well-man, on the subject. As a result' of their deliberations, he told us that as the tent fittings had not arrived, he must make other arrangements to get the men sheltered from the rain. They were accordingly set to work to clear out from the dry well the caked mud at its bottom and on the top to build a little circular wall round its eighteen-inch wide entrance. Thus, moderately dry, and with the water unable to find ingress, he considered it would be a suitable habitation for seventy-eight full-grown men.

Now this well, by actual measurements, was eighteen feet in diameter at the circular bottom, and had an extreme height of ten feet in the centre of the vault; ventilation there was none, except the tiny hole for entering it, Needless to say it was pitch dark as well, damp and moist, and the atmosphere, even to start with, was foul.

I hesitate to think that even Achmed, hateful little bully that he was, realised what he was doing when he condemned seventy-eight human beings to go down there. But at the first speck of rain, down the well they were driven, and, having wedged themselves round the bottom like sardines, there in that hole did they spend six nights!

On the first occasion the men were rather glad to go than otherwise; glad to be out of the wet and cold and wind. Inside the well they were, for a space, a little better off, comparatively dry and warm; but they soon changed their minds!

Outside the hole, at the entrance, was posted a sentry with a loaded rifle, who ruthlessly drove back any who put their heads up. The men were not even allowed out to relieve nature, and that with a great number of dysentery patients among them.

Is it to be wondered that the men thought they had been deliberately put down there for the purpose of killing them? Or that they expected that, in the event of a genuine rainfall, that the water rushing down in a torrent would drown them like rats in a trap? For to get the whole number in or out in case of emergency took quite half an hour.

I never spent a night in that well myself, but I have been in it many times, and I have seen the poor wretches who came up out of it, and I have heard their descriptions.

The first night was bad enough, but the men put up with it, believing it to be the only one they would have to spend there. They actually spent six nights in that foul dungeon! And the nights were thirteen hours long, from sunset to sunrise.

A sailor is fortunately more used to a confined atmosphere than most mortals; he is accustomed to the pent up closeness of between decks. That is the only way I can explain how nobody died.

Each night the hole became fouler and more poisonous, for it was impossible to create a current of air and ventilate it in the day time. Their heads throbbed to bursting, they got cramp in all their limbs.

Protests were no good; each night at sunset the victims were driven down by the grinning guards again. It made sentry go such light work, when only one guard was necessary to look after seventy-eight men!

By the fourth night it beggared description, so foul was the atmosphere; all were coughing and choking, some became delirious, while others rapidly fell into a state of torpor. On the fifth morning a number were hoisted out insensible. The sixth night was the last; many were obviously dying—even the careless sentry was impressed and fetched Achmed. He went down, and let it be counted to him for righteousness in the land to which he has now gone—the next morning the men were released from this noisome den, never to return.

A few more tent fittings had arrived, various make-shift arrangements were devised, and by the next evening the crew had rigged up some kind of covering for themselves above the surface of the ground; but even had this not been so, I think they would all have chosen to die at the guards' hands, or to soak for months exposed to the rain, rather than permit themselves to be driven once more into the terrible miry pit which they knew so well and dreaded so much.

That "one man's meat is another man's poison," I never saw more clearly exemplified than at Bir Hakkim. On the question of rain, for example, Holy Joe's views and our own were contrary and opposite.

Holy Joe, as head man of the wells, had one object in life and one only, and that object was to have his wells full and overflowing with water. To obtain this water he must have rain, and all day long he anxiously scanned the sky and direction of the wind, and became elated at the sight of the tiniest cloud.

We prisoners, on the contrary, were indifferent to the water supply; in fact, we would gladly have seen the wells dry up, for it would have compelled our being moved elsewhere, and we felt that no change could be for the worse. As for rain, a prolonged downfall would have meant our certain death. Our ancient tents were about as water-tight as a sieve, and the smallest shower caused us the most intense misery and discomfort. Shivering, we stood in our filthy solitary suit of clothes, while the elements did their worst. The weather was bitterly cold, probably a temperature of 40° Fahrenheit at night, and half-fed, soaked to the skin, with no change of clothing possible, and a puddle to sit or lie in, no human constitution can hold out for long.

Therefore we looked at the sky with an even greater intensity than did Holy Joe; rain to him meant no discomfort in his snug new tent, and it meant wealth when it increased his water-supply; but rain to us, a few days of it, meant death—nothing less,

As the clouds got bigger and darker, he redoubled his appeals to Allah for the bountiful supply that would fill his rock-hewn cistern; he augmented his daily prayer-meetings from three to five in number.

We, on the contrary, discussed our fears and hopes together, and offered up many a mute appeal to Him who looks with pitying eye on all prisoners and captives, that He would be pleased to avert the calamity which appeared about to befall us.

The clouds faded away again, and, human-like; both parties forgot the Providence which directs all things.

The old black priest, as a rainfall became less probable, abated his vocal efforts to reach the ear of Allah. By the time that the sky was clear again he had once more reduced the number of his prayer-meetings from five to three per day; his voice was almost gentle in the early mornings and hardly disturbed our slumbers.

We, for our part, had forgotten our soul's stirrings; once more we were engrossed in our petty wrangling, quarrels and disputes, as though a day of reckoning had not been so near at hand.

"Because man goeth to his long home, and the mourners go about the streets.

Or ever the silver cord be loosed, or the golden bowl be broken. Then shall the dust return to the earth as it was: and the spirit shall return unto God who gave it.

Vanity of vanities, saith the preacher; all is vanity." Somebody remembered these words from *Ecclesiastes*," and we often discussed them as prisoners.

## CHAPTER 17

# "Blessed are They. . ."

Our life at Bir Hakkim now began to settle down into a more or less steady routine. The extraordinary thing is that, looking back upon it, although I can remember much unhappiness, much travail of spirit, much physical pain and discomfort during most of the period, yet I cannot recollect a single moment when I felt actually dull.

We were so engrossed in our trivial occupations, in the struggle for existence, in trying to glean the least fragment, of news and in discussing it, that our minds in many ways became peculiarly active. We watched with the keenest interest every arrival and departure of caravans or of solitary individuals and small parties. Basil, dressed in Arab clothes as he was, with his sallow complexion, and speaking fluently most of the languages of Turkey, Syria and North Africa, was often mistaken by new-comers for one of the camp Senussi, and was thus able to gather much of the tittle-tattle and news of the desert, together with current reports and opinions, before his informants became cognisant of his identity. But, from such news as filtered through to us, I have little doubt that the simple Bedouin were very nearly as much in the dark about the true state of affairs as we ourselves were. Rumour has wings, and news in that country spreads with amazing rapidity, but, like the Genie of the *Arabian Nights* who was confined in a bottle, news, as soon as it was loosed, magnified itself without measure, and the most trivial events were exaggerated into matters of world-wide importance.

The Senussi, and I fancy most other Arabs partake of their characteristics, were an interesting study. They are true sons of Esau, as one reads of him in the Bible— generous, impulsive, careless, their hand against every man and every man's hand against them; although they are so extraordinarily efficient in their own sphere of life, in their ability to exist and multiply in a land where no other human being living under their conditions could exist, yet they are at heart but the simplest of children. Childlike; they are apt to be cruel and despotic, believing in brute force and power as opposed to reason. A very young child will inflict all sorts of cruelties on animals; dismember flies, decapitate snails; it does this on an irresistible impulse, although it knows quite well that it is doing wrong, and that the animal suffers; but there is with children a kind of morbid curiosity which impels them so to act; they love the sense of despotic power which they exercise over their lowly victims. The Arab mind is similar, and human life, especially that of an infidel Christian, it holds as cheaply as does the child an insect. A wandering stranger is likely to be shot on sight, just for the mere lust of slaying, and for the desire to possess his property, however meagre. The crew of the *Coquet*, marooned on this coast a few months later, was an example of this.

But here, at the camp, we saw the other side of the Arab character, his character at home in his own tent. And home life, whether in an Esquimaux hut, a working man's cottage, the cavern of the man of the Stone Age, is much the same all the world over. Once eat a man's salt, and, unless he is very bad indeed, you can for the time being consider your life is safe with him.

During the first week at Bir Hakkim, and until we got our own tents, I often used to visit the tents of our guards, and found them a kindly and genial lot. I was unable to speak more than half-a-dozen words of Arabic, but this seemed to matter not at all; we were companions in the same way as animals are companions to each other, or even as a dog is to his master.

Many a cup of tea did I drink in the tent of my friend the little Blonde Man, who always looked as though he had green hair, for reason of the emerald cloth which he wore tied around his head.

And the teapot! I like to imagine the effect it would produce if it were placed on the table of a West End drawing-room. The child-like Senussi had made many captures of goods and household utensils from the Italians, and of such trophies there were often many of whose original purport he had no conception; he therefore adapted them to such uses as seemed good in his own eyes, and to such utilities as, by their shape, they suggested to his tent-dwelling mind.

This teapot, in particular, had most obviously come from a hospital, and, at its inception, it was intended for purposes far other than that of drinking tea out of! It had, in fact, a large spout and no other opening, and had been used by patients confined to bed. Need I say more?

But, to the simple Senussi, who knows not bed nor sick patients, the spout suggested but one thing and one only; it appeared to him to be a novel form of teapot, and as such he employed it.

Readers will see by now that we were beginning to lose some of what we called the *refinements* of civilisation. We certainly were; the veneer had worn off; we were down to near the bed-rock of human passions and emotions. We had not reached it yet, but we were rapidly approaching that foundation upon which all else rests. Never more can I have patience with conditions and laws which have not some foundation on that bed-rock of reality. Many things which in civilised life I had believed to be of the utmost importance, I now found to be fatuous trivialities. Many things which I had looked upon as unessential, as *frills*, I now knew to be the verities of existence, no longer to be lightly brushed aside. And above all and everything else, the fair and square dealing of man with his fellow-man, of generosity, kindness, unselfishness, justice; these and the like were the *only* things that really mattered in the least; the rest was veneer, a house built on the sand.

How simple a man's needs really are after all! A handful of rice, a mouthful of water, a few rags to cover one's body, and, if possible, some shelter to creep under at night. These are all that are essential to material welfare, all that are needed by the millions who know no greater comfort—and are content.

Literature, amusements, exercise, change—they are quite in-essential. We had but to open out eyes and see the sharp-witted, intelligent, active Arabs about, us; they were undoubtedly better off in the way of health, morals, and happiness than the average European.

What curious subjects we discussed in those days! When we first arrived there were two schools of thought; one was of the opinion that we should all rapidly degenerate, and become mo-rose, taciturn, intractable, each holding what he possessed by force and craft, and not by moral right. The other school, though by no means religious men in the ordinary acceptation of the word, held that the ordinary rules of Christianity and civilised ideals would be maintained.

Let it be understood that these two schools were schools of argument, and not necessarily of action. The exponents of the *brute beast* theory were in most instances in actual deed shining examples of their opponents' views. They were, more often than not, the least selfish and the best doing of our party. While, con-trariwise, the *Christian Ideals* group, when it came to the actual living proof of their professed views, were, human-like, often apt to fall from grace. I believe that, in their hearts, the brute beast party were *afraid* that their own theories were true, and they only argued in support of them, in the hope that their oppo-nents would be able to convince them as to the falseness of their belief, whereby they might be able to take comfort.

One officer, at any rate, the fairest and justest of any of us, though ever stern in his manner, was never tired of tell-ing us of the experiences of a friend of his, whose ship was wrecked on a desert island, where he and his shipmates had to spend a considerable period. According to his account, these men *did* degenerate to a marked extent into savages. One of them, I remember, possessed himself of the only axe and, hav-ing cleared a certain area for himself with it, forbade any other to approach it under threat of instantly killing him with the weapon. We were all very impressed with this story at the time, but things did not so turn out with us. Bickering, quarrelling, disputes there were, intense jealousy, and at times suspicion on all matters of necessities of life, such as food and clothing; but, in the end, the *Christianised* party won hands down!

News of the outside world we had none, except the German-ised information which Achmed thought fit to impart to us, and the tales gathered by Basil from the natives; but our tongues seemed never to cease wagging, so keenly did we discuss everything. Of course, there was nothing to read either; but Mahomet Zoué had unearthed an ancient French schoolboy's primer of a date prior to the Franco-Prussian war, and this those who had a smattering of French read eagerly; another officer used its margin as a diary.

Politics and the war we had long ceased to argue about; we had so long been without news of either that we were reduced to vague speculation. One curious subject which we almost came to blows about was as to the precise times at which certain holiday trains started for various seaside resorts, and also what the actual cost of a return excursion fare might be. Themselves nearly all employees of the L. & N. W. Railway Company, my companions readily waxed very hot on this matter. We liked to talk about, and imagine, the wonderful things we would do when once we were free again.

For the first month or so we also conversed much about food, and what we would one day eat. Everyone described gloatingly the best dinners he had ever eaten, and lived over again those gluttonous hours when there was no food limit. But this prac-tice gradually fell into desuetude; the more we talked of what we couldn't get, the hungrier we got, and the more the craving and longing for it increased till it became well nigh unbearable!

Soon we learned to talk only of what we *had* got, to sit round in a circle by the fire, all eager-eyed, and watch the every move-ment of the one who was acting as cook for the day, advising and generally wrangling with him as to what he ought to do. The spoiling of any food was far too serious a matter to be left to the untrammelled intelligence of one person! Everyone wanted to be cook, and to do it their own way, and everyone else wanted to show them how to do it! Rice had been our only food for some time now, and we were all steadily getting thin-ner; no grain of it was ever wasted.

Each mess had one enamelled iron wash-basin only to serve as a dish, and we had no plates nor individual receptacles for our food. In the officers' mess, as soon as the cook announced that the rice was cooked, the basin was brought forward, and the pot containing the rice emptied into it. Only one-half of us could be cooked for at a time; the other seven cooked and ate their meal after the first seven had finished. The rice having been poured into the basin, it was levelled off, and Mr. Dudgeon, the Chief Officer, who by universal vote had been elected for the delicate duty, did the portioning. To divide a basin of rice into seven exactly equal portions is no easy matter. When he had done this, a thin stick used as a stirrer was employed to cut out the sectors. When the sector-next to your own was being removed you watched the operation with extreme jealousy and keenness to see that there was no undercutting of your own sector, and that no loose grains were detached and came away from it. On your own turn coming you brought up a flat stone to serve as a plate, and as you removed your portion you also became conscious that your every movement was regarded with keen eyes and the greatest suspicion. The least infringement of rules which we had evolved from experience was likely to lead to a free fight! Seated in the dust, we would eat our portions, and, having finished, hungrily watch the second seven partaking of theirs.

Paddy, the dog, always got sufficient. If the majority of us only gave him half a tea-spoonful of rice each, the total of it, lumped together, was ample for his needs, and he was by far the plumpest and best conditioned of the party.

We were supposed to be getting ½ oke (1½ lb.) of rice daily, but as a matter of fact we received much less, and were eternally hungry. But we no longer minded having no meat. Rice is a perfect food in its way; the only trouble was that we never got half enough of it.

By the time we had been at Bir Hakkim a week, we were already becoming reconciled to our life there, and we found the time to be passing surprisingly quickly. The officers and men shared exactly alike in every way; there was no difference whatever in the treatment, except that part of the men went every day to the *Red Doctor,* and worked at clearing one of the bir there of stones and mud, in order that it might be available in the coining rainy season.

We were allowed to wander about by day in sight of the camp, a radius of a mile or so, and at these times collected firewood and anything else which looked as though it might be useful.

The men had a kind of pitch down by the old graveyard, where they occasionally played rounders with a ball made from rags.

# CHAPTER 18

# On Camels and the Culinary Art

A few notes suggested by a perusal of my diary at this time may be of interest:

Sunday, November 28th—We were informed that the crew of another British man-of-war, sunk by submarine, would be sent to join us for internment. A little rain, the first we have had, fell in the afternoon.

With reference to the above, heavy rains on the coast began on the next day and transformed the desert into a quagmire, but providentially it never reached us.

I could not gather any information about this alleged sinking of the British man-of-war and the capture of her crew. It was probably, like so much else that we were told, pure myth; we certainly never saw this crew, or heard anything further about them.

Tuesday, November 30th—A party collecting firewood to the south of the camp came upon wheel tracks in the clayey-sandy soil. I went down to look at them, and felt much as Robinson Crusoe must have done when he discovered that human foot-mark in his solitary island. What vehicle could possibly have come clown here, and what on earth could it have come for? Discreet inquiries by Basil elicit a reply from Achmed, to the effect that they are the tracks of two Turkish Government motor-cars which visited the place a couple of years ago. We all know that Achmed is a liar and do not believe him, and Apcar, who is an expert motorist, assures me that the country would be quite impossible for motors. We remain puzzled, but they certainly look like motor-tracks.

Thursday, December 2nd.—A caravan of sixty camels arrived from Sollum, and stopped to water their beasts. Basil elicited the incredible information that the journey had only taken them five days, whereas it had taken us a fortnight from Port Bardia, a no greater distance.

The watering of a large caravan of camels is quite an amusing sight. The animals crowd up, snorting and bubbling shrilly, while the camelmen, with a loud "healy hauley" chant, draw the rawhide water-bag hand over hand up from the well; they then upset it on to the rocks. Though hundreds of years old, no trough of any kind has been constructed for animals to drink from, and the camels suck up what liquid they can from the pools formed; the remainder of the water, well-mixed with dirt and camel droppings, drips back into the well. The camels quarrel and fight for priority of place, but each gets his turn at last, and, as he drinks, swells visibly like a leech, or perhaps like the magic cat of the fairy tale.

We are all getting very used to camels now. At first we were all terrified of them, and the way they had of coming up with horrid snarling faces, frothing mouths, and savage jaws; we took very good care never to get within reach of the latter. But now, I personally take no more notice of them than do the natives, or than a groom does of a lively but un-vicious horse. A female camel with her young is, like all mothers, quite a pretty sight. It is difficult to the uninitiated to picture a camel with tender emotions, but the mother camel noses and licks her young just as does a cow her calf. Poor beasts, they get nothing from man but blows and burdens to bear, and just sufficient to drink. They forage for themselves all night after working all day. And yet people accuse the camel of being an ungrateful animal. Ungrateful for what?

When all the camels have been watered, they are driven off for their night's pasturage on the dried-up sticks and thorns which they love, one of the camel boys going with them. The endurance of the latter is a perpetual miracle; he has walked with the camels thirty or forty miles in a hot sun all day, he remains on foot all night in touch with them, and he covers another thirty or forty miles on the following day. During that time he gets no rest whatever, as camels once loaded are never allowed to stop, lest they roll with their packs. If a camel train is stopped for more than a few minutes, it must be unloaded.

All day long they meander along at a steady two or three miles an hour, from dawn to sunset, feeding as they go.

On the same day (December 2nd) I find from my diary that we got a special lesson from Mahomet (Achmed's cook) on the art of cooking rice properly. Hitherto we had been content to eat it wet, sloppy and glutinous, cooked in the manner which our inexperience dictated; but from now on we were able to partake of it dry, firm, and with every grain separate—a very different, much more palatable, and far more nutritious food. As the housewife in England is also often in the habit of spoiling her rice, perhaps a knowledge of the Arab way may help her.

The rice is first washed or soaked. Twice as much water (exactly) as rice is then brought to boil in the pot and salt put in it. When the water is boiling freely, pour the rice in, level it off, and put the lid on. Bring the pot to the boil again, then draw it to the side of the fire. (In our case we actually drew the fire, and only let a few hot embers remain.) Let it gently simmer for twenty minutes, then take the lid off and taste the rice, to see if it is soft and properly cooked. If it is cooked, leave the lid off, and let the steam escape until the rice is quite dry. If the rice is not quite cooked and is still hard, let it simmer for a little longer with the lid on: then dry off as before. In no case should any of the liquid ever be poured away, as it is the most nutritious part.

Thus cooked, the rice will be brown at the bottom, but not burnt, and these brown parts act as an appetiser I for the rest, which will be found to be surprisingly good eating, plain or with a little stock in it. We never tired of rice; though for months we often had nothing else. To hungry men such as we were, no Lord Mayor's banquet could have had more delicate and unexpected flavours, flavours quite unsuspected by those at home, who use it as a doubtful addition to their meat in the absence of vegetables.

We first ate rice with suspicion, having no belief in it as a food. We ended by believing rice to be the perfect food; only, some form of fat is necessary, if nothing else is eaten.

A tea-spoonful of olive-oil, brought to the frizzle at the bottom of the saucepan before the water is put in, and then left to mix with the latter, is all that is needed to make the perfect food.

When we got flour, which was always barley-flour, as we occasionally did in lieu of the rice, there were several ways of cooking it. The versatile Basil, our Admirable Crichton, was invariably our head baker. It was he who kneaded the dough in our combined bath, baking-pan and snail-boiler; it was he who portioned it out into equal-sized little biscuits for baking, and who retained a tiny lump (which we hoped would go sour, but never did) to leaven our loaves on the next baking day.

There were several methods of baking, the first and most popular being that in use by the Senussi. It consisted in covering a small area with flat stones, and upon these a large and fierce fire was lit, and allowed to burn for about an hour, until the stones were well heated. The fire was then raked off, and the dough poured upon the stones, and at once covered over again with a thick layer of ashes, taking great care that no live ember came actually into contact with the dough, for if it did it would burn it shamefully. An hour later, and the hot ashes were once more raked off, and the dough taken out—the most appetising and the most sustaining bread in the world, and one to which the ashes impart a flavour which cannot be obtained in any other way,

A second way was to make small thin biscuits, which were cooked in the baking-pan, one or two at a time very rapidly, it having a very hot fire under it. It is somewhat similar to the Scot's way of making oatcakes. But a third method was evolved by Basil, while we were at Bir Hakkim; it was a genuine oven.

First of all he gathered some brushwood, and with this as a support, he constructed a beehive-shaped dome of wet sandy clay. It had a little hole at the top to let the smoke out, and a small entrance on one side of the bottom for a door. These preliminaries accomplished, he set fire to the brushwood inside, thus baking the dome into a solid brick, and at the same time leaving the interior empty. Thus was the oven complete. When baking day came along the oven was heated for hours with burning brushwood inside, until it became very hot. The fire was then all drawn out and the barley-cakes put in, then covered with ashes as before, and the door and chimney hermetically sealed.

Our excitement was terrific on that first baking day with the new oven; even the Arab guards stood round in an amused and interested circle, and the prisoners leaped and danced like holiday school-boys. It was a great success; Basil, the head baker, was loudly acclaimed.

Of the art of cooking snails we were all now exponents. At first it was only the very young (and therefore most hungry) and the least fastidious who would eat them. But our gradually increasing hunger, and the necessity for more food as the weather got colder, brought us all into line. Escargots were on the bill of fare of every mess at most meals of the day. I brought the shells of some of these animals home to England with me, and am told they are of the same family as the French edible snail; but their shells are pure white, and as hard, thick and bony as those of winkles.

Our first method of cooking them was primitive. We simply put them on the fire. As the heat got to them, they emitted steam with a loud whistling sound. When this music stopped, it acting as a warning similar to that of the patent egg-boiler, you knew that the dainty was ready. You extracted it with a splinter of wood, and ate it—if you had the courage!

At Bir Hakkim, we had more time to study gastronomy. We generally boiled the succulent molluscs. The bath-cum-baking tin was requisitioned, filled with water, and under it a larger fire was lighted. Into this liquid we plopped our unhappy dinner, several of our number meanwhile squatting round the edges of the tin, occupying themselves by pushing back any of the horned delicacies who attempted to climb out. The water having boiled for ten minutes or so, and a green scum two or three inches deep having gathered on the surface, the water was poured off, exposing the snails to view—grey, limp, greasy and lifeless—their heads and horns hanging out of their shells. I cannot remember ever seeing anything much more disgusting to look at, but they were food, and we ate them greedily, with ferocity, without salt, bread, rice, vinegar, or any other accompaniment.

One of our number so distinguished himself by his zeal in the capture, cooking and consumption of snails, that he was popularly known as the Snail King. Seated by the fire he might be seen at any time with a cap full of snails and, accompanied by one or two chosen cronies, devouring them as though they were at a whelk-stall in Whitechapel.

One of the most treasured relics which I brought back with me from the desert was the Snail King's winkle-pin. It is a piece of sharpened bone with an eye in it, for it was used also as a darning needle.

These feasts were quite an entertainment for the officers, and our interest in them was by no means diminished by a little incident which we witnessed. Someone had evidently a down on the Snail King's weakness for slimy delicacies, and this individual, finding a live cartridge, extracted the powder there from and inserted it in a snail shell, filling the aperture afterwards with the head and horns of another snail. The Snail King, observing this extra fine specimen, placed it on the fire, and waited for the usual whistling music to commence. Not a sound. He was just putting his ear a little closer to listen when the foreseen occurred. Fire, snails and Snail King were precipitated in all directions; the banquet had to be indefinitely postponed!

Perhaps I cannot better close this chapter on camels and the culinary art than by telling of the first meat which we tasted after many weeks. Incidentally, it shows how we had descended in refinement since that afternoon of November 6th, when we felt such disgust at seeing the Senussi bearing off some disgusting looking (to us) pink camel meat. The entry in my diary now is for December 7th, just a month later.

A baby camel had been missing for several days, the loss causing the old priest, Holy Joe, to curse and to swear; but, as in the case of the Jackdaw of Rheims, nobody seemed a penny the worse. But on this morning he came to me with a long face and informed me, through Basil, that the young camel was drowned in the well, and he wanted one of the prisoners to get it up.

I suppose it was really the priest's own job, he being in charge of wells, to fish it out; but I do not think either he or any other of the Arabs could swim, and, in any case, they would be afraid to go in that dark and devil-haunted place, I suspect.

As the camel obviously had to be got out, or we would be compelled to drink and wash in camel soup indefinitely, I called for volunteers. The weather was then cold, and nobody being particularly keen, I determined to go myself. Having been lowered down into the dark chamber, I swam about for a moment or two, and then touched something soft and hairy with my hand; it was the camel's foot, and the animal was floating belly up, mostly submerged. I towed it to the centre, attached the rope to a foot, saw it hauled out, and then made my way up in the same way.

When I got up to the surface of the ground I saw the prisoners were gathered round the dead camel's body, their mouths fairly watering. We asked if we might eat it, and we were told "Yes"; the Arabs would not eat it because it had not been bled according to their law, so we might have it all. The carcase was already a good bit distended after two days down the well, and when we started to cut it up the smell was so nasty that we thought we had better bury it. But our appetites were clamorous at the sight of so much flesh, and we changed our minds. We lived on putrid camel for three days afterwards—camel soup, stewed camel, roast, fried, and boiled camel, camel liver, and snail stew.

Sudden death will never make me eat camel again! If you ask me what camel tastes like, all I can reply is that it tastes exactly like the live animal smells—rank, horrid and disgusting.

That camel gave me such a disgust of meat that I was practically a vegetarian during the remainder of the time we were prisoners.

# CHAPTER 19

# Holy Joe, the Old Man of the Wells

How differently do different individuals bear captivity! Some there are, and they form but a small percentage, who have settled down into a state of dull apathy. Being forcibly compelled by others to do so, they perform their tasks, but never willingly. They have always blistered feet, if the excuse will serve to get them off their share in the daily collection of firewood. They draw water, help to wash up and clean the rice, only on compulsion. Their own persons they have long ceased to tend; cold water does not appeal to them, and they never wash, but lay grey-faced all day upon their backs in the tent, or squat in a semi-comatose condition about the fire. Not only do they not wash themselves, but they shake their heads gravely at the more hardy and cleanly of our number, who daily strip in the cold wind and lave themselves, a process accomplished with a rag of canvas we have saved, and a pint of water in the boat's bailer. These hardy ones, they say, are on the sure road to death by dysentery and every other disease they can think of.

In direct contrast to these grey-faced melancholies are another group, about equal in number. It is they who are up at earliest dawn, busily engaged in blowing the embers of last night's fire into a flame, and who, having rekindled it, are busily boiling a kettleful of hot water. It is they who, in the chilly morning air, have filled the dripping water-skins, and dragged them the two or three hundred yards from the well to the tent door, a thankless, unpleasant task, in process of which they get chilled and wet. Making up the fires is no easy matter either, and one accomplished only after many a cough and choke. We always pile up the fires overnight, and in the morning one or two live embers may generally be discovered among the ashes. As we have no matches and no flint and steel, this is an important matter, and those whose fires are entirely out, are dependent upon other tents to be able to light up again.

Drawing water, by the way, is no very popular task, for, besides being wet, cold and fairly heavy work, it may also incur the penalty of a swim in the well. The well-bucket is hauled up by means of a grass rope, fabricated by Holy Joe, twisted skilfully between his toes and fingers. This rope very readily gets frayed and breaks, leaving the bucket at the bottom of the well. As Holy Joe refuses to provide another bucket, it is a matter of either going without water or of going down the well for the bucket; wherefore we have agreed, that in whose ever hand the well-rope breaks, on that individual shall rest the responsibility of getting the bucket back. Hence the great unpopularity of being water-drawer, for with the greatest care the rope generally breaks at least twice or thrice a week!

But there are some individuals, and one especially, who never seems to be worried about anything; he takes whatever comes quite philosophically. Always with a pleasant fatherly smile on his face he listens to what is being said; he even joins in the argument himself at times, and then, satisfied, he rolls himself up and drops off comfortably to sleep! He is of that phlegmatic, un-temperamental Anglo-Saxon mentality which so puzzles the Latins. We others, and especially those more highly strung, unable to sleep, envy him greatly. In fact, there are times when his good fortune fills us with rancour and all un-charitableness, so happy does his lot appear, when compared with our own. The stupefying midday heat, the bitter cold of the long fourteen-hour winter nights, during which our bodies are but an aching misery from lying on the hard, rocky floor of the tent, the tedium of the endless, aimless days, anxiety, home-sickness, hunger—all these mean comparatively little to him. He just sleeps!

But, to do him justice, when he really is awake; he is so bright and amiable that one can almost forgive him. We, at any rate, choke back our wrath and disgust, and temper somewhat the reproaches we have prepared.

How incredibly hard the ground is at night! It is true we have mats to lie on, but they are worse than a plank-bed, hard and glossy as the rock underneath thorn. After laying for an hour or so in one position, the pain in one's hip-bone becomes so intolerable, that one always has to turn over. We are packed so closely in the tent that this movement literally means that everyone else has to move. We recall an alleged humorous picture postcard we have often seen; it depicts Pa, Ma and a numerous family, all tightly wedged into one small bed. Underneath the picture is written the legend: "When Pa says all turn, we all turns together." Somebody repeated this joke for the first night or two, but the exquisiteness of its humour rapidly lost its point. Nobody laughed.

We made an effort of digging a little trench under the mat to ease some of this pressure on our hip-bones; but, whichever way one lay, the hip-bone always had a knack of moving somewhere else rather than to the prepared hollow; we were not a success as anatomical engineers. The trouble was slightly ameliorated by it, when one lay quite still in one position, but cured it never was.

Achmed, though still cynical, sneering and unpleasant with us as ever, had latterly ceased to be quite the same bête noire that he used to be. Practically his last outburst was on December 5th, a Sunday, when, after our usual hymn-singing service held after dark in the officers' tent, we so far forgot ourselves as to end up by singing the National Anthem.

Needless to say, the Senussi. sentry took no notice of this, To him all English tunes were alike, and it might just as well have been the Wild Man of Borneo that we were singing, for all he knew to the contrary, or cared.

But, with Achmed, things were different; the air caught his ear at once, and it certainly did not bring back pleasant memories. We had barely finished the first verse, and were just starting it over again (a repetition necessitated by our national ignorance of the second), when he bore down upon us an angry, spluttering whirl-wind. Paddy, noting the apparition, at once rushed out and barked at him, an incident which did not tend to improve the Egyptian's temper. Puffing, fuming and stuttering, a habit much indulged in by small vain men when aroused, he loosed his angry tongue at us. There was much in what he said about His Sublime Majesty the Sultan of Turkey, and vigorous threats as to what would happen if we further continued such an affront as daring to sing God save the King while still remaining in a camp of "His Turkish Sublime Majesty's North African dominions." I tried for a moment to ar-gue with Achmed, pointing out that our National Anthem was a hymn and a part of our church service, but he would have none of it. Achmed being the power with the big stick, I as usual got the worst of the argument and desisted. It was many a long day ere we were to hear that tune again.

At this time the crew were working daily at cleaning out the Red Doctor, the well a couple of miles to the northward of us, and Holy Joe always superintended these labours. At first he always carried a gun, and, accompanied by half-a-dozen guards, marched the party off. But presently he developed a new hab-it—he left the gun behind and, in its place, he took his elephant whip, a whip similar to the South African sjambok, and made from the hide of some great animal such as an elephant or a hippopotamus, the haft and lash being all formed from one solid piece of hide. This formidable instrument he laid impartially on both white man and black, whenever he considered that their conduct called for some such gentle corrective.

Our poor devils of sailors, half-starved and weak as they were, were unable to shovel earth continuously, wherefore, whenever Holy Joe caught them doing what he considered slacking, he laid it on to them most unmercifully.

The men came and complained to me, saying they would only be too glad of work to pass the time, but that it was quite impossible for them to do it on the food they were then getting. Some said, in fact, that they would down Holy Joe upon the very next occasion that he struck them. From this, however, I dissuad-ed them and induced them to grin and bear it as best they could, for, as to the result of striking the Holy Man, with armed guards about, there could be no possible doubt: it would mean instant shooting! This was a matter which could not be remedied; but I did get Achmed to say a word or two of caution to our nigger tyrant, about his being a littler gentler in his ways.

Holy Joe posed as a man of property, for, besides owning a palatial tent, a plump and pleasant wife, a numerous progeny, and a couple of grandmothers, he possessed also flocks and herds—that is, if I may be permitted to call two fine specimens of the Jerusalem donkey,—herds. These donkeys never appeared to do any work, but apparently their whole time was fully occupied foraging round for food. I can only imagine that the priest really retained them as augurs for foretelling the weather. When the asses brayed excessively, he hoped for rain, and he then put in an extra amount of time and zeal praying. When the asses were dumb, he noticeably reduced his devotional efforts to correspond more precisely with the probability of the Deity complying with his requests. For Holy Joe was no sportsman; he never prayed on the off-chance.

There being no grass for the donkeys to graze on, the poor animals had to be content with bushes, pieces of stone, and, I suspect, snails, and the arrival of us prisoners must have been a red letter day for them. Daily we collected great stacks of brushwood, and left them piled outside our tent door. In the morning they were invariably nearly all gone.

At first we suspected our guards, and rightly—for Paddy caught them removing our store more than once and stuck his small teeth vigorously into the pilfering hand; thereafter we always made him a bed in our wood-stack.

But Paddy was on friendly terms with the donkeys unfortunately, and we soon found that the latter were, more than our guards, the real culprits. Nightly they ate up our day's labours, and, not content with this, they tried to knock our tent down as well on more than one occasion, thereby adding insult to injury.

However, we had our laugh at Holy Joe. In due time his flocks began to multiply—all his nanny-goats kidded. There must have been twenty or thirty of these pretty little kids about, and as they increased in strength and agility they, goat-like, yearned for alpine-fastnesses to climb. Our desert being about as mountainous as a cricket-pitch, they looked around for a substitute to the rocks and pinnacles for which their goat-natures hungered. And then it was that Holy Joe's palatial tent came into prominence; in less than a minute the twenty kids were dancing over the sloping roof, like ants on a dead caterpillar! Out flew Holy Joe and out flew the two grandmothers; Mrs. Joe and all the little Joeys appeared on the scene. It was a great game of Tom Tiddler's Ground. And as fast as they chased the kids off one side of the tent, up they sprang on to the other. It kept the whole clan of Holy Joe hot and angry for a fortnight, and African curses fell like autumn leaves. But, for the prisoners, it was an entertainment and relaxation greatly appreciated, the best of all cures for sore eyes.

But Holy Joe, in his way, though stern, hard and fanatical, was not altogether a bad sort, and he was the only one who ever made even a pretence of sometimes telling the truth. According to his lights, he was just and honest, and, moreover, a person with whom it was as well to keep on good terms; for he it was who decided what we might do or not do, and he possessed also three articles of inestimable value, of whose existence we gradually came to know.

First and foremost he had a darning-needle! This needle had been at its birth a patent tin-opener. It was one of those pieces of wire which, with a loop at one end, and an eye at the other, are used to strip off the tin edging wound round a pot of pâte-de-foie-gras and other potted delicacies. I know not how it first came into Holy Joe's possession; probably, like most other things, it was by capture from the Italians. But now, with its loop straightened out and the other end of it sharpened to a point, it made a darning-needle six inches long and, being the only one, was so valuable that any of us would have given a five-pound note to possess it. And sometimes we were allowed to borrow this treasure.

The second valuable item possessed by Holy Joe, had once been a pair of scissors: but at that period there was only three-quarters of a pair, they having lost the half of one blade. Moreover, the blades were loose at their axis, blunt, and allowed objects to go between them in lieu of cutting them. But time being with us no object, we were enabled by their aid, using care and patience, to make some show of trimming our hair and beards; this was achieved by seizing two or three hairs at a time between forefinger and thumb, and then gradually sawing and masticating them off with the remaining portions of the scissor blades.

The third treasure was part of a dulled and cheap German looking-glass, two or three inches across. It partook of the nature of those curved magic mirrors I have seen at exhibitions, which distort the physiognomy of the gazer. But such as it was, by enabling us to look at ourselves in it, it became an endless source of interest, if not of delight. I shall never again laugh at my monkey cousin at the Zoo for doing this same thing in the future. This mirror was the most popular, if the least useful, of all the Priest's treasures.

Holy Joe was a useful man and a handy fellow, and I learned many arts from him. How to twist a rope from grass, holding it in my toes. How to darn, and also how to make a woollen thread which would draw, from scattered pieces of wool. My accomplishments increased mightily as the days advanced, and this last was not the least of them. Let any reader who doubts this try it for himself.

# Chapter 20

# Achmed Departs

Referring to my diary, I find that on December 2nd nearly all our shoes were already worn out, and that we were rapidly becoming barefoot. Most of us had been wearing the Arab slippers, supplied at the Caves only three weeks before; but we had marched several hundred miles in them and had no means of repairing them. I do not know if white men, accustomed to wearing boots all their lives, can ever become habituated to go barefoot. Certainly none of us ever did in this stony wilderness, and it was an exquisite pain to carefully pick our way over a hundred yards. We did not even possess rag which we could bind round our feet; hence walking was a slow and painful progress, except over the sandy patches.

That afternoon an old woman hobbled up to the camp with four or five sheep and kids for sale, and approached Achmed. Although he had more than a hundred pounds of our money, he informed me that her prices were prohibitive, and he refused to buy any of them. Dejectedly we watched the old woman depart with what we had hoped would be our supper, but apparently she did not go very far. That same night there was an uproar in the camp; a wolf had made off with one of the sheep! Immediately there followed a tremendous fusillade of rifles, amid which the scared wolf made off, dropping his prey. In the result we were given three-quarters of the sheep's: carcase. Achmed could now buy cheap, and we had our mutton after all, the first meat any of us had tasted for fifteen days. A desert sheep has little more flesh upon it than has a well-fed English rabbit, so the reader need not picture us partaking of a gluttonous feast, such as that on the camel; the ninety-five of us had each something under an ounce of meat and sinew per head!

The before mentioned feast on the putrid camel; who got drowned in the well, occurred nearly a week later, and for my effort in saving it Achmed awarded me (at my own request) a prize of a ship's biscuit, which I shared with no one. The joy of having something hard to bite, after living for so long on soft food, is a pleasant memory which still dwells with me.

Some of the men had an idea that the officers were getting more food than they themselves were receiving, and they watched our tent, and the ingoing and outgoings, with the utmost, jealousy. Representatives from each mess were always present when food arrived, and when it was portioned off, and this division was done with more scrupulous care than would even be the case with money payments. The officers shared exactly with the men, and there was no real shadow of cause for the latter's suspicion; but make a man hungry enough, and he will suspect his own shadow of trying to rob him!

We had a small one pound jam-tin for measuring out the rice and barley-flour. The meat we cut and tore up as well as we were able with a blunt and ancient sword bayonet and some sharp stones; it was no easy matter to divide it into exact proportions according to the number of men in each mess.

We were living very much after the customs of the men of the Stone Age, to whom iron was unknown, and there was not even proper flint in the vicinity, though some of the stones resembled it.

All our knives were taken away from us when we landed, but two or three of the worst ones were returned to us at our urgent solicitation; but they were little better than hoop-iron and almost useless. A stone was a more practicable cutting and scraping instrument.

Needles there were none, so again we had been reduced to the cave-man's methods. A shin-bone of a goat was about the best raw material, and, starting from this with a fragment three or four inches long, a hole was bored in it with a splinter of glass. This hole having once been bored in the bone, it formed the eye of the needle, and working with this eye as the central point, one or two days' hard work followed, while the bone was rubbed down on either side of it against a piece of hard rock into a pointed instrument; it formed a quite serviceable darner when finished. By means of it, the more naked were able to make themselves clothes out of old rice sacks. Mr. Marsh, one of the mates, was quite an expert at this sort of tailoring, and the blue stripe on the sack, when properly disposed, gave quite a natty if lizard-like appearance to the wearer; but he had many rivals. Buttons were made from stones, with a piece of sacking tied round them. For thread we used some priceless yarns drawn from an old sail. We also twisted up the sheep's wool gathered from thorns and from the fleeces of defunct animals.

These bone needles, by the way, I found to be absolutely identical with some ancient Roman ones dug up near Newcastle-on-Tyne. I have still got three of mine, of which one is broken. The very greatest care had to be used in their employment, as they were so fragile.

When we had meat, we generally stewed it with our rice, roasting being by far too wasteful a method. When all the goodness had thus been boiled out into the soup, the fragments of meat were carefully collected and portioned. This portioning could, of course, never be exact enough to satisfy everybody, and we therefore had recourse to chance for allotting it. One of our party went outside the tent, where, of course, he could not see what was taking place inside. The cook on the inside then held up a piece of meat, and cried out, "Who is to have this?" The one outside mentioned a, name, and so on with each fragment, until all had been portioned off. The same procedure took place when bread or dough-boys were distributed. It caused a pleasurable diversion for us, and the risk of a quarrel or fight was eliminated. Hard necessity was the force which compelled us to adopt these methods.

Even in the officers' mess there were those who were not above suspicion. Thefts of food occurred on more than one occasion. The culprit or culprits were never discovered. If they had been, though I do not think we should have killed them, we should certainly have flogged them within an inch of their lives, and driven them forth for ever out of the tent, to fend as best they could in the open!

Of course, none of us had anywhere where we could lock up things; but we all had some little corner, some stone, under which we could keep our treasures. But things of such value as food, thread, or needles were always carried about on the person. One took no chances with them.

For some time past, our small garrison had been out scouring the country for camels, which they commandeered from the unfortunate owners without any payment whatever; but if the owner liked to accompany his beasts, he got a small daily dole of rice (about half our starvation ration), in lieu of payment.

Achmed was never tired of expressing his contempt for the British, whose troops only fought because they were well paid to do so.

He, on the contrary, like the rest of the Turkish forces, lived practically on the promises of what they might hope to get at the end of the campaign, and any little pickings in the way of loot which came to them in the meantime. It struck me, though, that he had feathered his own nest pretty well already for the start, with what he had collected from us prisoners.

However, on December 15th, having raked together a caravan of forty camels, he departed about 11 a.m. He announced that his destination was Sollum (then in Senussi hands, though we did not altogether believe it), and he promised (promises were always cheap with him) that he would return in time for Christmas Day, bringing with him good store of food, and even luxuries such as eggs, for that festal occasion; for, having been baptised a Christian, he knew all about such things, a matter which the simple Senussi could hardly be expected to do.

We watched his caravan disappear out of sight to the east-north-east, speculating as we gazed as to what his journey would in reality bring forth. He was the first of the rats to leave the sinking ship of our hopes; we were to become used to seeing our rulers depart one by one, as our affairs became more desperate. Only three of us ever saw Achmed again; they were myself, Mr. Dudgeon (the chief officer) and Basil.

Achmed having gone, Mahomet Zoué, the magnificent but kind-hearted Senussi officer, whom I have already mentioned for his humanity, now became the supreme arbiter of our fate.

We all felt a sense of relief at Achmed's absence and, strange as it may seem, the days appeared to slip by surprisingly quickly. It was but two and a half weeks since our arrival at Bir Hakkim, that most desolate spot on earth, but we had already to a certain extent acclimatised ourselves to the surroundings. We had thrown off in great measure our fear and depression; the Senussi we had actually had dealings with, though rough and ready in their savage methods, were not lacking in kindness of heart. We kept ourselves fully occupied with our cooking, washing, vermin hunting, and the collection of snails and firewood. It was a dog's life, but dogs are not unhappy once they become used to it, and hope of release by exchange was not yet dead in our breasts. We were all lighter-hearted now than at any time since landing; one sometimes even heard a laugh, though no one could err from truth so far as to describe us as being gay. But our tempers, owing to the continuous strain of hunger, were deplorable. The least little incident, and everyone boiled over; but it did no harm and served to ease our feelings.

The men from time to time had a fight of sorts; invariably over the food question. Though officially I had a stern eye for such matters, I fear I also occasionally took up an unostentatious position on the outside of the ring, where, owing to my height, I could get a good view; but, to our regret, these tussles never lasted long. Mahomet Zoué or Holy Joe rapidly got wind of the affair, and intervened. I tried to explain to them that it was a British custom, and that the men were hitting each other in all friendliness for sport. But as apparently Senussi ideas of fisticuffs comprehended disembowelling and stabbing with knives, and sudden death, my plea was ineffective, and the combatants were separated by the priest with his elephant whip.

Perhaps, too, it was the lack of tobacco which was as answerable as anything else for our irritability. It was a month since we had our last smoke, and some of us felt it pretty badly. The pipe-smokers were the most philosophic about the deprivation, and had now got used to it. But the cigarette smokers were inconsolable, and so remained to the end.

Our minute daily dole of tea, having been boiled five or six times for a beverage, was then carefully collected and dried by the nicotine worshippers, after which it was carefully rolled in precious scraps of paper and smoked. The smell of this burning mixture, however, was so horrible that we sternly prohibited it being indulged in within twenty yards of the tent.

One or two of the men collected and dried mosses and lichens and smoked these, in many cases making themselves seriously ill by so doing; but the next day they were at it again.

# CHAPTER 21

# The Second Rat

On Friday, December 17th, Thomas Owen, the runaway, the man who escaped while we were on the march a month before, was brought back. Mahomet Zoué received him with every mark of indignation, and we were prepared to see him publicly flogged or some such similar punishment administered, after all we had been told of the Senussi by Achmed and the Turks. But to our pleased surprise, Mahomet contented himself with merely smacking Owen's face and then causing him to be confined in the dry well for a few hours. Whether the man was still wandering in his mind, or whether fear kept his tongue tied, I do not know, but I was never able to ascertain what his wanderings and adventures had been. Apparently, however, he had been at Sollum, and had been kindly treated, and was better off than ourselves in every respect; the piece of soap and the boxes of matches which he brought with him were sufficient proof of this.

On the same day that Owen returned a little rain fell. It was the second shower we had had at Bir Hakkim, but it fortunately did not amount to much. Mahomet Zoué was much more approachable than Achmed ever was, and I talked much to him through Basil, as he, unfortunately, had no English. He was at one time head man at Ben Ghazi, but left it when the Italians took possession, though his wife and family still remained there. He was a saddened man, and knowing something of civilisation, liked this homeless, barbarous life little better than we did; the task of doing gaoler to us prisoners was obviously distasteful to him. He indignantly denied that the Italian prisoners were badly treated or killed by the Senussi, and said that in reality their treatment compared favourably with our own. He held out high hopes of our release by exchange, and stated that if this had not taken place within six months, it would be the fault of the British, as the Senussi themselves were quite willing to effect it. He also pointed out that if it were really their intention to keep us as prisoners indefinitely, we should long ago have been marched into the interior, instead of being kept so comparatively close at hand.

With these and similar conversations I was much cheered and was able to cheer others. Not yet had we learnt the lesson that neither Turk nor Bedouin can tell the truth to save their own lives. Through lying so consistently to us, as will appear later, these poor and in many ways kindly folk, actually did lose their lives.

The desert scrub had already taken heart at the dampness of the atmosphere, the night fogs, and the sprinkle of rain. The stunted bushes are already putting forth sweet-scented and aromatic leaves.

We were now informed that Achmed was not returning after all as he had promised; our expectations of Christmas dainties begin to fade, but we did not yet abandon all hope that something might turn up.

On Sunday, December 19th, the last sugar remaining was issued to us, and we were told that there would be no more; by common consent we agreed to save this up for Christmas Day. Our minute dole of tea disappeared some time before, so there was no tiring to vary the rice except our two ounces of goat on alternate days, and the rare issues of barley-flour. How delicious these two cereals are, alone and unadorned, and how little folk at home appreciate them! But then, they had not our privilege of cooking them over a camp fire, nor of that "hunger which is the best sauce." Our tea we missed sadly, though the amount which at any time we got of it was always microscopic, and it always depended upon the humour of Mahomet's cook as to how much that amount was. We had got into the habit of making quite a social function of our tea-drinking, assembling together round the fire about an hour after sunset and brewing it

Arab fashion with the sugar in. Sometimes we only got one tiny tumbler each, more often two, and on one ever-to-be-remembered occasion, it worked out to three cups each. Those who had broken their glasses borrowed from others or used instead small Italian tomato tins, which they had somehow acquired, and the same size as the smallest of potted meat tins. These tins held as much as two tumblers, and were very carefully measured to see that none got more than his fair share. Seated on stones round the fire, we drank the ambrosia, and even at times burst into song, impelled thereto by the cup which " cheers but not inebriates." At such times, with burnous wrapped tightly round our persons, screened from the wind, soothed by the velvet sky and twinkling stars of a desert night, we forgot for a moment the solitude, the sadness, the squalor, hunger and danger of our position. I have had more unhappy moments surrounded by all the comforts of civilisation and the consciousness of a full stomach.

The Red Doctor well had now been thoroughly cleared out and cemented by the working party, and was ready for the storage of the expected winter rains. The only cement available was a small sack of Portland cement brought on a camel, and by some means it had got wet on the way, and was at first as hard as cement can be. But Mahomet was not easily put off a tiling once he had made up his mind to it! Half-a-dozen of the crew were daily put to work to break up this cement, which they did by hammering it on rocks with stones for hammers, after which the dust was passed through a string sieve. To my astonishment the resultant powder was then as good for cementing as before it had been wetted. I certainly never heard of this property in cement before; but as it took half-a-dozen men a whole week to obtain one sackful, I hardly think it will be employed on a large scale in England as a result of this discovery.

Five days before Christmas the men were put to work on another well situated between the Red and White Doctors in the open plain. It was entirely filled in and covered over with sand, and we had not hitherto suspected its existence; but Holy Joe, who knew of it, induced Mahomet to put our men to work on it. It greatly interested me, it being of quite a different pattern to those we had hitherto encountered, and I should imagine it was more ancient than the comparatively speaking modern Roman wells, which were the only ones we had hitherto seen.

This well was much smaller, and it had steps leading down to the interior on one side. It was blocked by large masses of stone as well as with sand and rubble; some of these stones were far too heavy for any rains to have washed them into it. From this, and from the fact that it had no mound marking it, I surmised that it had been deliberately filled in, a state of affairs which excited my curiosity as I could not account for it. When the men had excavated a certain distance, it was discovered that there was a fault in the rock which made the well incapable of retaining water; the original diggers had obviously then abandoned their work, and the well had never been completed. It was while employed in digging here that one of the men found an antique object which I never saw, but which he described as being an ancient Egyptian seal. The possession of this treasure-trove he kept secret and buried it under the floor of his tent. There it probably still remains, for in the excitement of our final good-bye to Bir Hakkim he unfortunately forgot all about it!

At last the long-expected caravan arrived from Sollum on the 22nd of December. It consisted of nine camels only, but at its advent our spirits rose at the thought that they carried our long-expected Christmas delicacies! To our very great dismay it brought rice and barley-flour only. No boots, no clothes, no sugar, tea nor biscuit. Bagged and barefoot our last hope of a Merry Christmas now fled from us.

With this caravan came rumours that we were to be transferred to another camp at Siva. Basil had heard of the place and could tell us something about it, but not much. Siva was a very ancient town, and as I know now, about two hundred and fifty miles across trackless deserts from our then position. Situated there is the ancient Egyptian temple of Amnion, and I fancy it was this place that Nouri Pacha had in his mind when he said he would send our men to an oasis where they would have every comfort, and would be employed in excavating the relics of a bygone age. An oasis Siva certainly is; but from all accounts it is an unhealthy one, where malarial fever is ripe. But how they could possibly have transported our wretched sailors, enfeebled, rotten with dysentery, such a distance at this date, does not appear. We were quite incapable of the journey.

On December 23rd we had five hours' steady rain, after due warning had been given by the loud braying of Holy Joe's asses the night before. The water poured through our sieve-like and rotten tent, and we all spent the day standing in order to keep as dry as possible; but we were all bitterly cold, wet and exhausted before it was over. Of course we had no change of clothes, and people with dry clothes, a roof, and a bed to sleep in, can have no idea of the utter discomfort and misery a little wet may cause. The have gots can never picture the feelings of the have nots, until they themselves have actually experienced some of the latter's privations.

There was no escaping the weather; no dry clothes; no warming food, no anything—we were just caged rats, almost without hope.

But a merciful Providence was on our side once more, though we, in our terror-stricken fears, knew it not. The winter proved to be abnormally dry at Bir Hakkim, almost rainless. The fate which seemed so near was averted.

On this occasion we lit our fire inside the tent, the smoke partly escaping through the tattered roof. Arabs never do this, and invariably have their fired outside, as the smoke and heat rot the tent fabric; but we threw care for the future to the winds, our present necessities for dryness and warmth being too great.

The next day, Christmas Eve, we put all our energy into building low walls round the tent and digging trenches outside them; by these means we hoped to divert some of the streams of water which flowed over us.

This day a Turkish officer, Lieut. Mustapha, visited us on his way to Sollum from the west. He took our mails with him, and was evidently impressed by the squalor, misery and want of our surroundings; and he promised to interview Nouri Bey on our behalf. He also had once been a prisoner of the Bulgarians; and one who has himself been a prisoner can never again be deaf to the sigh of other captives. These mails of ours were delivered in

England on February 15th, together with earlier letters we had sent, and they told our friends at home of our safe existence until Christmas Eve. These letters comforted our relatives as they had been intended to do, but it seems incredible now that no one could read between the lines. We well knew that nothing unfavourable to our captors would be allowed to pass the censor; our comments, therefore, were very guarded, but still . . .

Here are some extracts (with italics added by me at a later date) from the letter I wrote on that occasion:—

December 24.—This is Christmas Eve. A Turkish officer is passing through our camp on his way to Sollum, and has kindly promised to take letters for us. I have no idea when they will be able to go on from there; but General Nouri Pacha is so kind that I am sure he has made some arrangements by now through Geneva or some other way. We have had no news of our homes or the outside world for some weeks, and we long to get letters and to know that our dear ones know that we are alive. We shall think a lot of you all to-morrow (Christmas Day), and I know you will think of us. Our time is two hours earlier than yours. We have been starving ourselves for a week so as to have a good feed, and this is a list of our good things. Don't they make your mouth water?

Two kids (legs and ribs only) between ninety-five of us.

A pudding (rice boiled and mixed with flour and a long saved lump of sugar).

Soup made from the meat and thickened with flour and rice, and some salt if we can get it.

Boiled rice—half a pound each.

We were hoping for tea and sugar as well, but they have not arrived in time. But in any case we will have a lovely big feed and go to bed not a bit hungry. We will sing Christmas carols round the fire in the evening, or, at least as much of them as we can remember.

It rained yesterday—the first for eleven months—and we got very wet and cold, but in God's mercy it is fine again to-day and we are dry again. We are building up stone walls round our tent, so I hope we will not feel it so much when the rains really start.

I have kept wonderful health and have had no dysentery or anything the matter with me so far. But I shall be very glad when more clothes, shoes and some soap arrive, as it is very cold at night. We wonder much how the War is going on, but food is our main and nearly sole topic of conversation and engrosses all our energy. We have all got tents of sorts to cover us now, and the Senussi officer in charge of us is kindness itself, but he can get very little in this desert country.

The men eat enormous quantities of snails, but I have not taken to them yet, and am entirely a vegetarian. I exchange my half ounce of meat for part of another man's rice ration, an arrangement that suits both of us. I get quantity and he gets quality. We hope some day to get onion, oil, or tomato sauce to flavour our rice with; it will be a very great treat.

# CHAPTER 22

# Christmas

Christmas Day dawned sunny and bright, but with a very chilly feeling in the air.

We had our Christmas robin redbreast, for one of the natives had captured one, they being fairly common birds near the sea coast. And now Mahmoud, the bright-eyed merry foot-boy of Mahomet Zoué, was exhibiting it with childhood's usual indifference to the feelings of its pets; the poor little feathered captive had already lost its tail, but with our assistance it eventually escaped.

We had an extraordinarily tender feeling now for anything held prisoner; the sight of the bird moved me to tears, and one wondered with horror how one could have ever enjoyed seeing the Zoo, or have oneself kept wild birds and small animals in cages.

Christmas Day being a Saturday the men should have gone to work at well clearing as usual; but, by special dispensation, they were allowed the day off on condition that they worked on Sunday to make up for it.

Captain Tanner, Apcar and I began the day by paying a visit of ceremony to Mahomet Zoué—that is, if one may describe as a ceremonial call the limping procession of us three bare-footed, verminous, and shirtless derelicts, to the cowshed tenanted by Mahomet, and grandiloquently designated block-house.

Our reception was cordial, and it terminated, as we had all along hoped, by our being offered a light repast of Arab bread with sugar to eat with it, than which, for a hungry man, no mere pastry-cook's wares could for a moment compare. And what was more, before we went away, Mahomet dipped into a sack and presented us with a double handful of white beans; a gift for the officers' mess.

Those beans, so long as I have life and intelligence, I shall never forget them. We put them into the soup, and we all revelled in the un-hoped-for, un-dreamt-of luxury.

Following the custom of the Navy, Captain Tanner and I went round the various tents to visit each mess in succession at the dinner-hour and to wish the men a "Merry Christmas"—a pleasant persiflage which evoked many wry faces. The men had not yet learnt to be provident, and many, although it was then only midday, had already eaten their whole day's rations. This meant that they would have to go hungry until 9 a.m. the next morning, unless they had become habituated to eating the celebrated Libyan lily-white snails.

I have no doubt that these snails helped materially to nourish us and to preserve our lives, and the men ate daily increasing numbers of them. I myself have eaten them, but I never was able to overcome my horror of their repulsive appearance—the green slime of the water in which they were boiled, the grey, limp, inert masses of jellified gristle which emerged when the water was poured away, the eyed horns, the curled forefoot and tail. Ugh! With vinegar, with salt, with a taste of bread or rice to put with them, I might have managed. In Paris I was very fond of escargots of the same family, daintily cooked with herbs in their shells. But here we had no vinegar; salt was generally unprocurable; bread and rice were scarce commodities. To eat these lily-whites in their unadorned pristine nakedness was more than my nerves were equal to; my aversion to them would have made them into a poison; the ultimate and final stages of starvation could not make me do it.

But many of the men by now fairly gorged them, and I have no doubt that snails formed the bulk of their Christmas fare.

For readers who are interested I give herewith the recipe for cooking snails as practised at Bir Hakkim Abbyat. It, is copied from The Black Hole of the Desert, a book compiled from the diary of that stout Yeoman of Signals and trencherman, Allen, who served with me all the days of the captivity, and also subsequently in the Arctic Squadron. It runs as follows:—

"Take as many Libyan (lily-white) snails as may be required and submerge them in water which has been brought to the boil, taking care in the meanwhile that the snails have not escaped from their shells. Boil brilliantly for two minutes, when the snails will come out of the shells of their own accord. Throw away shells and boil snails for ten minutes. If hard-boiled snail is required much less time is needed. Serve according to what garnish is available. If no plates, saucepan should be passed round."

By this date we had tidied up the camp considerably. Each tent had a low wall or bank built round it to keep some of the torrents of water from running directly through the tents down the slope, as they otherwise inevitably did. Bach tent also had a small enclosure marked off with white stones, coastguard fashion, and this was brushed daily with a handful of twigs. The officers had, in addition, marked off a larger space known as the quarter-deck, which they reserved exclusively for themselves. These spaces were useful, as they were the only spot for miles round upon which you could walk barefoot, without stubbing your toes on the stones. In addition, there was a path we had also marked out to the well which was very useful in the twilight and dark, if one wished to avoid severe contusions and abrasions.

This Christmas morning the petty officers' tent, at any rate, looked quite festive. Quartermaster Abbitt, who had suffered more than any one else from dysentery, and was quite unable to move, had been carried out into the sunshine, and his pinched face smiled up bravely as we arrived. If ever there was a triumph of mind over matter, that triumph was his. For four months he was practically unable to move, racked with the most violent dysentery. But he never for one moment gave up heart; his courage and cheerfulness helped to inspire all of us, and he received even then his reward, for where others died he returned at long last to his home in Wales, safe and rejoicing.

We could not foresee this then, but we did begin to see the love and happiness with which such conduct always surround the man.

It helped me to understand in part the answer to that problem which had so puzzled me at the Caves when poor William Thomas had passed on. The question then was, as to what it profited a man to be kind, unselfish and forbearing, when in the end we would, as far as we could see, all be stuck in a hole in the ground, and the memory of our good deeds perish with us.

Loving shipmates always tended poor Abbitt day and night: Milward, the naval seaman-gunner, being always conspicuous by his devotion, as also he ever was to his naval work.

But to-day, the petty officers had made their surroundings as bright as the inhuman squalor in which we lived permitted. With white snail shells they had formed lettered inscriptions designating the different localities. For instance, their own shack they labelled Hope Villa, and the paths leading from it into the desert were Snail Alley and Rice Walk. Three other tents were labelled respectively Snail Villa, Cosy Corner, and Millbank. (Part of Holyhead is known by this name.) Even some of the more promising wild plants in the vicinity had been watered and cared for, and bordered by a neat little circle of white snail shells, as handsome in its way as a box edging.

In every tent there were a number of men prostrate with dysentery, many incapable of movement. To look at their companions, you would think the latter brutish, incapable of tender feeling; but never did mother tend her ailing child more gently and faithfully than did these poor wretches their stricken comrades. They would fight like wild beasts among themselves for their food, but the sick and helpless, who could do nothing for themselves, were the care and the first consideration of all.

Is this the triumph of the brute beast, of which we heard so much on our first arrival at Bir Hakkim? Or is this the apotheosis, the real meaning, of Christianity?

We were of many religions, sects and creeds; many, indeed, professed to have no religion at all; but we were all sailors in the same ship, and the same Providence ruled us all. We had started without chart or knowing anything of the course; full many a peril had our ignorance brought from storm and reef and sandbank. But now we were beginning to learn the course, the only safe course, and to watch the compass card which hid the invisible needle that guided us. That magnetic needle always pointed but one way, "To do unto others as you would be done by."

In the officers' tent we had made great preparations for Christmas. We had treasured up those few ounces of sugar given us the week before, and we had voluntarily saved a portion of our rice and flour from our meagre daily ration. On Christmas Eve we had stirred the pudding. Basil has always acted as master baker, and now our eyes fairly stuck out of our heads, and our mouths slobbered audibly, as we watched the final preparation for our feast.

First of all there was soup—our two ounces of goat go into it, also a small quantity of flour, and to-day the never-to-be-forgotten beans. Soup, we knew from experience, was apt to be a quarrelsome course as we had no plates, and only one enamelled iron wash-basin out of which we ate in common. Therefore the soup could not be distributed into portions as the rest, of our food invariably was; we had to make other arrangements. The liquid having cooled sufficiently, we formed a circle round the basin, and then dipped our spoons in together. Each had exactly the same number of dips, and we kept time like rowers, one selected acting as stroke. It was rare for us to get through our soup without a quarrel. Perhaps someone accidentally knocked another with his elbow, and spilt part of his spoonful. Or a super-sensitive individual objected that another was holding his head too much over the basin and dribbling into it. It only took a word, and all our tempers were aflame, such irritability does continuous hunger breed. But today, and with the anticipation of better to follow, the soup course is amicably passed.

Next came the fragments of goat that had been boiled in the soup, and also tiny dough-boys, distributed by lot. To enjoy these, we retired to various corners, and gnawed them as a dog a bone. When we had finished, there was always someone grateful if you would give him your gnawed bone; one of the men specialised in this, and was generally waiting at the tent-door; he could eat practically the whole bone, and if there was still any fragments of bone left when he has done with it, Paddy was the beneficiary.

Then came the piece de resistance, the pudding! Petty Officer pudding we named it, after its inceptor in the petty officers' tent. It was made from barley-flour, into which the precious sugar and a certain proportion of boiled rice had been kneaded, and Ave sat up late boiling it. It was boiled for five hours in Captain Tanner's spare pair of cotton Arab trousers, and was a gorgeous and colossal sight— as hard and as heavy as a cannon ball, weighing about twenty pounds. This gave us each nearly a pound and a half of suet-less dough, gloriously sweetened, and permitting twenty minutes of heavenly mastication!

Truly this may sound a formidable meal to civilised digestions ruined by indulgence. But to us, it will ever be memorable as the most enjoyable feast of our lives; whatever our other pains may be, indigestion is one that has long since departed from us.

Besides this titanic mid-day meal, we also had rations of rice for breakfast, and more rice with ash-cooked bread for supper. Such a day more than made amends for all the saving, scraping and starving we had gone through during the week.

After dark, when the stars came out, we gathered round the fire outside and made a lusty attempt to sing Christmas carols, but with the best of intentions they were a difficulty. We all knew, or thought we knew, the tunes, but the words, having heard them but once a year or less, had quite escaped us. For weeks before we had tried to recall *Hark, the Herald Angels Sing*, but no one could take us beyond the first verse. So that, sung over and over again, and followed by some of *When Shepherds Watched Their Flocks by Night*, had to satisfy us.

That night, as we lay down to sleep, with our ears to the ground, many of us believed we heard the distant rumble and mutter of guns. It was probably only thunder grumbling away to the north, where they had much rain about this time. But it helped to hearten us, and made us hope that even then our friends were taking steps to help us. It was sweet music in our ears. We wanted no angel harps that Christmas; we wanted the crash and roar of British cannon, the smoke and flare of battle, the glitter of bayonets!

Presently our ears were smitten by a loud howling which

came from the Arab tents. It was the voice of women, bewailing in their Eastern way the death of their bread-winners. A messenger had just come in, as we learned, with news of Senussi casualties, and our guards looked angrily and menacingly at us.

We lay down that night, and slept as we had not before slept, with hunger fully removed for the first time, and with it departed most of our persistent worries and anxieties.

And though neither we nor our gaolers then knew it, our salvation had drawn appreciably nearer.. Two hundred miles away the British troops had attacked the Turkish camp, and the Battle of Christmas Day had been fought and victoriously ended.

I like to think the rumbling we heard that Christmas night was the sound of British guns; it is just possible that it may have been so. In that flat and silent country, with the thin damp atmosphere, and an ear to the ground, it was possible to hear at incredible distances. But, unfortunately, I have also recorded in my diary several other dates upon which we thought we heard distant gun-fire, and on none of those other dates can I learn of any artillery action having taken place.

# CHAPTER 23

# The Battles of Christmas Day and January 23rd (or Halazin)

It is time for me to revert once more to the military situation, a subject which I last discussed briefly in Chapter 14. In that chapter I carried events as far as December 17th, 1915, and I will now take them to the close of January, 1916.

At Christmas time, and during the months which followed it, events of great importance to the prisoners' future were taking place on the western Egyptian frontier, although, like the man in the cellar whom I have before pictured, we were quite ignorant of what was really going on; only distorted echoes of events in the outer world reached our ears. For the rest, we lived in fable and imagination.

For the main incidents of these two battles of Christmas Day and Halazin, I am indebted to a most interesting article in *Blackwood's Magazine* for February, 1917, entitled 'In the Western Desert of Egypt'. I have also made use of press cuttings of the day and of accounts given to me by men who actually witnessed these events.

Shortly before Christmas, British scouting aeroplanes brought news that there was an enemy concentration in a deep and tortuous wadi—one of those ravines similar to the Dry Dock, which run down to the sea-coast. This ravine was only seven or eight miles west of the British lines at Mersa Matruh, at a place called Wadi Merjid.

Jaffir (or Gaafir) Pacha, the Turco-Senussi Commander-in-

Chief, had by now come to the conclusion that if his somewhat faint-hearted Senussi allies were to be kept actively on his side, it was necessary for him to do something more than sit down and watch the British lines at Matruh, and talk of the riches of Egypt. The advance must be continued at any cost; and he determined to resume the offensive. With this end in view, he made every preparation to attack on Christmas night, having a firm conviction in his mind that he would then find a great part of the British forces hors de combat as a result of their Christmas carousals. Unfortunately, however, the premises on which he reasoned were faulty, for, if he could but have known it, there was not a drop of liquor in the whole British camp. Moreover, Christmas Day was the very day selected by the British General himself to pay Jaffir an unexpected visit!

An hour before daybreak on December 25th, 1915, the British were already on the move—horse, foot and artillery—hoping to surprise Jaffir. But the wily Turk was not so easily to be caught napping; our troops had gone but a short distance, when, from a neighbouring hill-top, a beacon-fire was seen to blaze out. The cavalry sent- to investigate this phenomenon were received by a mixed fire from ancient weapons, jezails and the like, discharged by Jaffir's Bedouin scouts, which, however, did no damage to the horsemen. Dawn was now breaking, and its advent was heralded by a deep booming from seaward; it was the British sloops Annabel and Clematis beginning to shell the ravine of Wadi Merjid, where the Senussi camp was situated. The range was extreme, but the shells were dropping to a nicety in the desired location. As our troops advanced, they could see the smoke and dust on the hills in front of them where the naval projectiles burst.

The British land forces continued their advance, and, coming to some three thousand yards from the enemy, the latter opened fire with his nine-pounder mountain guns. The infantry then deployed and our own horse artillery battery got going, very soon spotting the enemy guns, and with their second round knocking out one of his weapons. This was proved when our subsequent advance discovered a dented shield and broken gun-wheels on the spot where our shell had been seen to fall.

While the artillery action was in progress our infantry were by no means idle, but advanced rapidly across the open plain, and started the steep climb towards the enemy in the hills: for a while it looked as if they might have a bad time of it.

But there was still another unpleasant surprise for Jaffir; he suddenly discovered that two mounted yeomanry regiments, supported by guns, had worked round in his rear. This discovery at once took the heart out of the Senussi defence; with the naval sloops enfilading the ravine, aircraft at close quarters dropping bombs from overhead, the British infantry in front, the yeomanry in rear, and their guns outmatched, they were very glad to beat a hasty retreat. In this, they were only saved from annihilation by the broken nature of the ground, which allowed of their rearguard to holding for a sufficient time the British infantry panting up the slope. By this means they were able to escape by the only gap left—the interval between the cavalry and the sea-coast.

The British then proceeded to burn the enemy camp, and captured there large quantities of ammunition, camels, prisoners and barley; the loss of the barley especially was a great blow to the enemy, in view of the shortness of food supplies caused by a vigorous blockade and the failure that year to sow or reap crops. Desultory fighting among the shelters and rock-caverns of the ravine continued until dark, the British bivouacking for the night on the scene of battle and returning to their base at Matruh the next day. The Turco-Senussi forces themselves made a hasty retreat westward, many of them in a state of panic, a state which was not diminished by the hearty shelling which they received from our sloops whenever the fugitives came within sight of the coast. The Senussi especially, who a month before had started the campaign with such rosy dreams of loot and the conquest of Egypt, were already beginning be sadly disillusioned.

It was during this battle of Christmas Day, that an incident occurred which directly affected us prisoners at, Bir Hakkim. It will be remembered that shortly after getting to the Dry Dock on November 15th, we had been joined by Lieut. Apcar and three other Europeans from the torpedoed horse transport

Moorina. Although at, the time we did not see them, there were also near at hand thirty-six other Indian natives, horse-keepers from the same vessel, who had landed with Apcar. The Senussi, discovering that these Indians understood the handling of camels, employed the majority of them as camel-drivers, and in this capacity many of them witnessed the battle of Christmas Day. the Indians, finding themselves unexpectedly near the British lines during a rapid advance, made a dash for liberty, and thirty-one out of thirty-six thus succeeded in escaping and rejoining the British. Of the remaining five Indians, three who were Mohammedans were not present, being regarded as honoured guests by the Turks and living in luxury at Sollum. But the other two, non-Mohammedan Rajputs, were sent, to join us other prisoners at Bir Hakkim. They arrived there on January 17th, and through them we were enabled to obtain a transitory glimpse of some of the events then happening in the outside world.

On January 3rd very heavy rains commenced on the coast, transforming the desert littoral into a sea of mud of the most clinging description, its constituents of lime, clay and sand making of it for the time a morass in which the naval armoured cars and wheeled transport wallowed up to the axles, and rendered their further movement impossible.

That the Senussi were much impressed by the—to them—unexpected results of the Battle of Christmas Day, was evidenced by one of their Chiefs presenting himself at the British camp on January 7th and suing for peace. But on January 16th he got his stern and final answer, that there would be no peace for the Senussi until the Tara prisoners were given up. I think it probable, though I have no definite evidence, that it was at this time that, the prisoners' letters home (the last of which were dated Christmas Eve) were then turned over to the British, and were sent to England, arriving there in the middle of February.

Shortly after Christmas, further news was received that the enemy was again concentrating, this time twenty-six miles to the westward of Matruh, and inland of the Khedivial road which runs along the coast. It was believed that his intention was to retreat to the oasis of Siva, and that he was only waiting until he could commandeer enough camels for his transport, before starting the journey. Siva (the Promised Land of the Tara prisoners) was nearly two hundred miles inland and directly south from the coast,; if once the enemy could succeed in getting his forces there, it would have been at that time quite impracticable to follow him across the deserts. If his retreat, to this safe harbourage were to be prevented, it was necessary to attack him at once.

In spite of our need for haste, the weather was so bad, with continued rain-storms, rendering the desert impassable mud, that the British were unable to move. But late on the afternoon of January 22nd, during a temporary improvement in the weather, a start was made.

Our forces, now comprising Territorials, Yeomanry and New Zealanders, marched to Bir Shola,, where they arrived about 10 p.m., and fortunately found a well of good sweet water. The night was black as pitch, the rain had re-commenced, and the weather was cold and stormy. Entrenching and making the camp secure after dark in such conditions was no holiday task, and all were rejoiced when, after a sleepless night, the force again marched at, dawn on January 23rd. There was no track, and the troops marched on a compass bearing towards the spot where aircraft had located the enemy, which was known by the name of Halazin. It was heavy going; the mud more than ankle deep, and the strain of the previous day's march and the disturbed night soon began to tell. The pace got slower and slower; many men fell out with sore feet or hobbled along as best they could. It seemed a wild goose-chase, and every moment the men were getting more despondent and helpless, when the cavalry, who with some guns were a couple of miles away on the left, sighted the enemy forces and fired a few rounds of shrapnel at them.

The sound of the guns at once produced a magical effect upon our tired men, who cheered and at once quickened their pace, many actually breaking into a jog-trot in their eagerness to attack. The enemy's position was on a slight rise above the level desert, and his strength was unknown, but believed to be considerable. However, our troops advanced rapidly across the two miles of open plain still intervening.

As the sun rose, the mirage raised by its heat caused observation to become extremely difficult, and to an European it was often impossible to decide whether objects seen were men, camels or bushes. Under such atmospheric conditions nothing retains its true outline, and objects are multiplied indefinitely. Our guns in the centre soon came into action, and every instant the battle increased in intensity. The British, advancing as they were in the open, had no cover of any kind against the showers of bullets which fell constantly even in the field-dressing station. During the morning, the enemy succeeded in driving in our cavalry, but failed in the attack on our right flank. Shortly afterwards it was seen that he was closing in around the British left rear. To prevent such a calamity, two of our guns concentrated against the threatened danger, and the infantry reserves counter-attacking, the Senussi enveloping movement was quickly checked and broken up.

But by now the main British attack had succeeded, the enemy's camp was penetrated and burnt. Unfortunately little booty fell into our hands as the result of this achievement, for Jaffir, profiting by the lesson of Christmas Day, had already taken the precaution of removing nearly everything of value before the action commenced.

Thus far matters had turned out fairly satisfactory for the British, but they were by no means out of the wood. Their casualties already numbered four hundred and seventy, and there was no means of evacuating them, for both transport and ambulances were stuck in the mire miles away, only two miles in fact from their last night's bivouac at Bir Shola. Hence the British were reduced to the ammunition, food and water they had brought with them, and it was by no means certain that the enemy was beaten. Should he get between the British and their transport, the affair might well assume a serious aspect. Swept by a gale of rain, the exhausted troops spent the night without blankets or great coats on the field of battle, more than half anticipating that at dawn they would find the enemy all around them. It was an anxious night.

But at dawn there was no sign of the enemy; he had probably

received as much punishment as he cared about, his casualties being estimated at eight hundred, including two Germans. The British were free to begin their return journey from Halazin, the featureless spot where the battle had taken place. With the more slightly wounded mounted on cavalry horses and gun-limbers, and the seventy severe cases carried on stretchers by the troops, they started back. The labour of carrying the wounded across that sea of mud was arduous in the extreme, and in six hours they only covered six miles. Fortunately, at the end of that time, the transport and ambulances turned up, and they were able to make better progress. Yet another wretched night they were destined to spend at Bir Shola, swept by a gale of wind and rain, ere, on January 25th, they arrived once more at Matruh; from thence they were able to send the wounded by hospital ship to Alexandria.

The battle of Halazin was the hardest fought battle of all the campaign and the least decisive, but it served to clear the enemy from within striking distance of Matruh. The British up till now had been mainly on the defensive, but they had already inspired the Senussi with a respect for British arms, although they had dealt no really severe blow at him, with the exception of the food supplies which he had lost on Christmas Day. Those tireless and wonderful marchers, the Senussi, had hitherto proved too slippery and elusive a foe for us to be able to administer the sharp punishment the case required. Up till now the importance of the light armoured car for this task had not been fully realised, for the naval cars then doing duty with the forces had been hampered beyond measure by the terrible winter mud. Although they had accomplished very useful work, their true potentialities had not yet appeared. The dénouement came about when the Duke of Westminster, with his brigade of light armoured cars, arrived on the scene, which they did at this period and at the same time that the finer weather made its advent.

The naval cars finally left on January 29th, their machines sadly battered and in need of repair, after their three months' desert campaigning at the worst time of the year and leaving behind them the Petrol Hussars, as they quizzically labelled their army confrères, whose officers were mostly drawn from crack cavalry regiments. It was thus that the Navy, to its intense disgust and regret, missed the final thrilling events of the campaign.

In the meantime, the British army at Matruh settled down to organise its transport, and to collect supplies for an advance and an offensive campaign in the spring.

# CHAPTER 24

# A Promise

The day following Christmas, our guards were full of vain-glorious accounts of a battle, in which they stated that the British loss was three thousand killed and nine hundred prisoners. News takes generally about a week to get through to us from Sollum, but there are often long lapses when no caravans are passing. Messengers had come through on Christmas night, but they certainly could not then have heard even rumours of the British victory of Christmas Day. The wailing of women which we had heard that night was probably for relatives killed in some earlier fight, probably that of December 15th. We all felt very uppish after our Christmas feed, which, I suppose, normally would have nearly killed most white men. But as it was, we merely smiled at the Senussi accounts of victories, and presently Basil elicited the information that the Senussi themselves confessed to a loss of a thousand men killed! Certainly the gloominess of our guards' countenances did not correspond with the alleged greatness of their victory!

Our provisions, from now on, were issued to us weekly instead of daily. The actual amounts were three sacks of rice and one of barley-flour to last ninety-five men seven days. We generally got an ounce of goat's flesh per head every other day in addition; or, very occasionally, in lieu of the meat, a minute proportion of olive-oil. With the exception of a very limited amount of salt we got nothing else.

Night after night at this time, we were cheered by what we

believed to be the sound of guns, and more than once we thought we saw searchlights against the clouds; but I have no doubt now that it was thunder and lightning up to the northward, where the rainy season had now set in in earnest, and where standing in the tent, for the smoke choked and blinded one; but lying down at full length, there was a comparatively pure stratum of air just above the surface of the ground. Captain Tanner had a marvellous memory for verses and recitations, and I don't know what we should have done without him in those long winter nights, while he gave us song after song out of Gilbert and Sullivan, and from Rudyard Kipling songs and recitations not a few. His and my ideas, as to tune, generally differed, but as his voice was infinitely the more powerful of the two, and as he could always remember the words, which I could not, I did not count for much in these musical soirées! Mr. Birkby, the wireless officer, was once a choir-boy and had a remarkable voice, and we all enjoyed *Where My Caravan Has Rested*, as sung by him. But the silliest of songs appealed to us most. There was one, beloved of the Pierrots in years gone by, whose chorus is, "Drinking cider through a straw-aw-aw." How we loved it and shouted it, till the tears ran down our faces. But I suppose *Mandalay*, (to a tune invented by Captain Tanner), *A Climbing Up The Golden Stairs* and *Hey Ho! Roll a Man Down*, the old sea-song, were the prime favourites. The officers' tent was by far the most vociferous. I don't know why; most of the men were comparatively silent. But the south tent, a very ragged structure, inhabited by Welsh firemen, occasionally indulged in Welsh glees, which they sang really beautifully. I have often sat entranced, looking out on the desert night, the cold wind soughing and pale stars peeping out from between the cloud rifts, while the red fires glowed through the great rents in their tent roof, and the Welsh melody floated to my ears. It seemed to bring back the world of two thousand years ago somehow, when mistletoe grew on the oak, the Druids sacrificed their victims, and the world was young and cruel, full of surprise and romance. We also felt cruel and bloodthirsty sometimes, and there was no recitation we liked more than that gory tale of Kipling's 'The Grave of the Hundred Heads', which Captain Tanner knew by heart.

Looking back at my diary, I find that on New Year's Eve it was exactly eight weeks since we had been landed from the submarine, and that, in spite of much travail of soul, the time had passed very quickly, and we were beginning to fit into our places. We had all become accustomed to permanent hunger, squalor, dirt and discomfort. Hope ebbed and flowed, but cheerfulness was becoming more frequent, and religion deeply felt by most, and no longer hidden by the cloak of shyness. Politeness, which at one time we had almost lost in the hunger of the beast, was now not infrequently seen, and discipline, though of a strangely patriarchal and republican mixture, was well maintained, in spite of the fact that officers and men were herded indiscriminately together.

We, or rather the majority of us, washed; but there had been no soap for over a month, and we were mostly of a complexion nearly as dark as the Arabs, and a great deal more ragged than they. The three empty sacks which we had left over at the end of the week were distributed for clothing to the most necessitous, after the matter had been very carefully gone into. We were never tired of abusing what we considered to have been our meanness, because when at sea we all wore our oldest clothes, with the result that we were all now in rags. We solemnly vowed that, should we ever be torpedoed again, we should be found dressed in our Sunday best.

The average number of dysentery cases was from ten to fifteen daily; there were six others with rupture and no trusses, one man in the last stages of consumption, and another, in purgatory from stricture, had now developed uric acid poisoning. The sick had the same food as everyone else—rice, and there were no bandages, medicines, change of clothes or comforts of any kind procurable for them, nor could we even get them camel or goat's milk. It was pitiful to see their pale, wan faces, and it hurt to be so totally unable to relieve their suffering. One told the men about all the promises we had had, of food, clothes, comforts and medicines for the future—and I tried to paint the picture as brightly as possible. But I fear such fairy tales no longer convinced or heartened the despondent; they already know too well the value of an Arab's promise! But even though our New

Year came at the coldest, darkest, and stormiest season, yet in it we could already see promise of better things, of hopes reborn. The sand-grouse, which, ever since our arrival, had haunted the camp in the early morning to get some of the water-drippings around the well, had departed; there was now sufficient moisture for them to exist elsewhere. Every morning Mahomet used to stalk them and have a pot-shot or two at them with his rifle, and the whirr of their wings as they flew off, was one of the first things we heard each recurring day. Finches, larks and wag-tails splash wherever there was a puddle; they were evidently already considering the question of mating. Many of the desert shrubs made brave efforts to put out a green leaf or two, and strange-looking tendrils and beak-shaped buds were pushing their heads from unexpected places in the sand. Even the celebrated lily-white Libyan snail, now sadly thinned in numbers, showed signs of waking up, and began to soften the celluloid-like door which, for many a moon, had sealed the entrance to his tabernacle. We were a surly-looking crowd, but in truth our hearts were soft. The cravings of hunger and the longing for meat, often caused me to wander for miles throwing stones in a vain effort to knock over a lark or other small bird. Basil, observing my fruitless efforts, had a brain-wave, one of many, for he was ever the Admirable Crichton. He still possessed the rubber life-belt in which he landed, and from this he cut several strips of elastic. With these, a piece of rag, and a forked stick, he soon contrived a quite serviceable catapult, and we amused ourselves for some days watching him practise with it, using small stones for projectiles; he even, greatly daring, went so far as to tickle up one of our dozing guardians! Then, one day, there was a shout, and I saw Basil striding proudly back, followed by a group of eager prisoners; he had knocked over his first bird! It was one of the little black-and-grey crested finches, of which there were quite a number about the camp, and he was holding its limp body up aloft, its eyes closed, the head hanging over the side of his hand. We gathered round the fire, the fierce, ravenous beast inside us yearning to spit and cook the plump but tiny little morsel. As we watched, the bird opened its eyes—it had not been killed after all, but only stunned—beautiful limpid black eyes, they seemed to search our hearts out. The bird never struggled; it just looked round in a dazed, pleading, pitiful way. We were mesmerised by it! Basil opened his hand and gently stroked the bird, then burst into tears. How could we, we who were hoping for life and liberty, destroy the happy existence of one such as this, this poor little embodiment of freedom and joy? In my heart to this day I feel sure, that if we had eaten that poor little wretch, as a moment before we had all so desired to do, we should ourselves never have obtained liberty. But as it was, we had already so learned by what we had suffered that, at the sight of the bird's mute appeal, we were all rendered physically incapable of perpetrating what seemed to us then to be no less than murder. I have killed hundreds, probably thousands of birds; I have slain human beings—but I never felt like that about it before.

Presently the bird shook itself slightly in Basil's open palm, then gave a feeble flutter; we all watched it in tense silence. Suddenly, with a happy chirp, it sprang into the air, flying at first slowly and feebly, then gradually gaining strength, until it at length alighted safely among a flock of its companions.

The catapult was put away, never to be used again, and we went on with our avocations, conscious of a promise—

"Blessed are the merciful, for they shall obtain mercy."

# CHAPTER 25

# Winter and Spring Time

The first week of January was a terrible one for us, for the long-dreaded rain was upon us, and we experienced it on the 2nd, 3rd, 4th, 5th and 7th of that month, accompanied by bitter gales which tore and wrenched at our crazy tents, and on the 5th there was hail in addition. As well as possible we had prepared against this rain; the loose stone walls we had constructed and the trench we had dug around our tent served to give us some manner of protection; we had also amassed a fairly large stack of firewood, which broke somewhat the force of the wind, and as the chill of the first wet blast came sweeping down upon us, we hastened to take cover beneath the porous tent roof. Shivering, we hoped for the best; but, as the blackness of the night gathered, shutting out the last glimpses of flooded camp visible through our tent door, so did we become cognisant of an ominous sound of dripping in the interior. First one and then another found himself lying in a pool of water. It was not long before we were all standing around the central tent-poles, hugging our tatters to us and holding mats above our heads. Thus we were wont to spend the night, sheltering the sick as far as could be contrived. At dawn, how happy were we if the rain had ceased; in that case we would sally out, clothed as Nature made us, stretch our stiff limbs and hang our sodden garments over rocks to dry. But often there was no sunshine; instead of the warm sun there loomed up but a dim, aqueous ball, framed in a colourless fog-bow and floating amid heavy mists. Or mayhap, sunrise showed no more than a cold, grey sky, mottled and mare's-tailed, through which penetrated no beam of heat to temper the keen wind.

Providentially for us, it was a very dry winter; after that first wet week of January, my diary only records two other subsequent rainy days at Bir Hakkim, and they were widely separated, else had we all perished. But such as they were, they helped to hasten the first two deaths which occurred among us at the White Doctor. On January 5th, Mr. Cox, boilermaker, passed away shortly after dark; and on January 10th, John Hodgsom, A.B., also got his ticket home. We buried both their bodies on the day following their departure, poor emaciated frames that they were. There were some ancient, graves in the desert to the south of the camp, and not far from these, we scraped and shovelled out a shallow hole among the sand and stones. I do not suppose many of my readers have seen the body of one who has died from neglect, cold and slow starvation. A healthy man could have held it in one hand with ease at arm's length, so light and thin had it become; probably not more than three or four stone in weight, just bones with a shrivelled skin stretched over them. To give them decent burial, we sewed the corpses up in one of the rice-sacks so sorely needed by the shivering crew for clothing; then we carried it down on another sack held by four bearers, and followed by a straggling procession of all the prisoners.

Captain Tanner always conducted these burial services, for I was entirely unable to control my voice, weak enough already, without the loss of power which such emotion brought to it. There are some hymn tunes which I can never hear again without a choke in my throat; they are those we used to sing by the grave-side under the grey and wintry sky, the stinging sand blowing into our eyes as though there were need to yet more augment the salt tears flowing from them: *Jesu, Lover of My Soul*, *Abide With Me*, and *I'll Nightly Pitch My Moving Tent a Day's March Nearer Home*. How they bring it all back to me, those memories of a time when we felt ourselves abandoned, starving, almost without hope, wondering if there would be any left to do these last rites to ourselves when our own turn came. A hymn in Welsh, and then we would gently shovel in the sand over the poor sack-sewn corpse; then place larger stones above this until there was a fair-sized cairn, and upon the cairn we would arrange white stones in the form of a recumbent cross, the symbol which now meant so much to us, and yet a symbol of which it is so hard to get the full meaning.

And then back to the camp, to follow once more our menial avocations, to start once more the round of petty squabbling and trivial disputes, as though such things could have any significance before the mystery of life in death, and the death which had become our life.

But with January 7th, the rains were for the time ended. Probably no more than an inch or two of water fell during the whole winter season of 1915-1916 at Bir Hakkim; yet what a miracle it wrought in a short time. Down to the south, where there was a shallow depression, there now arose the semblance of a vast lagoon. It was in reality hardly more than damp earth; but in the fairy mirage it became a boundless lake, extending out of sight. In the well, the water-level rose several feet, and in the other well next to it, the one which had been dry for centuries, and in which our men were forced to spend many nights on their first arrival, there were also several feet of water. With Holy Joe as slave-driver, the men had long been employed in clearing it out and cementing it, and in repairing the water-walls which guided the surface water into it.

We were very pleased to have water in that second well, as, besides precluding our being placed down there for punishment, it was right alongside the officers' tent and saved a journey to the other well. But two or three days later, drawing up some of this water from the new supply, we were astonished to find that it was teeming with strange fish-like creatures! They seemed to partake of the shape, liveliness and curly nature of hand-shrimps, but differed from the latter in having large, fish-like eyes. How they existed here during the long ages through which the cistern was dry, is a problem I am unable to answer. There were none of them in the other cistern, which bad always held water and had been kept in repair; but now, from this new source, every bucketful we drew up was simply alive with them, and they danced and skipped in the merriest manner when removed. The men not unnaturally did not relish this new addition to the food supply, but at first Holy Joe would not hear of our reverting to the old well, whose water he wished to keep in reserve. In fact, he appeared to be quite annoyed that we did not appreciate their undoubted value as nourishment when taken as a beverage, something in the nature of a clam-cocktail, or perhaps a soda-and-milk! But, in the end, we successfully protested against drinking them; they were merely employed to wash with.

The desert scrub had also taken heart of grace, and its dead-looking branches, revived by the welcome moisture, were everywhere throwing out clusters of olive-brown or blue-green leaves. Unexpected plantations of grass and tender green herbs sprang to life beneath every bush; the bush had mothered them through the long eleven months drought, had anchored them and kept them from being chafed out of existence by the ever drifting wind-driven sand, and had preserved them from being completely buried under it. A week or two later and many small perennials became a blaze of lovely mauve flowers, and numbers of butterflies went dancing past, whenever the wind was from the north. With them also came small hairy cockchafers, buzzing importantly; they looked much like bumble-bees, and evidently succeeded in impressing the men with the belief that they actually were such, for they treated them with the respect proper to a stinging insect. Fat and anxious beetles, with shining blue or brown coats of mail, scuttled from cover to cover, as though their very lives depended upon their ability to get as quickly as possible out of sight; a supposition not at all unnatural, with so many sharp-sighted and hungry enemies, both bird and reptilian, everywhere about.

Our white hard-shelled food-snails, now much depleted by our raids upon them, awoke from their long summer sleep. With the help of the external moisture they unsealed their gelatinous front-doors, and then, after putting forth a tentative head and horns, they climbed down from the rock or branch where they had been so long immobile, and walked abroad in hungry companies. A very short meal appeared to satisfy them, however; then they began to burrow assiduously in the sand. I disinterred a few of these lily-whites to elucidate the reason of this apparently un-snail-like conduct, and at once discovered batches of little pearl-like eggs, proof positive, if any were needed, that they, like all else, were engaged in the great game of Mother Nature.

Pulling up brushwood for firing at this season, at the roots one often found a scorpion hidden; but at the moment he was not very dangerous, his body being still soft and green and his movements sluggish.

Having something of a taste for entomology, I amused myself by collecting and breeding the caterpillars of a species of vapourer moth, common in this part of the desert. The female moth is wingless and practically unable to walk; in fact, she never leaves her cocoon, but lives, dies and lays her eggs in it, though her male partner more than makes up for the sedateness of his spouse by his nimbleness and winged activity.

But where to prison my insect captives was somewhat of a problem. In the whole camp there was not a single box, and all my worldly goods were contained within the folds of an old red-rubber tobacco pouch and half a pocket handkerchief; but I had, in addition to this luggage, a battered Italian potted-meat tin, which did duty for a drinking cup. This latter much-prized utensil, with a piece of rag tied across its mouth, was, I decided, just the thing I required for a caterpillarium. If needs be, I must suffer in the cause of science, and my craze for collecting pets! But this employment of my drinking cup for a dual purpose was not altogether felicitous, for the vapourer moth caterpillars were lavishly adorned by nature with tufts of bristle-like hair, which was very brittle; it broke off readily in contact with the skin and then partook of the nature of stinging-nettles! Wherefore, in the end, I had regretfully to allow my caterpillar friends to depart, for in those days, being perforce a stern teetotaler, I did not relish their somewhat gin-and-bitter flavour. Not till then could I again enjoy Holy Joe's only vintage, as it came straight from the cool dark depths of Bir Hakkim.

On January 7th we discovered a second batch of the tiny

onions, or garlic, as we called them; and from that day on, they gradually came up in increasing numbers, so that later on in the course of a day, twenty men by diligent searching might hope with luck to bring home between them two or three dozen of the roots; but, like children collecting blackberries, I suspect many of them were eaten on the spot, instead of being put into the mess-pot! We had had no meat latterly, but had been given a little sugar in lieu of it.

On January 12th, Mohammed, the Commandant's cook, left for Sollum, with the avowed intention of fetching back provisions, of which there seemed to be hardly any left in the blockhouse. Our guards had been steadily diminishing in numbers, and those left were mostly old men or boys.

Next day the news began to leak out about the fighting with the British on Christmas Day, though of course we did not know then the exact date upon which it had occurred. But Basil was able to glean that the Senussi had had a pretty rough time of it, and Mahomet Zone, the Commandant, himself a Senussi, spoke much about our being released before the summer came along.

On January 17th, a small caravan arrived from Sollum, and each of us was supplied with a, small piece of soap, the first which had come our way for two months. A busy washing-day resulted, and many of the men were so changed in appearance by the application of a little soap, that they bore little more resemblance to their old selves, to which we had become accustomed, than does a butterfly to the grub from which it is derived. For a day or two, it was quite difficult to recognise these new individualities, and the supply of an additional baking-tin, in which we could boil our clothes when the weather permitted, completed the metamorphosis.

With this caravan also came the two Indian horse-keepers, the only two of the thirty-six from the *Moorina* who had failed, to make good their escape during the battle of Christmas Day. They were Rajputs, and were the hundred and thirty British cavalry prisoners we had heard so much about. They were unable to speak a word of English at first, but Apcar, who spoke their language fluently, gradually extracted their story from them.

They had been incomparably better treated than ourselves from the beginning, having always ample to eat and tents to sleep in.

They described to Apcar how the naval shell had searched them out in the ravine where the Senussi were hiding, and how aircraft had come close overhead and dropped bombs on them, until most of the Senussi fled in panic, going as far even as Sollum, and being bombarded by the ships as they went. During this panic the Indians with their camels, finding themselves near the British lines, made a rush for them, and all escaped with the exception of these two, who were shortly afterwards sent to rejoin us. They stated that they had met no one else on their journey from Sollum. Thus we learned our first authentic, but still very vague news, of the outer world; it was the first we had had in nearly two and a half months.

## CHAPTER 26

# Two Departures

On January 18th, Mahomet Zoué, who had been our Commandant ever since Achmed's departure in the middle of December, left in his turn.

From the first, the duties of gaoler to us poor wretches had obviously been distasteful to him; he longed for the companionship of his equals and to take a more active share in the war. And he was aware, moreover, of a fact at which we only guessed—the extreme food shortage of this land of Libya, a country which was already beginning to experience the first spasms of famine. Since the commencement of the war with Britain, crops had been neither sown nor reaped. It was blockaded also from the sea and on the two Egyptian and Franco-Algerian land frontiers, so that no food could pass into it. And perhaps worst of all, a very large stock of its army's food supplies had been captured by the British from the Senussi in the battle of Christmas Day.

We, as prisoners, could only guess at most of these things by our own state of abject want. But Mahomet must have been aware of the real facts of the situation, and he, like many other Senussi; already regretted the hasty action which had brought them into conflict with Britain. Too late, they now saw that Turk and German alike cared nothing what suffering resulted to the country, so long as they could induce the Senussi to remain a little longer in the war. The Senussi had already put out independent feelers for peace, but the British had sternly told them that, as long as the men of the Tara remained prisoners, there could be no peace. The Senussi would even at this early date probably have been only too happy to make peace on these terms, but the Germanic power of the Turk in the land prevented them from releasing us. It was a question of "Pull Devil, pull baker," and we prisoners were the unfortunates likely to be rent in twain between the two combatants. For the Turk, we were out of sight, and therefore out of mind. I have no doubt the Turks felt sorry if they ever thought of us, and then, philosophically shrugging their shoulders, they would soothe any qualms that remained by remembering that such things were the fortune of war. The Senussi had no option but to continue the war as best they could, and Mahomet Zoué, humane man that he was, being unable himself to avert the death from starvation which he foresaw for us, desired, by going elsewhere, at least not to be a witness of it. He was the second rat to leave; Achmed before him had already feared to incur further responsibility for our safety.

Before Mahomet left, I handed him a letter which I had written for Nouri Pacha; in it I withdrew my parole, and gave as my reasons for doing so the facts of our abominable treatment, and his own failure to make good any of his own promises to us. Through Basil, I endeavoured to explain to Mahomet what the contents of the letter were; but, impatient to be off, he took no heed, and I do not believe that he even mentioned the matter to his successor. The fear of anyone escaping was, in his opinion, so remote a contingency, as to be hardly worth considering.

Personally, I had latterly been seriously studying the feasibility of escape at some future date, but, owing to the undoubtedly great obstacles and the peril of the attempt, I did not intend actually to carry it out while there remained any reasonable hope of our release by exchange. But I already saw clearly that unless something could be done, it was merely a question of time before we all died from slow starvation, dysentery and exposure. The recent arrival of the two Indians had also greatly inspired me, for besides gleaning from them some knowledge of the country between our camp and Sollum, it also led us to believe that the latter place was once more in the hands of the British. In any case, I wanted to feel that whatever steps I might decide upon in the future, my hands would be free and that I was no longer bound by a bond of honour not to attempt to escape. Achmed had gone, and with him had gone my chief fear of sharp action for withdrawing my parole. I judged that now was the opportune moment, while a new gaoler was taking over, to loose myself from these moral fetters; and therein I judged rightly.

Seven days after the giving of the notice I should be free to act as I liked. So Mahomet Zoué, for five weeks our Commandant, departed, and Selim, also a Senussi, reigned in his stead.

Selim himself was quite a different type of man from any with whom we had hitherto had to deal. There was nothing of the bold bluff soldier about him; he was of rather poor physique, with a dark, sallow complexion, a black moustache, no beard, and yellow teeth. He might have passed for an impecunious Spanish medical student or a monk, and he was reputed to be learned. We were also told that he was high in favour with the Grand Senussi, and that he had actually at one time been one of the latter's secretaries. To look at him would, at first glance, have been to condemn him, for he had the shifty, elusive ways of the man of words and not deeds, of the accomplished liar, of the diplomatist; there was no square-jawed determination about his character. But, for all that, he was the most truly forgiving and gentle of all our gaolers, one who abhorred force and brutality, and in his aptitude for lying he merely inherited the tradition of his race and country.

Soon after his arrival, Selim informed us that a two months' armistice had been arranged between the Senussi and the British, and he gave us many details of a peace conference which was to sit at Sollum, a conference in which the representatives of Britain and the Senussi alone were to sit, the Turks apparently being left out in the cold. I fear Selim's personal desires that such a happy consummation might take place, caused him to state for fact what was merely his own wish; the one tiling certain is that no such conference ever did take place, nor was any armistice at that time ever arranged with the British. But such a statement, coining as it did from a man who was supposed to be the Secretary of the Grand Senussi, had a tremendous effect on us prisoners. Excitement for a time was at boiling point, and we looked upon it as only a matter of a few weeks before we should be free. Personally, I did not feel as optimistic as most of the others, for I did not see how the Senussi were going to act in this way over the heads of the Turks, and I was studying more closely then ever the question of possible escape.

On January 23rd was fought the battle of Halazin, the least decisive battle of the war, in which, although the British remained victoriously masters of the field, their own losses were very heavy and their situation for some time was most precarious, until they got safely back to their old lines at Matruh. No news of this battle, nor of any subsequent one, reached us prisoners, and the absence of news served to confirm us in the belief as to the alleged armistice, pure fiction though it was. We also believed that the British were back in Sollum, for the Indians had said that the Senussi had fled in panic as far as that place after the battle of Christmas Day; if we had known that the British were in reality still on the defensive at Matruh, more than a hundred miles further east, our hopes would not have been so sanguine as they then were. But Selim was persuasive; we heard much of the Senussi and little of the Turk; we were told that the latter had only a dozen or so of officers in the country, who could easily be disposed of, and that the Grand Senussi was negotiating direct. Moreover, the supposed gun-fire, which we heard so often after dark, ceased after January 18th, and this still more confirmed our belief in the armistice. I have no doubt now that the sounds we heard then were distant thunder, which ended with the rainy season. The road to Sollum, from all accounts, was now under water. Camels brought twelve more sacks of rice on this day. They were just in time, for the supply in the block-house, which had been getting smaller and smaller, was within a day or two of exhaustion. It was a wet and stormy night with us as on the coast, but our hopes had been raised so high that we could bear it better. One sack of rice now had to last the ninety-three of us two days, and we got nothing else but a pinch of salt and a half mouthful of goat's-flesh every other day. This gave us about three-quarters of a pound of rice each every day.

Towards the end of January, many strange Arabs arrived at the camp, refugees for the most part, even solitary women being among the number. They are all unarmed and in rags, and appear to have but one object, to beg a small dole of rice. Our guards regarded these vagrants with much suspicion, and an armed party was sent to reconnoitre them ere they were allowed to approach; but having once satisfied our gaolers as to their bonâ fides, they were allowed to wander unmolested about the camp. It was then that Basil seized the opportunity to glean the latest news, which they, mistaking him for a Senussi, often imparted freely. They all alike assured us that the war was over (which, I suppose, from their point of view it was), and then made a sign, placing their two forefingers side by side and repeating the words Leglise-Saynoos, which we interpreted to mean that the English and Senussi were once more side by side working together.

Captain Tanner and I were much amused about this time, by a specially verminous old tramp coming to U8 and importuning us to write our names on a scrap of paper—the idea of a Senussi collecting autographs appeared too ludicrous. As a matter of fact, I believe the vagrant in question was a spy of the British, and that our signatures eventually got into our friends' hands.

At about 10.30 p.m. on January 28th, the third death among us at Bir Hakkim occurred. This time it was an officer, the poor old Chief Engineer, Mr. Robert Williams. We had all lain down soon after dark as usual, a few to sleep, when we were aroused by the watchers, who told us that yet another had got his ticket home. We all knew what that meant, as we waited in the dark gazing at the stars which showed through the rents in the tent roof, until someone had blown the embers of the fire into a blaze. We could then see the still figure in the corner, supported in the arms of Mr. Davies and Mr. Hughes, the two who never left him, and the young probationer surgeon bending over the group.

The smoke, blinding and choking, drifted to and fro, but every now and then it lifted, and in the flickering light we could see more clearly the silent figure of our old shipmate; little more than a skeleton was it, haggard and grizzled, but with the firelight playing on the features they had a strange look of peace and quietude.

We felt sure that he had gone to his Home.

For months we had watched, unable to do anything really to help, while the flame of life waxed dimmer and dimmer. At first, the old Chief had been one of the most cheerful. Deprived of tobacco, and at the same time losing his glasses when the ship sank, he had to his surprised delight found his eyesight gradually but so greatly improve that before long he could read without any artificial aid—a thing he had not been able to do for years. But as the months rolled by, the privation, the hardship, the anxiety told on one no longer young, and he lost hope. For those who have lost hope, dysentery finds an all-too-easy prey, and for six weeks now he had lain on his back in the corner of the tent, silent, staring with unseeing eyes, too feeble to move. At first he had eaten his daily handful of rice, and when little fragments of meat came our way he had always been given the tit-bits. The two young engineers had always waited on him hand and foot with unremitting care. It was they who bore him out into the sunshine; they who washed his clothes and his enfeebled body; and they also who twenty times each night faced the bitter winter wind and rain to help his infirmity. No mother could have done more for ailing child, nor with less hope of any earthly reward. And it was but a day or two back that one of them had helped him write his farewell letter home, and we knew that the time of his release was near.

We all tried to rally him with cheerful conversation, we told him of British victories, of Selim's story of the armistice, of the food and medicines coming, of an early release. But he heard with expressionless face and answered never a word, and now for days scarcely a morsel of food had passed his lips; he could not manage even broth made from the water our rice was boiled in, which was our substitute for beef-tea.

And now he had gone—Home.

No more was he a prisoner, chained to a hated land, separated from all he loved. At dawn, we should be sewing his body in the sacking so badly needed for our own clothing.

But he? His soul, his happiness, were dependent on us no more. He was free. He had gone Home. He would inhabit a house not built of hands, for he was already in a City where there is no more crying and where the prisoners are loosed.

Those who can walk will soon carry his body along in slow, barefooted procession, singing with feeble voice the hymn that tells of moving tent, that's nightly pitched a day's march nearer Home. Unheeded tears will stream anew down faces no longer ashamed of weeping. Throats will gulp and sob, as though made only for grief. From their posts our Arab guards will look on somewhat contemptuously, their women openly deride and mimic.

But what matter? They can pain him no longer. Nor Turkish General, nor Grand Senussi, nor all the German plots and scheming, can longer keep him prisoner. Round the grave we will gather, and when the sobs can be controlled a voice will pronounce: "I am the Resurrection and the Life."

Silently for a moment we shall stand. Then a tall, gaunt figure will step forward—one of the crew who was deacon of the little chapel among the green hills of Wales, the chapel where the old Chief was wont to worship. A passionate speech in the ancient tongue of Britain falls from his lips, and, though I understand no word, yet I see again the little village and the mountains sloping down to the sea, and the sunshine with the gulls flying overhead. Yet again our tears flow; happy memories and present sadness come upon us with the words. Then we stumble back once more to our tents, to divide those poor things which the old Chief left behind him on his journey, things which he no longer needs.

We indeed are still prisoners, having need of many things. But the old Chief is free. He has got his ticket, he is already Home.

And we—are left behind in the desert, and are crying.

Such thoughts as these came into mind that quiet silent night of January 28th when the old Chief made his departure from Bir Hakkim.

# CHAPTER 27

# Wheels Within Wheels

The last few days of January and the first week of February, were full of excitement for us prisoners, for optimism as to our release or exchange was at boiling point, and our hopes, which on our first arrival at Bir Hakkim had been so low, now were always at fever heat.

By my diary, I find that on January 30th, Selim entertained us to soured camel's milk, and afterwards discussed the situation; he appeared more confident than ever about our release, and also of the early arrival of the caravan which we had been expecting ever since the middle of December, and which was to bring us boots, clothes, food and medicines. I could not help being impressed by what Selim told me, and some of the pessimism I had hitherto felt began to leave me. At the same time I could have no doubt that Selim was a skilled if friendly liar, for, on the very next day, I ascertained through Basil that two messengers had arrived from Sollum with letters for Selim, letters which I imagine very greatly altered the situation, though Selim denied the very existence of the letters, or even the arrival of the messengers. But of their coming there was no doubt, for Basil had a conversation with them, before they discovered his identity as a prisoner, and shut their mouths.

February 1st was a fateful day for us, had we known it. On Selim's importuning, I wrote letters to the Grand Senussi, Tarrick Bey (Turkish Commandant at Sollum), Mahomet Zoué, Achmed the Egyptian, and also the British General, all imploring the hastening of a supply of food, medicine and boots. I was loth to write these letters, as I had written many similar ones before, and they had been entirely without effect, and we all firmly believed that Achmed was in the habit of destroying them, letters in my hand-writing having been seen torn up in his tent. But Providence, by the hand of Selim, persuaded me to try once again, and Providence also did something more: it caused me to do a thing which I had never done before. In my letters to Tarrick Bey at Sollum, I gave full details of our numbers and pitiful condition, and at the head of the letter I put the name of our camp, Bir Hakkim Abbyat. To do such a thing at the time appeared foolish to me, for Tarrick Bey was already fully aware of all that had happened to us, and such stores as we received came from him. The name, Bir Hakkim Abbyat, was never mentioned in our letters home, nor in any other document, for we feared that its insertion would mean the destruction of the whole letter by the censor. But on this letter to Tarrick Bey I did put the fateful words, and it was the only occasion on which they were ever thus put in writing; something, which I call Providence, made me do it in spite of myself.

A messenger left with these letters, and the letters which we had written home, for Sollum the same evening. None of the letters were ever delivered, I believe, yet the one I had written to Tarrick Bey eventually led to our deliverance. So does Providence, with a touch, alter the whole fate of men!

Eight Senussi notables were encamped half a mile to the southward of us, obviously people of importance. They visited our camp and were decidedly friendly, though I do not know what their purpose was in coming to this isolated spot. But I could not help thinking that at this period it was the Grand Senussi's wish, or at any rate the wish of his leading chiefs, to obtain peace with England, and thereby food, by setting us at liberty. The fly in the ointment was the German-Turk, who was by no means the negligible power in the land which the Senussi wished us to believe. For the Turk had officered and disciplined a Senussi army, which held the temporal power and the food supplies. Sayed Achmed, the Grand Senussi, was no longer in control of the destinies of Libya.

On February 4th, I again interviewed Selim to try to find out what food still remained, as it was obviously very little. We were many days' march from anywhere, and, with the large number of sick, were quite incapable of covering even ten miles a day, bare-footed as we all now were. Should the supply on the spot run out, we should in a very short time all perish from starvation. Fortunately the weather in the next few days was sunnier and warmer, and Holy Joe (Osman the Wellman), who, being a priest, was supposed not to tell lies, raised our optimism once more to boiling point by assuring us that we should surely go in four or five days' time.

On February 8th, a messenger arrived from Sollum, and I was ordered by Selim to write at once a letter in French to Nouri Pacha, saying what clothes, boots and food we required, stating also how many were sick and how many had died. The messenger departed in great haste immediately on receipt of my letter, and there were general rejoicings among the prisoners in the camp, who looked upon it as a good augury of an almost immediate release. My own feelings were entirely different, and I did not at all like the look of things. If Nouri Pacha were still in charge of us, then Selim's story about superseding the Turkish officers and of being able to regard them as of no account, was an obvious lie; and, by the way in which Selim himself hastened to obey Nouri's orders, it obviously was so. In my opinion the Senussi were as much as ever the servants and tools of the Turks, and the letter did not mean our release, but more likely that we were to be marched even further into the interior. From what I have learned since my release, I have no doubt that the opinion which I then formed was correct: it was intended to move us elsewhere. But at the time, the reader must realise that all con-clusions we came to were formed from the vaguest surmises and distorted fragments of news; we knew nothing of the true military or economic situation of the country.

About this time one of the sheep fell ill, so, to save its life, or rather to carry out the Mohammedan law that no animal must be eaten unless it has first been bled, it was hurriedly killed, and we gloried in an extra meat ration. Sheep skins did not appear to be so extensively used for carrying water as those of goats, which were invariably saved for this purpose, To get a goat's skin off in a manner to render it fit for a water-bag was an art in itself, for the whole body has to be got through the neck, in order to avoid making holes. To do this, as soon as the animal's throat has been cut, and even before it is dead, a small puncture is made near the hock. To this hole an Arab applies his mouth, and blows with all the vigour of which he is possessed, so that the whole skin becomes inflated like a football before it has time to stiffen. By this means the removal of the carcase through the skin of the neck is much facilitated. Once the carcase is out, the skin is pulled inside out, and rubbed over with saffron and pepper, and the limbs, where they have been cut off at the knees and hocks, are bound round, and a rope for carrying spliced on to them. The water-carrier is then all complete, ready for use.

With the warmer weather in the second week of February, butterflies became very numerous indeed. Hares were very much in evidence, and a little while back the petty officers captured a baby one, which they speedily transferred to their pot. But of late our movements had been more restricted, and for some days we were not allowed to go to the northward of the camp, nominally on account of wandering Bedouins who might murder us. At that time we believed that there must be an army on the move in that direction, but I believe now that the reason given us was the true one, and that refugees, driven by famine, were making their way westward in large numbers. Some of our soldiers went out commandeering camels, and there were mysterious comings and goings, and movements of boxes and provisions. These our guards tried to conceal from us, but we were as keen-eyed as cats, and a camel, like a city set on a hill, cannot be hid even at night; the loud-voiced protests in which it indulges either at being loaded or unloaded, speedily awakened the whole camp. We were full of conjectures, anticipations and hopes, and spent our time try-ing to fit together the pieces of our jig-saw puzzle; but it was in vain, for most of the parts were missing. We lived in such a web of falsehood, mystification and concealment, that none of us had yet succeeded in giving an explanation that would satisfy more than a moiety of the objections it at once suggested.

We had no working parties after February 9th, so the men had all the more time for conjecture. All the wells within reach of us had now been cleared out and repaired, and, as a matter of fact, the men were incapable of doing any more manual work; we none of us ever got accustomed to going barefoot over the jagged stones, and to pick our way painfully along to collect firewood and snails, was about as much as any of us could manage. The rice issued to us at this time was almost uneatable, for it consisted only of broken grains and rice flour, filled with mouse droppings, evidently the sweepings of a granary. To cook it was well-nigh impossible, for it at once turned to glue when put into the water, stuck to the pot, and burnt badly.

On Friday, February 11th, a letter was handed to me which gave the final blow to our hopes of release. Basil, in a state of great excitement (for he was always an optimist), brought the letter to me from Selim, and everyone gathered around to hear it, fairly trembling with hope that it would at last give definite news of our release. It was from Tarrick Bey, written in French, and dated February 11th. I give here a rough translation, the original handwriting being difficult to read, and my own knowledge of the French language (especially its Turkish form) being somewhat weak; but I retain the original letter to this day. It runs as follows:

*Monsieur le Colonel,*
I have received the letter which you sent to His Excellency General Nouri Pacha. I will send it at once to the General. I have read it and understand it. I hope you will be repatriated in some months, at least two to three months. Because of the general war, this fatality to the civilised world, will be finished in the next summer. As soon as the General has accepted your demand, I will send you all—whatever it is—to your destination. The General is at Matruh. I am going to see him and after my return [1] (I will do the necessary).
Receive my respects,
*Commandant Tabik*

---

1. This part is indecipherable.

This letter took me some time to decipher and explain to my messmates, and many of them at first flatly refused to believe in its genuineness, so loath were they to give up their hopes of an immediate release. They preferred to believe it was a forgery of the Egyptian Achmed, that scapegoat upon whose unconscious head we were wont to unburden our curses and attribute our sorrows. Absurd as this may seem, some colour was given to it by the discovery that the "C" of Commandant just before Tarrick's signature, had originally been another letter, apparently a capital "A" There was a yell on the discovery of this, and the majority loudly proclaimed that this was proof positive that Achmed was the real author of the epistle, and that the "A" was where he had thoughtlessly begun to sign his own name!

However, in the end, the other officers reluctantly came round to my point of view, and realised that our release was not near at hand as they had hoped; that, in fact, we were still in the power of the Turks, and that the latter had no intention of letting us go before the end of the war. The letter confirmed my worst fears; and from that moment I decided to attempt to escape on the first opportunity.

This was another Friday, and Friday seemed to me to be a day big with fate right through our captivity. On a Friday we were torpedoed; on a Friday we arrived at the Promised Land of Bit Hakkim; on a Friday the first of us died in the officers' tent, our old Chief Engineer; on a Friday we received this fateful letter, which meant so much to us, and on a Friday, though it was yet hidden in the mists of the future, we were to receive our freedom.

On this Friday I determined, somehow, at some time, to make a bid for freedom; but for the present I kept this resolution carefully to myself.

# CHAPTER 28

# I Prepare for a Journey

The morning after the receipt of Tarrick's letter, I interviewed Selim and asked him for an explanation, demanding to know how he could reconcile what he had himself told us with what the letter stated. Selim was polite and conciliatory as usual, but skillful beyond measure in changing the conversation, and I got no nearer the point I was after. However, he modified his original statement as to our almost immediate release, into a vague personal opinion, which was, that he did not think we should really be kept so long as two or three months, the period to elapse, within which, according to Tarrick's letter, we might anticipate the ending of the European War. Selim then attempted to give us more soothing syrup, by telling me to have further lists of food, boots, etc., made out to have ready for Mahomet Zoué, our late Commandant, whose cook had returned on the previous night and had stated that Mahomet himself would be back in a few days time.

On February 14th, the sick had all taken a turn for the worse, due no doubt in great measure to the wave of pessimism which had now spread over the camp, and also to the still dwindling rice ration, which was of the same bad quality of dirty and broken grains. Our hunger was very much greater than ever before, and officers and men alike now ate enormous quantities of snails. After a day or two of great depression, we began to cheer up again, for it is one of those curious anomalies of human nature, feat the more wretched and painful existence becomes, the more does one desire to prolong it. We reasoned, moreover, that our gaolers would surely not have taken the trouble to keep us alive for three months and more, merely to let us perish now. We even welcomed the pangs of starvation, for we felt convinced that the very shortage of food would, in the end, compel them to release us.

The possibility of one or more of our number escaping, was now a common topic of conversation in the officers' tent, and one or two had loosely expressed an intention of trying to do so; but the general opinion appeared to be that it was quite impossible.

Various schemes were discussed, and for a time we almost settled upon what appeared a very simple expedient.

We had often noticed the extreme dislike of the Arabs to approaching a dead body. Once one of our number was dead, or even known to be seriously ill, no Arab would go near the tent where he lay.

What could be easier than to report that one of our number was dying, and a day or two later to give out his death? We had already had three funerals at Bir Hakkim, and the mournful hymn singing procession to the graveside was now familiar to all our guards. We would have a mock funeral, and bury something, or at least appear to do so. Then, as soon as it was dark, the alleged corpse could, with ordinary luck, make good his escape, without the least fear of being missed and pursued.

But there was one fly in our ointment. Should the runaway, as was more than probable, ever be recaptured and brought back, his escape would at once implicate the whole of the other prisoners, who were likely to have a very slim time of it as a result of their little deception. The deception itself, too, in the first instance, would mean that every sailor in the camp would have to be warned beforehand, a necessary preliminary which would not help the cause of secrecy, and, among so many, there might well be one traitor, one who, to save himself from after-punishment, and to curry favour, might divulge the matter to Selim.

If only one could get through and make our pitiable plight known to the British, we felt assured that something would then be done.

But how? For the time being there seemed no practicable

way. I cautiously approached the one or two officers who had expressed an intention of escaping, but when I directly moot-ed the subject, I found that it was an intention only, and that for the present, at any rate, they had no clear determination to carry it out. Wherefore I held my peace, and for the time being confided in no one except Basil and Apcar, who were neces-sary for my purpose.

Basil I employed to teach me a few words of Arabic, sen-tences which I thought might be useful to me, and these I wrote down carefully and phonetically, with their English equivalents, in a spare page of my diary.

Apcar was invaluable to me, for, through him, I was able to interrogate the two Indian horse-keepers, our fellow-prison-ers. These men, having come all the way from Sollum, could give me a very good idea of the country lying between us and that place, a route which they described as being dead flat all the way, and they also stated most emphatically that they had encountered not a single human being in the whole journey. They could also give me some idea of the appear-ance of Sollum from inland, from Bir Waer, the Senussi Camp which overlooked the place. I wanted to be able to recognise the latter at a distance if possible, so that on sighting it I could hide, and then endeavour to make my way through the be-leaguering Turkish lines after dark. But in all matters which we discussed through the Indiana I had to use the greatest caution, in order that they themselves should get no inkling of what was toward.

For the past two or three weeks I had steadily been get-ting into training, so far as was possible. I was always out with the firewood and snail collecting parties, and every evening I walked for some hours barefoot on a sandy patch near the camp, Basil acting as trainer. My Swedish and Sandow exercises amazed the guards, who took my prostrations and kicking as some new form of religious mania, and were deeply impressed thereby; one youth especially had always had great hopes of converting us to Islam, and I fancy he thought he had now at long last succeeded!

For a week I saved daily a quarter of my rice ration of three-quarters of a pound, a real test of fortitude in a person with naturally so hearty an appetite as myself. None of my brother officers said anything about this at the time, but I fancy the more observant noted it and began to suspect my intention. By this means, and by eating my stale rice, I had at the end of the week two days' freshly boiled rice saved. The trouble with the rice is that, once boiled, it readily turns sour, and becomes fermented and poisonous, and will not keep eatable for more than a very few days. It was necessary for me to take my food with me already cooked, for besides the danger there would be in lighting a fire, there were also the two additional difficulties that I had nothing to cook the rice in, and also that I should be able to obtain no water on the way, as every well was sure to be guarded by soldiers.

Apcar also helped me in another material way; he had been sick practically ever since he landed, and therefore was virtually the only one of us who had not worn out his boots. His Arab shoes were also still in good order, and, himself retaining his European boots, he turned these native shoes over to me. With my bone needle and some thread from an old sail, I was able to repair them sufficiently for a journey, and I had in addition the remnants of my own European shoes.

Ever since the day we had landed, I had kept a very careful, if brief, record of all events of importance which had happened to us. Among these, I had put down the number of hours we had been on the march each day during our journey to Bir Hakkim, and the general direction we had taken, and I also knew approximately the number of miles per hour we had moved at. These I plotted out carefully on a piece of ruled foolscap which I possessed, and for a sailor accustomed to navigation, it was an easy matter to get a good general idea of the direction and distance we had come from Port Bardia, the place where we had landed.

The trouble was that it was not Port Bardia I wished to get to. It was, in fact, the place which I particularly wished to avoid. Sollum, which I believed (erroneously) to be once more in British hands, was my objective.

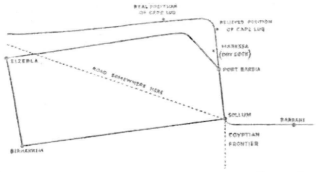

With the greatest care I checked all the information available, both that obtained by Basil from camel-rivers, and that which the Indians could give me. But the latter had taken little or no note of the direction, and the former always went on a more or less circuitous route along the line of the wells, whereas the path by which I wished to go was the most direct route available. My trouble was that I had only a very rough general idea of the configuration of the coast, and that I had no notion how far Sollum was to the south of Port Bardia. I guessed the distance at forty miles, whereas in reality it was only fifteen miles as the crow flies.

Another thing which also put my calculations somewhat awry, was the situation of Cape Lucq, the spot where we had spent the afternoon on November 18th, and whence we had obtained our last glimpse of the sea. I believed it to be the north-eastern point of Cyrenaica (the spot where in reality Ras el Mehl is situated), when, as a matter of fact, Cape Lucq is the northern point of that part of the coast and not the north-eastern, and is some twenty-four miles further to the west-north-west than I believed.

These two false premises biassed my calculations as to the first part of our wanderings, and made Bir Hakkim appear closer to Sollum than in reality it was. Since those days, I have been able to check the real position of Bir Hakkim with some degree of accuracy, yet I find that my original calculations, based as they were on next to nothing, were surprisingly correct. The direction of Sollum east-north-east northerly was very nearly right, and the distance which I estimated at eighty miles, though in reality it is a hundred and fifteen miles, was only ten miles wrong when taking the believed position of Cape Lucq as a departure point.

This old map with which I made my attempted escape is still in my possession; or rather, the greater-part of it still is so.

My one great fear was that I should get into territory north and west of Sollum, which I suspected to be swarming with Senussi; but in this matter I had one sheet anchor to help me in avoiding it. I knew that a road ran somewhere to the westward from Sollum, and that, if I struck this road, I should at once know that I was too far to the north, and should therefore keep a little further to the south on my easterly course. My main object was to strike the sea somewhere east of Sollum, and once I had crossed the Egyptian frontier, which runs south from Sollum, I hoped I should be safe. With this idea in mind, I determined not to strike north for the sea until I believed I was well to the eastward of Sollum. If I overran Sollum it would not matter much, as I hoped I might then encounter somebody, once I had reached the coast, and I believed that I should then be in friendly territory across the Egyptian frontier. But if, on the contrary, after turning north, I struck the road running west from Sollum, I should know then that I had not yet gone far enough east, and should continue on the south side of this road, which I knew eventually must lead me to the coast in the vicinity of Sollum.

To my companions in the officers' tent, when I first broached this project the evening before starting, it at first appeared madness, and they tried their best to dissuade me. To wander for five or six days in a waterless desert without a map looked like sheer insanity, in which I must inevitably perish. But presently the logic of my argument began to tell with them, and they saw with my eyes, and began to hope, like myself, that such an escape really was feasible. What they doubted most was my own powers of endurance, but of these I never had the least qualms. Thanks to the best of mothers, and a life free from excess, I was, at the age of forty-one, in the prime of manhood, Bad and insufficient rice, with snails, may not appear to be an ideal diet to train on, and I certainly had not much reserve of energy; but it was probably much better for athletics than the life of the average town-dwelling European, with his tobacco, alcohol, vitiated atmosphere, late hours and fancy dishes. I was lean and muscular, accustomed to the climate, exposure and want, and above all, I was filled with hope and enthusiasm, that which no season ticket is a better passport for touring the surface of our globe. I had calculated the distance at eighty miles, or four days' march, averaging a minimum of twenty miles a day, which I felt positive I could accomplish. And, supposing the distance were a hundred or even a hundred and twenty miles, I still felt confident that I could manage it. For I was now as inured to hardship as the Arabs themselves; I could go for a couple of days without water if necessary, and even without roots or snails as auxiliaries, I hoped I could endure four days without food. Latterly, we had discovered several edible roots, and they were of assistance in staving off the more acute pangs of hunger.

Matters then stood thus. I had saved two days' full rations of my own rice, and as Sunday, February 20th (the day on which I had determined to make my attempt), was the day on which rations were issued, I was able to draw an advance of two days more. I also spoke privately to Mr. Morris (the Chief Steward, who did the issuing), and obtained from him another t ration from the general stock. The officers also gave me a ration, so that I had in all six days' rice rations. Unfortunately, when boiled, this was food of a terribly heavy nature to carry, for rice absorbs exactly twice its own weight of water, and the combined mass resulting weighed anything from twelve to fourteen pounds.

Two or three days anterior to the Sunday, I had it given out that I was seriously ill, knowing that those sick were occasionally allowed a little flour by way of medical comfort. The ruse was successful, and, by keeping out of sight, I obtained nearly a pound of barley-flour, which Basil quickly made into biscuits for me. My assumed sickness was also likely to keep any Arab from visiting our tent, and my absence would in all probability not be noticed for some days after I had left. Holy Joe, the well-man, had also gone off on a journey for a few days, and, as he was by far the most observant of our gaolers, his absence gave a much greater freedom to my preparations, of which most of the officers, and none of the men, knew anything until the day itself.

Thus I had six or seven days' full food supply, including half a pound of cooked goat with which the officers' mess presented me, and also some fragments of biscuit, about a pound of dates, and a little sugar which Basil had somehow acquired in his visits as interpreter to the block-house. This food I did up into six portions in my spare pair of Arab cotton drawers, tying a string between each, and hung them over my shoulders, like two rows of sausages. Rice was in the two top cannon-balls, and the biscuit (which would keep) in the lower ones. I suppose this food weighed, with the dates and sugar, which I kept in a bag round my waist, some sixteen pounds. It was a very awkward kind of pack, but the best which, with the means at our disposal, we could contrive.

The other difficulty was water. I had to carry with me enough for six days. I have by me as I write the actual calculations which I made at that time, and I find I carried thirty-six of my little tomato-tins full with me. These tins run slightly under four tins to the pint, so I had something under nine pints, probably exactly a gallon. In the whole camp we could not find a single water-tight goat-skin bag. The new goat-skins, which had been prepared at Bir Hakkim, had, I fancy, been sent off for the use of the troops; at any rate, there were none to be seen anywhere. However, we selected the best small skin available, and into it I carefully measured my gallon of water which I proposed to carry on my back, Basil skilfully fitting loops to go over my shoulders, so that it was held something after the manner of a grip-sack. As the water skins were always wet on the outside, it was impossible to tell whether this skin was really leaking badly, as we did not finish fitting it until the last moment, it being always in use. But, in any case, it was the least porous skin available, and, as such, I had to use it and hope for the best.

I now had some sixteen pounds weight of food and ten pounds weight of water, and I carried in addition to these various odds and ends. An Arab horse-shoe for luck and also to use as a frying-pan for snails, my diary and pencil, a list of officers and men, half-a-dozen treasured matches and a stump of candle for night signalling, in case I should get in sight of friends near the sea, my pipe and tobacco pouch, in which latter I kept my bone needles and some thread, tomato-tin drinking cup, my spare worn-out pair of shoes, a few letters and the map I had prepared. I also carried Tarrick Bey's letter for use in case of re-capture, to prove that he had received my notice of withdrawal of parole, for I did not fancy being shot off-hand for such a disgraceful offence.

Altogether, I felt very well equipped for a ten days' journey if need be. I went through matters carefully with Apcar before leaving. He had the advantage of much clearer reasoning powers than most of the others, and never allowed his judgment to be warped by optimism; but even he had come so far round to my view, that he agreed the chances were at least even that I should not be at once shot, in the event of my falling into Senussi hands. Of this latter contingency I had little fear, for the Indians had assured us that they had met no one on the whole journey; the real danger, it seemed to me, was death from thirst and exhaustion, had I miscalculated the distance and direction of Sollum.

The day before I left, Owen Roberts, one of the men, passed away from the accumulated effects of starvation, dysentery, and consumption, and we added a fourth cairn to the other three already there on the desolate wind swept plain to the south of the camp. Poor fellow, his limbs were but pipe-stems when we buried him; there seemed not an ounce of flesh left on his body, in spite of the tenderest care from his companions. I had often been touched on visiting his tent to see how these starving men had set aside for him practically the whole of their combined day's meat ration.

The day before he died, we were given a small date ration, in addition to the bad rice. The sweetness of the dates, half caterpillar and dirt though they were, was a very great joy to us all, and the sick in particular were immensely benefited by them; but they came too late to help poor Roberts.

His death was the final link, if any further had been needed, to complete the chain of events that impelled me to act. If by any deed of mine I could hope to bring help, then I would endeavour to do it.

# CHAPTER 29

# Off!

As before stated, Sunday, February 20th, was the day I had decided upon to make my bid for liberty. There were many reasons for going at that moment. I would not defer the matter longer, for I felt that my strength was diminishing every day; it was now or never, while the nights were long and the weather still remained cool. In the heat of summer, and with lengthening days, to have attempted it would have been sheer insanity, even if my strength held out until then. Hitherto I had been quite free from dysentery, but I could not be sure that this immunity would always continue, though I felt very fit.

Of my ability to keep in one direction in a straight line all the time I had no doubt. Every evening, when the stars were visible, we had spent hours in studying them, and I knew to a nicety at what points of the compass the principal constellations rose and set, and also the times at which they did so. It was obvious that I must travel by night, for the Bedouin of the desert had the keenest eyesight, and an ability for observation which puts to shame our telescopes and binoculars. To move in the daytime would be merely to invite capture; at night I should be more on an equality with my Senussi neighbours. Let not the reader imagine, however, that the nights of the Red Desert in February are cloudless, scintillating with stars. The contrary is the case, and more often than not the stars are veiled by clouds. Having no compass, I had to depend on some other means than the stars for telling my direction. There was one other—the moon.

It was upon the moon only that I finally depended, and on Sunday, February 20th, 1916, the moon was at, or near, her full. However cloudy it might be, unless it was very bad indeed, I might hope to catch glimpses of the moon shining through the clouds during the greater part of the night, and thus shape my course. Her light, in addition, would make the painful journey over that sea of stones somewhat easier, and it would not materially increase the danger of detection.

Everything seemed to be propitious for a journey. A number of our guards had left a week earlier, and there now appeared to be very few but old men and boys left to look after us. We were rarely mustered, and an Arab's arithmetic is so weak, that if half-a-dozen of the men had been gone, they would probably have been unable to detect the fact. Of course, owing to my rank, I was a more conspicuous figure, and my absence would ordinarily soon have been noticed; but the pretence of my sickness would probably now defer this discovery for some days.

On that Sunday morning we were again encouraged to send letters by a mail ostensibly leaving for Sollum; for all we knew to the contrary none of our letters had ever reached England, and we had never had a reply to any of them; but I took this opportunity to send along my last will and testament before escaping. We were practically unguarded, the Arabs evidently regarding an escape as impossible; we had been marched to Bir Hakkim two hundred miles round three sides of a square, and trigonometry being to the Bedouin mind an unknown science, it never occurred to them that anyone would be able to find their way along the fourth side of the square.

Having seen the caravan with our mails out of sight, and got Basil to report the exact direction it took, I spent the rest of this, my last, day in resting. Up till the last I was in doubt about one thing—should I steal the Commandant's horse? The old white horse which had come with us all the way was nearly always somewhere about—hobbled, poor beast—and eking out a precarious livelihood on shrubs. If I could catch him, he would undoubtedly give me a good lift on my way during the first night. But the danger was too great. We could not catch him until after dark, and even then there would be great risk of his hoof-beats being heard. Moreover, his track would be clearly visible, and, when I abandoned him at dawn, he would be a beacon to all the world to point out the way I had gone; a horse in the level desert is more visible than St. Paul's Cathedral! In the end, therefore, I decided to trust to my own legs, and hoped that even if I were pursued, they would think I had made for the Italian port of Tobruk, a place one-half the distance away that Sollum was, but one of whose location I had only the vaguest notion.

I was now very lean and sunburnt, with a brown and ragged beard. With my Arab clothes I could well hope to pass for an Arab myself, except on very close inspection. I would travel by night as far as possible, and if I found it necessary to travel by day, on sighting anyone, I would very slightly alter my direction to avoid the other. If, in spite of this, the stranger should close with me, I would pretend madness, religious devotion, or to be a dumb mendicant, whichever pose best seemed to suit my purpose at the time, By these means I hoped to avoid interrogation, and, if all failed, as a last resource, I should have resort to bribery. The Arabic sentences I had so carefully written down at Basil's dictation, explained that, though I had no money, I was specially under the protection of the Grand Senussi and the Turkish General, and that, on my safe arrival at Sollum, my guide would be rewarded with a bag of gold.

I could think of no other contingency, and it was with a light heart that I stole out an hour after sundown on the Sunday evening, bearing with me the hopes and blessings of all such of my fellow-prisoners as were aware of my venture. I was much touched at the heartiness of the hand-grips as I left the officers' tent. Do not imagine we were all always friends, for we were constantly quarrelling; there was much jealousy, bickering and malice among us. But at that moment all our past feelings were wiped out, and I do not think they ever returned. All and every were with me at that moment, half regretting for their part that they were not accompanying me. Personally, I was very glad to be alone in the journey. A companion is a help, a moral support when one is cornered; but with two people there are always two opinions, and on such a matter of life and death I cared to defer to no one. With another with me we should have been like two greyhounds in leash, hindering, and not helping, each other. When one was tired the other would wish to press on. When one wished to go straight the other would seek to turn aside. Besides, the chances of two people being seen would be much greater than was the case with one, who could easily and quietly take cover.

Before going, I had arranged that, if I got safely through, I should get the ships at Sollum to turn their searchlights on to the clouds; we hoped that this would be visible, even at a distance of eighty miles. I had myself seen the glare of searchlights at sea, when more than two hundred miles distant from the port of Queenstown in Ireland.

Thus, with a stout staff in my band, I stole out into the darkness. The camp fires were heaped high, the flames shot up, and the glare dazzled the sleepy and un-suspicious guard. In some twenty minutes I had lost sight of the last gleam from Bir Hakkim, as I rounded the slight rise to the east-north-east. The sentry had no ghost of a notion that I had gone, and I was stumbling cheerfully over the pitiless stones in the darkness.

All had indeed gone well.

# CHAPTER 30

# Half Way

My first feeling of exhilaration at so easily getting away un-detected soon began to wear off, and it was not long before I became conscious of the ropes from my water-skin bag, which were cutting into my shoulders. I had padded myself against this contingency so far as possible, but even rags at Bir Hakkim were too scarce a commodity for me to have been able to borrow any from others, and my very leanness made the ropes bite into me all the harder. My back also was rapidly soaked through by the wet water-skin, and I greatly feared that my precious water-supply was leaking away, but of this I could not as yet be certain. However, the stones were so terrible in the dark that I soon forgot every other trouble and the pain of the ropes; all my energy and attention were required to prevent stumbling and falling.

Besides my Arab costume I wore also my naval uniform, not only for warmth, but also in anticipation that it might be of use to me as a protection if I were recaptured. At night I wore the dark uniform outside, but by day it was my white Arab shirt that I donned like a smock externally. They both were in the nature of protective colouring, smeared as they were by the soil of the desert. I had also, in addition, about ten feet in length of my fourteen-foot Arab burnous; four feet of it I had cut off, and left behind for lightness, at Bir Hakkim, before starting.

In less than an hour's time the sky began to lighten, and the full moon presently rising walking became very much better. I could avoid most of the stones, but the dim light was full of alarms. I am slightly deaf, and so had to trust more than ever to my eyesight, which, fortunately, is of the best; but at all times in the desert objects have a terrible monotony of appearance as well as of colour, and distances are always deceptive. At the unexpected appearance of any dark object I had to throw myself full length on the ground, and look at it against the sky-line, to observe whether it moved or not. After a time, feeling reassured, I would again rise and continue my march.

That such precautions were more than justified I soon had ample proof. It was about 4 a.m., and I suppose by that time the edge was getting worn off my vigilance. The moon was already low and behind me, so that I must have been sharply silhouetted against the western sky-line, whereas objects ahead of me were dim and misty-looking. Without the least warning I suddenly found I had tumbled right into a caravan of eighty or ninety camels, their ghostly shapes stealing silently down upon me both from ahead and on either side. It was too late then to avoid them, but I instantly did the next best thing, by throwing myself flat on my face, and drawing my sand-coloured burnous right over me. I suppose that by now my personal odour was similar to that of an Arab, for the animals went trailing solemnly by, without taking alarm or any notice of me. The camel-man himself (I only saw one) followed chanting in high pitched nasal tones, and he passed within a few feet of me, but failed to observe me, although I was lying quite unconcealed in the open. Probably his thoughts were turned inwards, and were concerned mostly with his bad luck at being on night dirty; if he saw me at all he probably thought I was some dead bush or sand heap; but, while he was passing, I was wondering all the time whether, if one of the camels trod on me, I should be able to avoid moving or crying out. It was all over in a quarter of an hour, and the last of the slow-moving grazing animals had gone past and faded once more into the silver grey of the skyline; but by then the moon had become so totally obscured by clouds that I could no longer determine my direction, and had perforce to waste yet another hour until the sky had once more cleared.

I had taken rests of a few minutes at 9 p.m. and midnight,

during which I had eaten a few dates, and licked the dripping hairs on the outside of my water-skin; but I think I was all the better for this extra compulsory wait of an hour, for it gave me time to survey damages. The shoes that Apcar had lent me proved to be a little too small, and I found when I took them off that, as I had for some time suspected, both my big toe nails had worked loose at the roots. To prevent them being turned right over backwards, I tied pieces of rag around both toe and nail; but this, though better than nothing, proved to be a very painful remedy, for the rag strips quickly cut into the flesh of my toe, so that both my feet were continually bleeding. I had, in addition, some pretty bad blisters on my heel, owing to not having worn foot-gear for nearly two months.

The rice also, which I had started out with, slung from my shoulders in front, I found hampered my movements a great deal, by banging to and fro against my body at every stride. I therefore alternately carried it in my hand, or hung it from my staff over my shoulder; an irksome and awkward arrangement, but a very much better one than my original method. My shoulders also gradually became accustomed to the cutting ropes of the water-skin, which at first I had found so painful.

As I journeyed, I found that the country was by no means so flat as the Indians had represented it to be; but then, they had probably gone by a different route to myself. It was about 1 a.m., I think, that I passed over a low range of boulder-strewn hills, from whose summit I gazed down on to the wet, shimmering desert, which in the moonlight had the appearance of the sea. But I could find no pool of water in spite of the recent heavy rain, though there had obviously been puddles quite recently, and in places my feet sank deep into mud, leaving behind an unmistakable track, which caused me to take the precaution of keeping, so far as possible, to harder, stonier ground.

But what amazed me and disquieted me most was the fact that there were numbers of other tracks, well defined paths through the desert, which, to judge by the fresh appearance of the cam-el droppings, had apparently quite recently been used; most of these tracks ran south-east and north-west diagonally across my own easterly course. The Indians had been most positive in their assertion that they had encountered no one on their way from Sollum; how then was I to account for this phenomenon, which seemed to betoken a much frequented neighbourhood?

Towards morning I began to feel very done with the heavy weight I was carrying, and the awful stones stubbing my mutilated toes; but the camel caravan incident helped to freshen me up considerably, and I managed to keep going at a steady pace.

At dawn I found myself in an absolutely flat and cover-less plain, with nothing of any sort in sight, whereat I stumbled on yet another couple of miles, until I got to a place where there were shrubs some three or four feet high growing. There I set me down to make my calculations, and write up my log on the back of my map. I found I had done very well. It was as follows:

Sun., 6.30 p.m. to Mon., 6.30 a.m. = 12 hours.
Stopped to hide from caravan,
4 a.m. . . . . = 1 hour.
Stopped by clouds to rest. = 1 hour.
Total, to 6.30 a.m., at 2½ miles per hr. = 10 hr. = 25 miles.
Drank 4 tins of water; ate 1 day's rations.

I spent all that day, Monday, hiding among the low shrubs; a very anxious day it was, and sleep a luxury quite out of the question, for, as soon as it was fully light, a number of large caravans passed quite close to me, with much noise and shouting of camelmen, and isolated groups of pedestrians often came within easy speaking distance; one group, a man on a horse-i and two women, I could easily have lobbed a biscuit on to, as they passed my frail cover. Luckily for me, they were busily engaged in heated argument, and therefore were not very observant, for the average Arab eyesight would certainly unerringly have detected me lying in hiding, the bush being too small to shut me out completely. I spent the whole day dodging round this bush, the largest of its kind, and dragging my water-skin and belongings after me, in my efforts to keep out of sight. By good fortune no two parties ever passed my bush from opposite sides at the same time, or I should inevitably have been seen by one or the other of them.

But my chief anxiety now was my water supply. There could no longer be any question that the skin was leaking terribly—there was no visible hole in it, it was simply a question of its age and general porosity; drip, drip, drip it went, and the precious fluid was lost in the sand. As I watched, I could see its bulk grow steadily less, already half of my whole stock appeared to have thus been lost. I put my mouth to it and kept licking the hairy outside, but this was really very little of an economy, for, what with loose hairs and congealed dust, I got more dirt than liquid into my mouth. Later on in the afternoon the stream of passers-by began to diminish, until at length there was no one in sight. All tins time I had not dared to sleep, but nevertheless I felt much rested and refreshed; so an hour and a half before sunset, after a good look round, I got on the move again, wearing my Arab clothes over all. It was fortunate for me that I had done so, for I had gone but a short distance when, coming to the edge of an invisible shallow wadi or valley, I found myself unexpectedly in the immediate vicinity of eight Arab tents stretched in a row along its course, and about which there were several people moving. It was too late then to turn back, as they must already have observed me; I therefore bad to trust to my disguise, and, by making a gradual detour, without going any closer to the tents, I gradually circled round them until I could once more proceed directly on my easterly course. Somebody at the tents actually waved to me, and shouted a something which I did not understand, probably a salutation. To him I replied by also waving and shouting in a similar manner; but it was with a very thankful heart that I at last lost sight of this camp astern of me. It must have been from thence that the caravans I had seen had taken their departure in the morning.

But where was the uninhabited country of which the Indiana had spoken? This, which I was in, certainly could not have been it, and I now felt sure that they must have come by an entirely different route. But, the solitude of the route was a matter of vital moment in all the calculations which I had made for a successful escape, and I already saw that my chances of getting through were greatly diminished.

There was rather a strong mirage before sunset on that afternoon, and I had several more scares before darkness finally set in, caused by my sighting some heaps of stones, the graves of long departed Bedouin, and a ruined building or two, which I took for another village. Distance in the desert where everything is much the same shape and the same khaki colour, is extremely difficult to judge, and consequently one is often unable even to guess at the size of an object when first seen. A large saddle shaped well-mound, an Arab tent, a humped camel, a grave cairn, a rock, a bush, a jerboa-mound, all look alike to the European eye. For a time, it is impossible to feel certain whether the object looked at is a well-mound forty feet high five miles off, a tent ten feet high one mile off, or a jerboa-mound showing just above a slight rise only a hundred yards distant; for there is nothing to compare them with, and they are identical in shape and colour, moreover, the mirage and the skimmer of the atmosphere cause the distant object often to show up more clearly and distinctly than the nearby one.

With nightfall, my troubles again began; fortunately the stones were not quite so bad as on the preceding night in the immediate vicinity of Bir Hakkim, and there were in addition more .bushes, which generally indicate firm, level going; but, with my feet in the condition they were in, and nearly all my toe-nails now secured in place with rag and pieces of thread, any walking at all was an exquisite agony.

There were, however, many fires visible after dark, and the necessity for avoiding these helped to divert my thoughts from the mere physical pain; the sight of them was most disquieting, and I appeared to be in about as an uninhabited a neighbourhood as Hyde Park. Every now and then a dog barked at me, but fortunately Arabs are not, if they can help it, night walkers, and I encountered no one. I continued to tramp steadily along at about, two and a half miles an hour until midnight, when I took a short rest.

From then on I continued with very short rests and occasional licks at my water-skin, at a gradually diminishing pace. There came a time when I could no longer lift my feet over the bushes and stones, my thighs got cramp from exhaustion and no longer responded to the impetus of my mind. I stumbled and fell every now and then, and for a few seconds would be unable to rise. But I went on, somehow, until the first pink dawn showed in the eastern sky. It was the release I had been waiting for, and I literally fell in a heap into the nearest bush, unable further to move hand or foot.

Some beast of prey was coughing and snarling near at hand, love-making in the manner of the felidœ. I did not see him, for he was in a clump of bushes a hundred yards or so away; but I think he was a leopard by the volume and catlike quality of the sound. It may have been only some large wild cat, but Colonel Snow had told me that leopards occasionally, though rarely, visited the vicinity of Sollum. However that may be, I took no notice of the animal, nor he, for that matter, of me; we had both got better occupations. And presently, recovering somewhat, I ate some of the rice and wrote up my log. My entry is as follows:

Started 4 p.m. and walked until 6 a.m., east by north, 2.3 miles per hour, with 2½ hours' rest.

Drank 5 tins water.

Total at sunrise on Tuesday=11½ hrs. at 2.3 m.p.h. = 26½ miles.

This appeared to be a good neighbourhood for hiding in, for it was uneven and covered with shrubs, some of the bushes being as much as five feet in height. Dragging myself to my feet, I hung my water-skin in the nearest bush, and put my drinking cup under it. The skin was now three-quarters empty, but not, leaking quite so fast as before, and I hoped by this means to save some of the precious drops.

Then, in the dim twilight of the early dawn, I lay down once more, in the joyful consciousness that in two nights I had accomplished more than half my journey. I had come fifty-one and a half miles, at a conservative estimate, out of the calculated eighty miles. I at once fell into the dreamless sleep of utter exhaustion.

CHAPTER 31

# I Become a Star Turn

It must have been about an hour later that I awoke suddenly, conscious that something was happening; possibly it was a human voice that was borne to my ears. The sun was well up, and everything bathed in dazzling sunshine. Cautiously raising myself on my elbows, I gazed at my surroundings, the which the dim light of dawn had prevented my properly seeing before I went to sleep.

My heart gave a rebound and seemed to stand still. On every side of me were men and droves of camels moving in various directions; quite close at hand was a collection of twenty or more tents, with herds of sheep and goats, and I could see other similar groups in the distance. I was literally trapped, and had lain down almost in an Arab village; and, as I watched, I saw the children come out to play. Possibly I might even now elude the herdsmen, but sharp-sighted children, invading every quiet spot to play at hide-and-seek, I could hardly hope to escape.

But fortune had favoured me so much hitherto that I did not even then despair; laying as flat as possible on the ground, from behind my leafy screen I watched anxiously the course of events. I had not long to wait. A group of men with guns was passing by, when one of them suddenly stopped and looked intently in my direction; he then shouted to his companions and pointed towards where I was hiding. Feeling quite sure that he could not possibly see me, I looked anxiously round to discover a cause for this action on his part. I was soon enlightened, for there, plain for all the world to see, was my fatal water-skin hanging from the bush above my head and still drip-drip-dripping its precious drops away. I knew then, that I had thus unwittingly made a signal which would seal my own fate. It was only the dull stupor of utter exhaustion which could have made me do so foolish a thing, or have caused me to lie down so near a village; but now it was too late to remedy it.

The men—there were three of them—began to run in my direction. Covering myself all over with my burnous, I lay at full length, pretending to be asleep, having at the time some faint hope that they would hesitate to arouse an individual of whose identity they knew nothing, and who appeared to be an Arab even as themselves. But an Arab has little sympathy with anyone who is found asleep after daybreak. I felt sharp fingers clutch into my shoulder and drag at me. I snorted and turned over again, as though wishing to continue my sleep. It was useless, and I felt myself dragged roughly to my feet.

I opened my eyes. At once there were loud ejaculations of astonishment; for I have blue eyes, and blue eyes are not seen among the Arabs. On the contrary, they are an object of derision and hatred, the sign of the accursed foreigner!

The three men, as I now observed, were of the most villainous and cut-throat type, quite the worst I had yet seen. Having got over their first astonishment, and examined me and the water-skin, they started to shout questions excitedly at me. As I was unable to understand them, they shouted yet the louder, emphasizing the importance of an answer with pokes of their rifle muzzles. As I was still unable to answer them, they then settled the matter for themselves, by rapidly going over my person with deft lingers to see if I had any belongings of value, and they were evidently much astonished at the discovery of my tattered old naval uniform under my outer Arab garments. I seized this opportunity to impress them with my great personal importance, pointing out my tarnished gold lace and the shreds of medal ribbon still remaining. I also got out my book of the words and started to recite to them my prepared sentences of Arabic, dwelling lingeringly upon my present poverty, but emphasising the immense quantity of gold which would accrue to the happy individual who conducted me in safety to Sollum. But my captors were much too excited to take heed at the time of what I was telling them, and I soon found myself stripped stark naked, for the better examination of my property; they then noticed that I was neither Mahomedan or Jew, and I began to see my death warrant written in their avaricious eyes, as they lovingly-fingered their rifle triggers and looked meaningfully at me.

It was at that moment that a diversion fortunately occurred. In so populous a neighbourhood, such an incident as my capture could not go unnoticed, and other groups were quickly making their way to the scene. Before my first captors could proceed any further, some twenty or thirty other Senussi had come up, with the evident intention of participating in the spoils. I and my belongings were pulled this way and that, and I was seized by a new group who drove off. my former owners, intimating to me at the same time by a sign that the former would undoubtedly cut my throat, a matter of which I had by then not the faintest doubt. But my new captors were themselves little better; they also maltreated and jeered at me, and the whole routine of apprising and valuing my belongings on their part, and of Arabic sentences and promises of future reward on mine, was gone through once more. For the moment I averted death; my Arabic speeches were gradually understood, and, perhaps, had some effect, and everything of mine which the natives touched, I roundly asserted was the special gift of the Grand Senussi to me, or, failing hint, of Nouri Bey. But I was by no means out of the wood yet. Hardly able to walk from exhaustion, but with a very sharp eye on my personal belongings, I was driven forward towards the tents, while every now and then, one of the Arabs in advance turned round and fired a shot at a few feet range in my direction. These shots were probably not intended really to hit me, but were meant to startle, and, if possible, to scare me; I fancy it was their idea of humour, a similar one to that used by the cow-punchers of the Wild West, when desirous of making a tenderfoot dance. If this were its purpose, it most signally failed, for by this time I was reckless with exhaustion, and openly jeered at this intimidating process. I felt, in fact, that it was time to assert myself and my importance once more. Among my most valued possessions there was a steel needle, a special gift from Selim to myself. One of the brigands, happening on this at the moment, at once annexed it. Instead of meekly submitting, as he evidently expected I should do, I at once seized him and shook him, and forced him to give it back. This done, I explained in pantomime to him that it was my own property. Having made him understand this, I then took the needle, and, with a great show of ceremony, solemnly presented it to him. So strange a thing is human nature that this cut-throat whom, only a moment before, was, I have no doubt, not only willing but eager to shed my blood, now felt a sense of shame. At first he would not even accept the gift; but, when I forced it on him, he reluctantly accepted it. It was a good move on my part; the rifle firing ceased, and my new friend, whom I took care to keep close at my side, kept me from, a good bit of unpleasantness.

For the remainder of the morning I was dragged round and exhibited at the various tents, much as dancing bears used to be in England, and my uniform, and the tattoos with which my arms are covered were displayed with much pride. I smiled and endeavoured to ingratiate myself with the inhabitants, but my first smile was almost my undoing—for I have a gold tooth! The sight of so much wealth (for to these incredibly poor people, a gold tooth meant real riches) at once excited their cupidity, and they appeared to consider that the removal of my head was the simplest method of obtaining the treasure. Seeing how the wind blew, I thereupon hastened to assure them that the object of their avarice was not gold, and I intimated that it was in reality brass or some such base metal; they believed me, for they could not credit that any human being would employ gold so extravagantly, but the display of my tooth was added to my other assets for showing-off purposes from that moment on.

It was now late afternoon, and I kept dropping from exhaustion and heat, when, approaching a new group of tents, there emerged from them two individuals arrayed in tattered khaki uniforms, who had evidently been aroused by the shouting from slumber. They were armed with somewhat ancient Martini carbines which they held in readiness, and at sight of which the Senussi began to slink away. I soon tumbled to it that these were two Turkish soldiers billeted in the village. They themselves were evidently puzzled by my appearance, and at the facts which the Senussi vociferously gabbled to them of my strange discovery. However, they at once annexed me as their own property, intimating to me by the usual gesture that my late companions intended to cut my throat. They then, like the others, proceeded to go once more dexterously over my person, with all the experience of old campaigners; but from this they soon desisted, realising that what such past-masters of the art of pilfering as the Senussi had left untouched, was unlikely to have a value which amounted to anything. My new Turkish friends then proceeded to interrogate me, an ordeal which, owing to mutual lack of knowledge of each other's language, consisted mainly of pantomime. I, however, worked off all my prepared Arabic sentences, to which they appeared to listen sympathetically. Perhaps, if Sollum had in reality been then in the possession of the British, as I believed, they might even, on the promise of unlimited gold, have taken me thither.

But, as it was, I got off very well in the end. The uncertainty as to my identity, and my own assurance in continually quoting the Grand Senussi and Nouri Pasha as my friends and patrons, prevented anything of real value to me being taken. Even my diary was treated with the greatest respect and returned to me; for the Moslem mind appears to reverence written characters in any form, more especially when it cannot understand them.

In those days I had not witnessed that dramatic British work of art, The Bing Boys; if I had done so, I should certainly have recognised in my two Turkish captors beings eminently fitted to fill the title role of that play. They were both Cretans, I believe, one being called Ali Hassan, and the other Mahmoud. Of the two, Ali Hassan was short, thick-set, as broad as he was long, essentially vulgar, and of a dark and Negroid type of countenance. The other, Mahmoud, was slim and good-looking, with regular features, of a more refined nature and able to read and write

Turkish with facility. Never did two men work better together, each supplying the qualities that the other lacked, their talents being complementary and not opposite. They played up to each other like the two comic villains of a pantomime, and they had become to each other so indispensable as to be inseparable. If it were a matter of robbery, intimidation or threat, then the bad old campaigner, Ali Hassan, with his bull neck, threatening brow, and ready rifle, was the chief actor; but when it was a question of gentle diplomacy, of trickery, or of sex dalliance, the pretty boy, Mahmoud, became the central figure, and the burly Ali Hassan kept his ugly bulk out, of sight. As I was destined to spend a whole week in the company of these two gentlemen, I had much opportunity for studying their merits. We three became very fast friends, and I was indeed sorry when we had to part. But I am anticipating.

My pantomimic interrogation having finished, and my uniform, ribbons, tattoos and belongings having been duly studied, Hassan looked at me and said the one word Leglise. Having repeated it several times, I gathered that he meant that I was English, and to this statement I assented. They then both whistled loudly and flapped their arms after the manner of a bird in flight. There was no mistaking the pantomime this time; they were obviously gently suggesting that I was an escapee. To this I again gave my assent and mentioned the word Bir Hakkim, whereat Ali Hassan, with his forefinger, drew down the lower eyelid of his right eye, exposing the red eyeball. This is the Eastern method of winking, or showing incredulity, and I responded by myself making a grimace. To my surprise, they both roared with laughter, and I was made to repeat the gesture, which was evidently new to them. Seeing their unfailing delight at its repetition, I then assumed several other facial expressions—hauteur, disdain, withering contempt, superciliousness, vanity, and the like. I was a made man! Never was Charlie Chaplin half so appreciated as I in that Bedouin camp of the Red Desert. My fame at once spread through the village, and I was once more taken from tent to tent, my uniform and tattoos now becoming only a side show; but as a facial contortionist, I at once rose to fame as the Star Turn of the Libyan Desert. No more did I squat humbly in the dust. I was gives the seat of honour, and, having duly performed in turn to each delighted family gathering, I was liberally rewarded with handfuls of dates and bowls of milk. Even then, I could not help smiling to myself at the thought of how those grave and stately gentlemen who adorn the Admiralty at Whitehall, would regard this novel method of earning a living, especially by one in their employ, and who held, moreover, the exalted rank of Captain in His Majesty's Navy! But so it was, and I have many a time done far harder and less pleasant work for smaller reward. With all my other accomplishments, however, my gold tooth still continued to be an asset of value; thus are misfortunes often in themselves a benefit! Civilised dental treatment was in itself a marvel in that land of perfect teeth. I remember once, at Bir Hakkim, the amusement we prisoners all derived when Captain Tanner, sitting with some guards round the fire, allowed the upper plate of his false teeth to fall. The guards, seeing the teeth only and not the plate, suspended thus inexplicably without apparent support in the middle of his open mouth, at once fled in terror, as though the devil himself was after them.

That night I slept on the floor of a tent with my two Turkish guardians, each with a hand on my shoulder, his loaded Martini rifle sticking into my side, and a big camel rug over the three of us; for with all their rough kindliness, they evidently still suspected me of an intention to escape. As though I had not already had enough exertion in the past forty-eight hours! As a matter of fact I was quite incapable of further movement, and could only feebly resent their notions of etiquette as to bed manners. My shoes I was compelled to take off, and my head-rag I was made to wear; against this dictum there was apparently no appeal, although my brow was burning and my feet were icy cold!

# CHAPTER 32

# Lodgers and Life in a Tent

That night of February 22nd-23rd was not all joy, in spite of the hitherto unknown luxury of a warm rug and a tent to cover my bones. The truth was, my two bandit Turk companions were a bit unsavoury, due to a many years' innocence of ablution and to the multitudinous hosts of vermin which inhabited their persons and clothing; these insect *lodgers* evidently considered my person as *fresh fields and pastures new*, and a general migration from both sides set in towards me. I was none too squeamish in those days, as may be imagined; three and a half months as a prisoner had somewhat acclimatised me to the third plague of Egypt, to which I fear Moses would have found both Turk and Senussi quite indifferent. In fact, for a long time we had been infested with pests, but, being by ourselves, we could keep their numbers in some kind of check after the manner of our monkey cousins. But the present invasion was on such a scale that I found myself quite helpless against it, and, for the third night, in succession I got not a wink of sleep, even had not the barking of dogs, the squealing of camels, cold feet and the knobby parts of two rifles in my ribs, been sufficient to abolish it. When one is already weak and exhausted, this nightly loss of sleep and blood, is a somewhat trying matter.

In the next few days I was to have much opportunity of studying the Arab at home, and the first thing which impressed me was the ideal nature of his habitation, the tent, for the climate in which he dwelt. Hitherto I had only lived in the rag-

199

ged and overcrowded tabernacle with which we were supplied at Bir Hakkim, but the tents which I saw now were a different proposition altogether. They were all quite new, they appeared rich and luxurious, filled with magnificent carpets and rugs of wonderful texture and thickness. Seen by the bright light of the fire burning at the door, the dark and cavernous recesses of the roof had quite a Gothic aspect.

A Bedouin tent is of the simplest construction; merely an oblong carpet made of camel or goat's hair, or of sheep's wool, and formed into natural-coloured bands of black-and-tan broad stripes. To erect it, two light poles are placed under the longer centre, where sockets have been fitted, about six feet apart, and the poles having then been raised and the sides pulled out by ropes secured to stones or pegs, the roof is complete. Around the under-edge of this roof a detachable flap is hung by wooden skewers; the lower edge of the flap on the ground being weighted with stones. The house is then complete, one side generally being left open, and the superabundant portion of the flap hauled out to serve as a screen to break the wind. It is within this sheltered enclosure outside that the fire is lit, and the family congregate to watch the cooking and discuss the news of the day, and it was here that I learned what little I know of Arab manners and customs. The village doctor was generally one of the first guests to drop in, invariably a powerful and saturnine-looking man. I always knew he was the doctor, for my Turkish soldier friends introduced him by drawing a finger across their throats; an intimation that he combined the gentle art of medicine, with the equally important duties of Lord High Executioner, and amputator-in-chief of the hands of malefactors.

The lack of bridge and other games appeared to pass quite unnoticed. The host and all the guests invariably opened the proceedings pleasantly by a lodger hunt, a sport at which they were all very adept and which hardly seemed to require the use of eyesight, for they merely had to put their hands into their bosoms to be sure of a good haul, which they nonchalantly threw into the fire; the ladies of the company being similarly engaged in the background. The Bedouin women I saw were never veiled, but on first meeting them, they customarily made a show of putting one hand before their faces, immediately afterwards to peep between their fingers, and then forget, all about such formalities. The Senussi women, as a rule, are naturally comely, full-bosomed, and of graceful figure, but terribly marred by the universal custom of tattooing their faces. They are generally well dressed in black or red clothes, whereas the men are mostly in white, or what passes for white in a soap-less land. The women, from all I saw of them, were treated with the greatest kindness and consideration, squatting somewhat in the background, but taking an animated interest in the conversation; they have a very definite place in the order of things with which they appear to be content, and never attempt to exceed. In height they are disproportionately small as compared with the men.

It is curious how the duties of the sexes appear to be reversed in this country. It is the man who stops at home, does the mending, cooking and cutting out, and a pleasant time he appears to have of it. The women and children wander out, gather the firewood, and till the fields when there are any.

Married life, though I know our Anglican bishops will disagree with me, appears to be very happy, in spite of the facility of divorce. A man has only to say, "I divorce you" three times, and he has got his *decree absolute.* But, strange to say, he seldom says it, for a wife is a real help-mate in this topsy turvy land, and an asset for which he has had to pay a large sum of money. It is his job to make life as pleasant as he can for his wife, for. if he does not, she is apt to run off and leave him, in which case "all the king's horses and all the king's men" cannot get her back again. Although the wife cannot divorce the husband, it is the custom and the proper thing for him to release her on such occasions. And to get another wife will make a nasty hole in his pocket! Hence this conjugal felicity.

Again, the Senussi being Moslems, *may* have more than one wife; but, excepting the very wealthy, few of them possess so much happiness. But when a wife gets very old, and is no longer able to add to the juvenile population of Senussi-land, the husband often pensions her off, and adds a second bride to his *ménage,*. This appears to give satisfaction all round, and I was unable to observe that it led to any jealousy. Man being in charge of the domestic organisation at home, as might be expected washing–up and suchlike extravaganzas are reduced to the simplest forms. There are no plates, crockery, nor silver, merely one or two large wooden bowls, out of which all eat with their fingers, and a large iron or brass pot, in which the food is cooked. These cannot be broken and are apparently never washed, and as the floor is the. sand of the desert with a rug over it, the servant problem has been much simplified in Libya; it also being a land where no one does any work if they can help it, there is no need for stamp licking nor of unemployment doles.

Table manners are simple. If there is rice (at that time a very rare commodity, owing to the blockade) it is placed in the large unwashed bowl in the centre of the group, and each grabs that portion directly in front of him and pushes it down his throat in one or two mouthfuls.

More generally the meal is dates. These are served in a similar manner to the rice, but you may only grab them one at a time. You then eject the stone with the forefinger and thumb of one hand into the bowl, and with the other hand, you throw the stoned date down your throat. This requires as much skill as shuffling or dealing cards, and, owing to my original lack of proficiency in it, I got hardly anything to eat for the first few nights, and broke my best tooth on a date–stone in addition. For, unless you can eat dates as fast as a hen picks up corn, you do not stand a dog's chance.

Camel's, goat's, or sheep's milk, sometimes soured and sometimes fresh, is often served round in the same unwashed bowl. It is passed from hand to hand, each guest taking a suck with a loud in–drawing of the breath. This is not done to make it taste like milk and soda, but to limit the quantity you can swallow at one gulp; when your lungs are full you have to stop drinking. Greediness is, therefore, limited to lung capacity, and not to the dimensions of *little Mary*.

But at the time of which I am writing, there was great scarcity throughout the land; rice, barley-flour and dates were becoming a rare commodity, and the poorer part of the population was driven to subsisting mainly upon snails and roots.

It was a revolting sight to see the huge iron pot filled to the brim with slimy snails, while the family gathered round and watched them boil and afterwards gorged them, cracking the shells like nuts upon stones, their faces and hands smeared with the brown juice.

I have seen it on many occasions. We prisoners at Bir Hakkim were not the only wretches in an abject state of starvation. Black famine lay on the land; only with the Turk, and his Senussi army, was food to be found.

But, strange as it may seem, with all their squalor and filthy ways, these Bedouins always gave me the idea of being aristocrats. Many a time the firelight reflected from their faces, I have sat and fancied myself in a West End drawing-room. There was the same old dowager, the same marriageable daughters, the same match-makers, the man with a tip, the bore, the courtly gentleman, and the man with a dog round the corner. These sons of Esau have most patrician features, and an engaging, devil-may-care generosity of manner. I never felt with them somehow that they were Eastern, as I should with Armenian, Indian or Jew. I could enter into their feelings, understand and sympathise with their ways. Living the life they lived, suffering the things they suffered, a feeling of kinship seemed to grow up between us.

# CHAPTER 33

# I Learn to Live on Nothing a Day

Wednesday, February 23rd, the day after my recapture, was an interesting but exhausting one for me, for I had no idea at that time as to what the real intentions of my two Turkish guardians, Mahmoud and Ali Hassan, with regard to my disposal might happen to be, or even whether my profuse promises of gold had prevailed with them, and they were considering the matter of conducting me to Sollum.

However, they roused me out at earliest sunrise, an action which I strongly resented, for I was by then so stiff and sore that I could hardly move, and the lodgers who had feasted on me all night had pretty well absorbed what little energy I had still remaining. From about 6 a.m. until 2 p.m. the Turks continued taking me round from tent to tent, after the manner of the previous days' proceedings, and having pulled faces and performed my tricks, we were generally rewarded with either dates or milk. So far as I could see, the country was covered with rows of tents in every direction, and with each row of tents were great vertical frames, upon which the Bedouin weave their carpets and tent cloths. Countless flocks of camels, sheep and goats covered the plain, feeding upon the pasture and foliage which had sprung up everywhere since the rains, and I began to realise how entirely hopeless my chances of escape had been in reality from the very first, and to understand the wherefore. For nine or ten months of every year this part of Libya is practically uninhabited; only a rare caravan or two passes across it, and this was probably its condition when the Indians had come through five weeks previously. The inhabitants of the land, during the long drought, live mainly in the west, where there is more water and some rivers; but with the first coming of spring, they migrate eastward, moving up and down with their flocks as did Abraham and Lot, and quarrelling for the rich but temporary pasturage, even as did those two patriarchs. There appeared to be few permanent water supplies available, the innumerable bir or Roman cisterns, with which the desert plains is dotted, being at that date nearly all choked to the brim with rubbish, and therefore useless; but both the camels and the flocks could go for long periods without water, and the Bedouin themselves subsisted to a great extent on the milk of these camels and goats. As the pasturage grew more scanty, and died off in the month of March, the Arab camps would be shifted once more to the west, and even at this early date (February 23rd) the majority had already begun their movement in a westerly direction. But famine had already gripped the land, and every site upon which an Arab camp had rested was plainly advertised by the huge white heaps of empty snail-shells—a monument of whose meaning we prisoners from Bir Hakkim needed no explanation.

Our courses this day were so very diverse, as we moved from tent to tent, that I found it very difficult to keep an accurate account of them. We were going much too far to the north to suit my taste, and I kept pointing my guides to what I believed to be the true direction of Sollum, but at this Ali and Mahmoud only smiled. However, I comforted myself with the thought that at any rate we were still going easterly, and that they showed at present no disposition to turn round to the west and take me back to Bir Hakkim. In the end I came to the conclusion that Sollum must in reality be further to the north than I had calculated it to be, and that we were probably heading in its direction.

Passing a tent where there were some beautiful hawks, Mahmoud, after the display of a little gallantry, succeeded in persuading the fair house-mistress to lend him one. We had gone hardly a mile, when we put up a hare at which the hawk was promptly launched; but after hovering round in the air in an undecided manner for a few moments, the bird made off, and we saw it no more; a fact which seemed to trouble no one, nor did the gallant Mahmoud appear the least disturbed about the loss of his borrowed property. Presently the country became more and more deserted, until there was no longer a tent nor a human being in sight, when to my great surprise in a slight depression of the ground we suddenly came upon a camel escorted by two armed men and accompanied by a graceful Arab girl of about eighteen years of age. My delight was immense, for I felt sure that now my two Turkish friends really did intend to take me to Sollum; they had not wished to appear to acquiesce before the other Senussi, but had secretly arranged this camel for me, in an out of the way spot, where we could make our departure unobserved. My spirits, however, were slightly damped when the two soldiers themselves got on to the camel's back, and left me to trudge behind; riding side saddle, with a loose rug thrown over the animal's back to sit on, they laughed and joked as the beast shambled along.

The two camelmen who accompanied us I did not quite like the look of, they appeared to me to be too interested in my personal property; but the soldiers took no notice, Mahmoud himself being too busily engaged in ogling the fair camel-girl, who herself assumed an air of only being interested in searching for tortoises, a table delicacy especially dear to the hearts of Arab women. These animals, although quite gaily coloured in black and white, need extra sharp eyes to detect them in their hiding places under the bushes.

We went on like this for a few miles in various directions, when, to my surprise, the two Turkish soldiers got down from the camel and made off, leaving me alone with the two strange and malevolent-looking camelmen. I once more began to be filled with suspicions that I was to be murdered in this isolated spot, and that the soldiers did not, as representatives of Turkey, wish to be present or complicated in the deed, but that they would presently come, back to participate in the spoil. However, a little reflection reassured me, for I felt confident that if such had really been their intention then they would never have brought a woman with them as a witness to the crime, and once more I began to hope that the camelmen were the selected means for bringing me to Sollum.

We wandered on in this manner for another mile or two, and then sighted a fire with a couple of men near it; as we got closer, I recognised to my great surprise that it was the two Turkish soldiers again, and with them, to my great joy, I found they had the biggest and fattest lamb which I had yet seen in the country.

They had just killed the animal, and the thorn-fire burned clear and bright. In an incredibly short time the lamb was skinned, hewn in pieces, and cast upon the flames. As each part was cooked, it was hooked out with a stick, portioned and devoured. The first part to be ready was the feet, then the liver, lights and kidneys, then the entrails, stomach and head. By the time we had finished eating these, the carcase and limbs were well roasted. The whole animal disappeared in less than half an hour from the time of my arrival, and, though we had neither salt nor bread, neither knives, forks, nor plates, there are few meals which it comes to man in life to enjoy as I enjoyed that one.

The Arabs tore the flesh like wolves, and cracked the bones with their teeth to extract the marrow, and I followed their example as well as I was able. So cooked, the entrails (quite uncleaned) of this sucking lamb were by far the best part of the animal, cut into lengths of about a foot and deliciously crisp and tender. I was able to understand why at Bir Hakkim when a goat or sheep was killed, our guards invariably took this *offal* and relegated to us the lean and sinewy carcase. The liver and lights, too, thus roasted in a white flame, have a seductive flavour which no civilised frying-pan can impart, and even the feet (hoofs, hair and all) were decidedly tasty and the stomach palatable. In fact, it was all uncommonly good, and I felt very much better and twice as much a man after such a quantity of nourishing food. I therefore began to have a real feeling of affection for Ali and Mahmoud, tempered with admiration at their having been able to provide such a feast in the wilderness, though how they had done it I could not imagine; but I never thereafter had the least doubt of their good intentions towards me.

Before the last strip of flesh was fairly down our throats, we were on the march again. In the distance, the yellow mound of the bir was showing up, and the camelmen were sent ahead with my goat-skin bag to see whether they could fill it with water there. We ourselves pursued a devious course in another direction. At first I could not follow the reason for this, but presently I spied a large flock of sheep and goats which we were overtaking. As we got nearer to it, Ali ran forward with his most threatening air, his bloodshot eyes flaming murder and his Martini pointed at the shepherd's breast.; the latter, after one startled look, fled helter-skelter for his life, leaving his shepherdess on her knees in a state of great terror, with the flock. The gallant Mahmoud at once proceeded to reassure the lady, and, having torn a blank page from my diary, presented her with a neat little I.O.U. for one sheep, written in Turkish. Whilst Mahmoud was thus pleasantly engaged, Ali had been inspecting the flock, and suddenly sprang upon the fattest lamb, which he seized, and bore off on his shoulders wildly bleating and struggling. We then proceeded to join the camelmen again, followed at a distance by the shepherd and his wife, who pursued us with loud acclamations and curses, and much shaking of fists. From time to time Ali would sally out and drive them off again with his gun.

During this scene of brigandage, not being then hungry, and having just eaten about ten pounds of mutton, I looked on with horror, and the cries of the two plundered shepherds filled me with pity. This was the answer to the provisioning problem which had for some time apparently weighed on the minds of my two soldier hosts. Again and again they had asked me for money, and finding that I, like themselves, had none of that unnecessary commodity, they had been driven to finding another solution of that ancient riddle of how to live on nothing a day.

Its unravelling appeared to give them the greatest satisfaction; a mile from the scene of the robbery, with the shepherd's cries still resounding in our ears, we killed and cooked the sheep, and commenced a second orgy, all within an hour of the completion of the first. Not till his pet lamb was finally dead did the shepherd depart, calling down curses on our heads, to the great amusement of us bandits. But this time we did not eat the whole animal, and merely consumed the *innards*. The greater part of the carcase we slung over the camel (whom I had nicknamed *Lizzie*, a name which eminently suited her), and departed.

Never was there a more cross-grained or slower beast than Lizzie proved to be. Her best pace seemed to be limited to a mile and a half per hour, and she never went more than her own length in any one direction, but zigzagged and tacked like a schooner with a drunken pilot; every living thing which came within reach of her she bit and kicked at.

Our progress was consequently somewhat slow, but, about an hour after dark, we sighted the fires of an Arab camp, wherein we made our abode for the night. Observing the fat lamb's carcase upon the camel, we were well received. An enormous black iron pot was brought forward, and the lamb was put into it and boiled. The resulting broth, about two quarts, looked uncommonly good, but my Turkish friends evidently despised it, and gave it with sundry pickings to the owner of the tent and his women-kind. The remainder of the animal we ate up ourselves within a very short time.

Thus, within four hours, we six individuals had entirely consumed two complete sheep, less the hide, horns and bones. That night I felt no hunger, but very decided pains; thus does conscience make cowards of us all, for I straight-way vowed never to eat mutton again! My Arab friends, however, being in no way inconvenienced by their gluttony, apparently experienced no qualms of conscience, and they were obviously surprised and annoyed when I wished to curtail the usual evening pantomime, the fame of which performance had preceded our arrival at the village, and to witness which an eager throng had already gathered. My excuses were of no avail, and I had to go through the show as best I could! Although we had been afoot over thirteen hours, from sunrise until after sunset, we had apparently only accomplished some sixteen miles to the north-east during the day.

At sunrise the next morning, Thursday, February 24th, I was again dragged out, feeling very *piano* as the result of excessive mutton, the debauch having affected me probably more than it would otherwise have done, owing to the fact that for the previous three months I had practically been a vegetarian.

For some hours we wandered from tent to tent, where, having duly performed my tricks, we were as usual rewarded with several bowls of camel milk, but no dates. I fancy there was no food left in this village but the flesh and milk of the herds, and the inhabitants were in the main existing upon roots and snails. But the result of this purely liquid diet was that I soon began to get hungry again, and to cast an anxious eye about the horizon to see if by chance there were any more sheep on the move.

We had not long to wait, and overtaking a flock, the usual simple process of acquisition was gone through. On this occasion, however, the shepherd was of tougher metal than his predecessors, and his wife a virago of the most outrageous type. She would have none of Mahmoud's signed papers, nor was she to be cozened by his gallantries; but, on the contrary, she tore the paper up and threw it in his face, and appeared to be about to use her claws upon his person, but, changing her mind, burst into tears instead. The shepherd himself was sour and dour, and would not leave us; only when we had actually killed and eaten the whole sheep did he depart, with muttered and long-drawn vows of vengeance.

How strange a thing is that feeling which we call conscience! Only yesterday I had looked on with horrified pity at this despoiling and open robbery of poor people. Today, I found myself entirely in sympathy with the brigands; it was I who had first espied the flock of sheep. And, although I had taken no actual part in this robbery with violence, yet I should have been more than indignant had it not gone forward, and I was only too happy to share in the spoils. I felt myself filled with contempt at the attitude of the owner in endeavouring to prevent our eating his sheep; it seemed a dog-in-the-manger policy when we were hungry, and he had all that mutton just waiting to be eaten. Quickly I was bubbling over with righteous wrath at such unheard-of and unwarranted obstruction to our just and natural demands. How dare he?

Stolen fruits had already become sweetest, but Lizzie the camel, I felt sure, had been acquired honestly. While we feasted the beast strayed, taking our water supply and my burnous with her. Three hours tramping in the blazing sun we had before we found her, and, when at last we tracked her down, she was lying full length on the sand, dozing with a seraphic smile upon her Satanic countenance.

We were still in the vicinity of yesterday's yellow well-mound, which I could see faintly down to the southward, but our long search had given us prodigious appetites. Just then a flock of sheep came into sight, and this time we waited to give neither explanation, apology, nor signed paper. Ali merely sprang upon the fattest lamb (our fourth), and, placing it upon the camel, we started at a great pace for the north-west. Truly the appetite had grown with the eating, and we already tasted in anticipation delicate mutton savours, as we bore the bleating captive away; but the old adage that "there is many a slip 'twixt the cup and lip," we unfortunately soon found applied also to mutton. Happening to look behind, we observed a line of armed men rapidly overtaking us; it was a local levy of shepherds, who, objecting to this our necessary commandeering, were coming up in skirmishing order, determined that we should no longer prey upon them.

We increased our pace to about six miles an hour, and showered blows upon the writhing Lizzie, but it was obviously no good, for we were being rapidly overtaken. After a hurried council of war, the Arab girl was put upon the camel and given the sheep to hold, while I, having been duly refreshed with a good kick or two (for I was by then nearly dropping from exhaustion), was turned into camel-driver, and limping, sweating, and swearing, flogged on the reluctant Lizzie from behind. The two Turks and the camelmen hung back a little, and a general action commenced.

I had been in action once before, at the storming of the Taku Forts, but this was an infinitely more humorous affair, for nobody seemed to get hurt! There was indeed a tremendous banging from the Turks' Martinis and the camelmen and shepherds' more ancient weapons, and spurts of yellow sand from dropping bullets were soon squirting up in all directions as the rear-guard action progressed. But somehow one had no sense of danger, and the situation was so ludicrously like a Drury Lane melo-drama, that I unexpectedly found myself roaring with laughter. The camel girl, too, did not appear in the least bit put out, and showed her rows of pearly teeth as she smiled back at me, and clutched at the struggling lamb.

But all good things must come to an end, and in a very short time it became obvious that our further flight was impracticable. Mahmoud and diplomacy won the day! As the enraged shep-herds came up to within thirty or forty yards of us, Ali brought up the camel with a jerk, and Mahmoud, taking the lamb, placed it in my arms with gestured intimation that I was at once to return it to its owners. Firing had by now mutually ceased on both sides, but I did not feel at all certain as to the nature of the reception which I would receive at the hands of those whom I now felt convinced were after all the animal's rightful own-ers. Whether it was my uniform that impressed them, I do not know; they may have taken me for some grandee of the land, some personage of importance, who had an hereditary right to steal sheep. However that may be, I was received with the great-est respect and many salaams, and I felt the virtuous glow of a Sultan bestowing a favour, as I handed over our intended supper to those humble supplicants.

The gift once received, the shepherds immediately turned round, and made off in the direction from which they had come. But Ali and Mahmoud were evidently still feeling sore about the matter, and at the unexpected reverse their plans had suffered. Before the shepherds had gone another hundred yards the Turks recommenced firing at their retreating backs, and continued this fusillade for as long as the shepherds remained in sight. The latter did not, however, return the fire, but moved along as fast as they could, as though fully aware of their guilt, and of a mean action successfully accomplished.

But fortunately, again, there were no accidents, and for all the firing, no one on either side suffered so much as a scratch.

We resumed our journey, lighter by the loss of a fat sheep.

## CHAPTER 34

# Hagar

After rendering up our sheep, we moved off to the north-west in a very hot sun, and at 3 p.m. we passed across the road running from Sollum to the westward. This was the road I had, at the time of my escape, made up my mind not to cross over, and it was to have served as a mark to warn me if I were getting too far to the northward of my course. But now, I was being taken across it against my will to I knew not what place; only this fact began to be obvious, that I was not to be permitted to proceed to Sollum; but I comforted myself with the reflection that at any rate neither was I being taken back to Bir Hak-kim. The country rapidly became more sparsely populated, and only very occasional flocks did we sight, all moving westward. Fortunately the surface was good going, with firm clayey sand and a good show of bushes. There were an immense number of bir or Roman cisterns, all choked and broken; I counted as many as a dozen of their yellow or white well-mounds in sight at one time, but there was not a drop of water among the lot; but in past ages, this must have been a well populated and fertile district.

I more than once pointed out flocks of sheep to Ali and Mah-moud, as by this time I was getting very hungry again; but they were evidently very sore about their recent failure, and were not to be easily drawn by me into further brigandage. Moreo-ver, my knowledge of Arabic was still limited to a dozen or so of words, and there were two words in the East with which I always seemed to get terribly mixed up, both with Basil and my new Turkish friends. The words were the two more often than any other on our lips—*ship* and *sheep*.

The Oriental invariably pronounces both those words alike as *sheep*, and the curious thing is that the native word for both has also practically the same sound, ship being *babor* and sheep *babar*. As we were always expecting food by a ship, pronounced sheep, and also the arrival of sheep pronounced sheeps, we prisoners were from day to day thrown into a state of wild excitement by an announcement from Basil that a ship had arrived for us. So now with my Turkish companions, I had again and again to describe the torpedoing of a sheep and the eating of a ship; it was confusion twice confounded!

Before dark, we got to an Arab camp, where we spent the night, and got also an excellent supper of dates and milk. Mahmoud always goes through some rigmarole of sending for the head man of the camp, giving him a signed order in Turkish, and, after these preliminaries, we are billeted out for the night, and given what food happens to be available. The wretched Lizzie had been unable to keep up with us, and did not arrive until long after we had gone to bed, so I had rather a cold night of it, as the beast was carrying my burnous for me.

The next day, Friday, February 25th, we were on the move before sunrise once more, this time on a more westerly course. On the previous day, although we must have done thirty miles on foot altogether, I calculated that we had only made good some sixteen miles to the north-west. Today, having cadged three lots of dates or milk, we headed at a great pace (some five miles per hour) to the west-north-west, taking, as usual, neither food nor water with us. My feet were still in a terrible condition with blisters, chafing, and the loose toe-nails and lacerated toes; in fact, I had practically no soles left to my feet, and my shoes were completely worn out and tied on as best I could manage with priceless pieces of rags and wisps of grass. I therefore found this pace very killing, though, fortunately, the sun was obscured by clouds, and I had no longer to carry the heavy pack with which I had first escaped.

We continued all day at never less than four miles an hour, and, as our hunger increased, we pulled up roots and ate them as we went; they were *Scorzonera Alexandrina* (as I subsequently ascertained), having a nutty, fibrous bulb the size of a small bean some inches below the surface, of a quite pleasant flavour, and a great help and comfort to me in my extremity. My Turkish friends appeared to have no sense of direction; when we overtook a rare shepherd or caravan, they would make inquiries and our course would be pointed out to us; but, within half an hour, they would be circling and zigzagging wildly towards other points of the compass, and I think it was only due to me that we ever got anywhere at all.

All this time the soldiers were merrily seated side by side on the camel, laughing and talking, and flirting with Fatma, the camel girl. As I was now on very good terms with the whole party, I at length succeeded in persuading them to let me have a ride myself. I rather fancy myself on a horse, and a camel looked an easy animal to navigate; but it was a matter about which I was soon undeceived! Lizzie was equipped with neither saddle, bridle, nor stirrups; a short rope was secured about her sneering Roman nose and brought up on the off side of her shoulder, and my burnous was lightly thrown over her much vertebrated back; but of secure holding there was none. How my two Turkish friends had poised so easily and so lightly upon this animated earthquake was a marvel to me! At the first blow from the stick, Lizzie slithered sideways, and off I came, rug and all, hung for a moment round her neck, then got trodden and finally rolled upon, as I came under the animal's feet. Fortunately a camel's feet are pneumatic-tyred, and both soil and camel soft all over; wherefore I suffered no harm from this attempt to loop the loop, and the incident but served as a cause for merriment to all parties, I. was content, after that, to limp along as best I might, and to watch the two Turkish *Bing Boys* pursue their acrobatic career upon Lizzie's back.

Fortunately the surface was still good going, the same firm sand and clay soil covered with low bushes, and now, as we approached the coast, there were a number of shallow valleys running in a northerly direction, quite green in places with grass and sappy-looking bushes, and with many signs of recent Arab encampments. To the south there was a low range of hills, but the only inhabitants we met were in an abject state of starvation, unable to supply us with food of any kind, however willing they may have been to do so. On we tramped to the west-north-west; the sun went down and it became pitch dark, and I felt thoroughly done, having eaten nothing except the handful of dates at sunrise. Apparently we were utterly lost, when, topping a low rise, about an hour and a half after dark, we saw fires gleaming in the depression beyond. It was a small Arab encampment, and the head man, a refined, kind-looking old gentleman with a long white beard, gave us his hospitality, which consisted of the bowl of rice which he had prepared for his own supper. It was the first rice I had seen since making my escape, and a great treat; but there was very little of it, perhaps a pound's weight, for this portion, which had been prepared for only two individuals, now had to suffice for the whole eight of us. Wherefore I went to bed very hungry.

We spent the early evening round the fire, the old gentleman petting and caressing his infants, to whom he appeared to be very devoted. As usual, besides my tricks, I was made to produce my map, and then was asked questions as to the direction in which various places lay. My ability, after a glance at the stars, to tell them correctly the bearings of Sollum, Tobruk, Bir Hakkim, and the like, seemed to them nothing less than black magic. The Arab guide is a marvellous individual in the way in which he can follow for hundreds of miles a route which he has once before traversed; it is, I fancy, a faculty shared by all animals of the wild, and is best known to us in the way a horse can find his way home on the darkest night. But, from all I have ever seen of the Arab, he is quite incapable of finding his way across a new district, or of even moving in a direct line, and he is entirely dependent upon having been there before, and on small marks and signs, which, for the most part, are invisible or unnoticed by the European. My Turkish companions were themselves like lost children in this desert, and, as the days advanced, they became more and more dependent upon me to guide them in an unknown direction to an object which I had never seen, and, for that matter, of which I did not even know the name. We had covered some thirty miles that day, and had made some good twenty to the west-north-west, as compared with sixteen in the previous day for the same mileage. But I spent a very comfortable, if hungry, night after it, under luxurious warm rugs in the old sheikh's tent.

Our first arrival at this camp of the valley had been very picturesque. The blazing fire we had seen we found to be lighted outside a white army bell-tent, and from inside the latter came a sound of melodious chanting, the first real music that I had heard in the land of Libya; it was the Koran which was being intoned by sweet, childish voices. There then fell a reverent pause, followed by a deep voice obviously invoking a blessing, and, as I squatted in the dust outside, I listened and looked up at the stars twinkling overhead, and, for a moment, became quite oblivious to my own pain, hunger, and misery. Presently there was a rush, a sound of light feet and excited tongues, and out bounded the makers of the melody—some twenty dusky urchins—bright eyed, ivory-mouthed, and merry as one of our own packs of English schoolboys just released from study. There is something very charming about these Arab children, and Moslems are by no means the stern fathers and husbands that I had imagined. The children are as cheeky as can be, yet not *enfants terribles;* but they take with impunity liberties with their seniors which would in England certainly involve condign punishment, yet which here meet with the mildest of reproofs, or with none at all.

The next day, Saturday, February 26th, I saw the sun rise once more as we started on our journey, after receiving our host's parting benediction, but accompanied by neither food nor water. I fancy his camp, like all the others, was pretty well cleaned out of these commodities. But, in spite of my hunger, I had had a most refreshing night's sleep, and we gathered and chewed roots as we went along on a wild zigzag and at a very fast pace. For some reason the camel was not with us, and I and the soldiers were alone. Apparently it was not I alone who had sore feet, for Mahmoud, taking off one of his boots (apparently a British Army one removed from some dead soldier), I was able to see that nails were projecting through the sole, some to a distance of nearly half an inch, and it seemed incredible to me that he could have worn them all this time in that condition. But apparently he regarded internal nails as the usual accompaniment of European foot-wear, and was delighted when I showed him how to knock them down by the use of two or three small stones as hammer and anvil, a method which had never occurred to him. This day I also witnessed what was to me a novel form of repairing foot-wear; it was a Senussi, who was sewing on to his shoes the rubber-like leather pads from the underside of a deceased camel's foot; it struck me as being an eminently suitable, hard-wearing and resilient form of sole leather.

This was a very bad day for me in my exhausted condition, as we covered at least thirty-five miles without food or water; but it was still good going underfoot, and the shallow valleys had flattened and broadened out. The range of low hills to the south gradually receded out of sight, while to the north-west the horizon appeared more rugged and uneven, and gave me the impression that we were nearing the coast. In the extremity of our hunger we tried to dig out some jerboas, those kangaroo-like rats with which the whole desert is peopled. The little mounds thrown up by their burrowing cover the desert plain in every direction, looking exactly like what we had at first believed them to be, mole-hills. But the jerboa, unlike the mole, is, I believe, purely a vegetarian, and its flesh is considered a great delicacy by the Senussi. However, our efforts to dig out the little rodents, which are slightly larger than a rat, were quite unsuccessful, and we had to continue on our meagre diet of herbs. In the course of the afternoon I became utterly exhausted, and threw myself on the ground, refusing to go further. Mahmoud and Ali then endeavoured to get me on by threats, pointing their rifles at me, and gently prodding me with the muzzles. But I knew by this time that they were much too fond of me to do me really serious harm, and I replied by merely winking at them in the approved Arab fashion; whereat, after a time, they desisted.

It was then that, like Hagar in the wilderness; I prayed that a well of water might be shown me, for we had seen no one that day, and were utterly lost, arid, as far as I could see, I should in all probability die on that spot from thirst, hunger and exhaustion. It was then, like Hagar, that my eyes were also opened. We had been going in a north-westerly and latterly in a northerly direction, but down to the west-south-west there was a peculiar formation, humps of land, which at the time I took to be tents. With renewed courage came strength, and taking matters into my own hand, I arose and insisted on my companions following me towards these objects. As we drew nearer, the objects on the horizon resolved themselves into a number of well-mounds, centred by a low hill upon which was a land of Pharos, and surrounded by the ruins of a town of some magnitude, which I have no doubt was Roman in its origin, but which, at the time, I was in a far too exhausted state to examine critically. My companions evidently recognised it, and gave vent to their feelings by shouts of joy. On the far side of it we came upon a solitary Bedouin shack, whose owner, having overcome his first fear at the sight of armed men, supplied us with water and directed us on our route. From thence we proceeded some two miles to the south-east, when we entered a valley where tiger-lilies grew waist-high in the wildest profusion, and, there being a water hole, we again slaked out thirst. A second valley like the first succeeded, and then we passed over a road, upon which were erected a number of telegraph posts, and I knew that our destination was near.

A mile or two further on, and we came upon the first signs of the Turkish camp, a ramshackle collection of huts and ragged tents. Judging by the debris, this camp had apparently at one time been a post of some importance; but, at the time of my arrival there, it contained probably no more than twenty or thirty soldiers, who, clothed in tattered khaki uniforms, came out to see us pass. I was conducted forthwith to the officers' quarters, a boarded two-storey building of the roughest description, looking like a miniature and dilapidated railway signal-box, from whose upper storey ran telephone wires connecting with the posts I had seen.

On the western side of the box, in line with the upper storey and reached by a ladder, was a small balcony. From it a cloud of pungent tobacco-smoke blew down, and smote my nostrils. Looking up, I saw a plump, self-satisfied and important little figure; it was clad in English khaki uniform, and the original defunct owner having been evidently a person of larger dimensions than its present wearer, the latter had equalised matters by buttoning the knees of the breeches round his none too slim ankles.

There was no mistaking that healthy glowing olive skin, that trim black beard, that self-assured cock-sparrow carriage. It was Achmed—Achmed the Damned, Achmed the arch-Egyptian traitor and renegade Christian—our late tormentor, task-master and commandant at Bir Hakkim. Beside him lounged Mahomet Zoué, his successor in command. Together they two looked down on me with stern and puzzled faces, news of my flight of six days previously probably not having yet come to their ears. Ali and Mahmoud rapidly blurted out the news and the locality of my capture, at which their brows assumed yet more a frown of threatening and incredulous ferocity. My ability to have got clear away such a distance undetected, at first evidently appeared to them to be improbable, but of the fact of my escape there could be no question, and their looks thereat boded me no good.

Truly had the lines fallen to me in unpleasant places.

# CHAPTER 35

# How, Like Daniel, I Saw the Lion's Mouths Stopped

Achmed, followed by Mahomet in a more leisurely manner, bounded down the steps from the little balcony where they had been, until they stood level with and confronting the culprit, my tired and dejected self. The ominous silence was first broken by Achmed, who hissed in the best melodramatic manner: "But why you try to escape? You are mad, I believe! What shall I tell ze Englishe Government if you had been kill by Senussi?" Mahomet, less theatrical in his manner, contented himself by looking at me, in disgusted amazement, and repeating over and over again the phrase, "Captain no goot! Captain no goot!" which I imagine to have embraced his whole stock of English.

Having a feeling that I was pretty sure to be shot in any case, I replied hotly, with the desperate courage of utter exhaustion that, "In case I had been killed, it would have given him a chance to tell the truth for once in his life!" I told him, moreover, that I was no more mad than he himself was, and that the reason why I had tried to escape was that we had had no news from our homes since the moment we had landed, and that I had tried to get to Sollum, to tell the British there the real state of affairs, and the manner in which we were treated by his enlightened Turkish Government. At the mention of Sollum, Achmed pricked up his ears, and asked derisively: "You believe then that Sollum is in ze hands of ze Englishe?" To this

I replied that I was *sure* that it was, and, at this, he smiled more sardonically and derisively than ever.

His relief at my recapture was, however, obviously genuine, and the atmosphere gradually became less electric, as we both began to regain our tempers. I was pushed up the steps to the telephone-room on the upper storey, to await his decision. In this room there was a mattress, and a bundle of a dozen or more of modern Russian magazine rifles, under the guard of an officer who was apparently always on telephone duty there, and who lay upon the mattress. He was civil to me in his Eastern way, as I collapsed into a huddled heap in the corner, where the cold wind, whistling through the chinks of the boarded walls, chilled me through. The news of my recapture was joyfully passed up and down the line, and the last words which my semi-somnolent ears caught as darkness stole over the scene were place names, such as Matruh, Barrani, and Sollum. This, at the time, I believed to be a bit of bluff, tried on for the purpose of impressing me, for I believed that these places had again become British since the Battle of Christmas Day. But I was too worn out to take much notice, and soon fell asleep. I seemed to have been hardly asleep a moment, when, in the dark, I was gently aroused, and I felt the smooth outline of a bowl being pressed into my hands. It was full to the brim with glorious peppered rice, and presently, as I ate like a cannibal, an oil wick was lit, and I was given several glasses of the strong, sweet Arab tea. I looked around in surprise at my visitors, and at this unexpected kindness, and I then saw that it was Mohammed, the somewhat Machiavellian-looking cook to our late commandant at the Wells. He grinned apologetically at me, and, behind him, smiling encouragement, was a good-looking and gorgeously attired Senussi officer. This latter individual was absurdly like the late Lewis Waller in appearance, and while I was regarding him with wide open eyes, he produced a packet of cigarettes and held it out to me. My astonishment was great, and I almost burst into tears at this unexpected, courtesy. In my pocket I still carried the pipe which I had when the *Tara* sank, and which I called my *liberty* pipe, for I had sworn not to smoke it again until I was a free man. This resolution had been easy to keep at the time, for no tobacco had ever come my way; but now I felt that my two days of liberty had earned me a respite from this vow. I accordingly gratefully accepted one of the cigarettes and rammed it into the bowl, and was soon enjoying the fragrant aroma of My Lady Nicotine, a lady in this instance of the most penetrating and soul-stirring potency, for the tobacco was of the rankest and vilest Albanian brand. But I was not in a critical mood, and could then imagine no greater happiness than to make myself sick with it! Later on in the evening, I was actually allowed downstairs to the lower room, where Achmed and some five or six Turkish and Senussi officers, mostly elderly men, were collected. They were extremely civil to me, Achmed fairly beaming, and I, having been regaled with more tea and further cigarettes, was asked to give them an account of my adventures, which Achmed translated to the rest of the group. I related to them such parts of my escapade as I considered advisable, and they were all, especially Achmed, much entertained by my account of how we had commandeered the sheep, and had managed to subsist for many days on nothing at all. I concluded by emphasising how good the soldiers had been to me, and specially commended their loyalty in having refused all the bribes which I had offered to them to conduct me to Sollum.

That night I slept with the other officers on the ground-floor, in the room in which we had dined, my head pillowed on what I could feel was a bag of macaroni, a substance which seemed to give some colour to Achmed's frequent assertions that he was receiving bribes of food from the Italians not to attack their Port of Tobruk. But, from subsequent investigations I have since made, I believe Achmed's statement to have been a lie, like nearly all his others and having no foundation in fact.

Ere I fell asleep, I tried to puzzle out the seeming contradictions of my treatment. When I had first arrived, most of the signs appeared to point to my early demise. As I had drowsed off, the telephone had been working frantically, and when I had again waked, the whole atmosphere had changed, and I seemed to feel myself almost an honoured guest. Had I, after all, misjudged Achmed, and was the Devil after all not so black as we had painted him? It seemed uncommonly like it; and without being able finally to solve the riddle, I fell asleep.

On this day of Saturday, February 26th, had been fought the Battle of Agadir, well to the westward of Matruh, and in that battle the Turks had suffered a crushing defeat, losing machine guns and their Commander-in-Chief himself, Jaffar Pacha, who was taken prisoner. The Turkish losses were very heavy indeed, and they had to beat a hasty retreat; Barrani itself, only forty-eight miles from Sollum, fell into British hands just two days later as the direct result of the action.

For once Achmed had spoken the truth, when he had said that Sollum was not in the hands of the British. It was not yet, but its fall was imminent. On the same day on which I had escaped, February 20th, the British advance had itself begun, and on February 26th, the clay on which I fell into Achmed's hands, the battle of Agadir was fought and won. At the hour when I came into his power the battle was still in progress, my fate in the balance. Achmed was in direct telephonic communication with the battle area, and while I slept he had learned the worst. It was he who then trembled for his own safety, for his own neck should any harm befall me, for he knew that the power of Turkey, the power for evil to which he had attached himself, was even then being rent in twain and broken in the land of Libya.

The next day, Sunday, was a blessed day of rest for me, and I spent it in washing and in endeavouring to lessen the multitude of vermin which were swarming about my person; for much as I liked my two Turkish guards, Ali Hassan and Mahmoud, I had no desire to keep their memory permanently green by retaining these insect mementoes of our friendship.

Later in the morning, these two worthies were brought before Achmed in my presence, and, after the delivery of a suitable speech, the latter presented each of them with a large silver dollar. They grinned delightedly, saluted, and turning to go, each gave me a hearty hand grip, to which I warmly responded. It was the last I was to see of them.

The day was one full of surprises to me, mainly on account

of the courtesy with which I was treated. Even Achmed so far unbent as to give me one cigarette, and to chat with me in a patronising, manner. Of war lies he told me no end. These I did not believe, but in hopeful expectation of another *fag* I assumed an air of respectful credulity, which I afterwards regretted when I found the hoped-for smoke was not forthcoming. He was full of lachrymose speculations as to what the gentle and paternal Turk would have done, had only be been left in undisturbed possession of his African dominions. According to Achmed, if only the Turk had been given half a chance, the desert would have been made to blossom like the rose, the wells would have been cleared out and repaired, and the poor benighted Senussi have been educated and taught the latest refinements of scientific agriculture! I was so moved by this narrative of beneficent intentions, that I scarce forbore to shed a crocodile's tear.

But a companion who was far more in harmony with my present mood, was my kind Senussi friend, the astral double of Mr. Lewis Waller. He fairly showered cigarettes upon me, and his pockets were ever full of dates, to which I was allowed free access. Presently, he and I and Mohammed, the cook, repaired to the upper room, where I sat down and smoked and watched the two gentlemen beautify themselves. From a gaudy-coloured bag they produced an enormous razor, reminiscent of a hay scythe, with which, having first sharpened it on a piece of paving stone, and without the use of any soap, they proceeded to remove their beards.

The spectacle was both gory and entertaining, but they mistook my enthusiasm for a desire to do likewise, and for a moment I was in danger of being shaved by the same painful process. But by this time I was quite proud of my silken whiskers and, having once witnessed the process by which Neptune initiates novices who cross the Line for the first time, I did not wish to undergo a similar baptism.

The shave completed, and having arrayed themselves in divers gorgeous silks and satins, the two presently departed, a self-conscious smirk upon their faces. I had no need to wonder where

*they* were going; such pains to be beautiful bespoke its own answer, and a man so much like Lewis Waller must be irresistible,
even in Senussi-land.

Achmed, as I saw him now, appeared to have an air of great
affluence and prosperity. He also appeared to have the handling
of much money, and was exposed to neither danger nor hardship, a state of things which obviously well pleased his mean
little soul.

Truly was the wicked flourishing like the green bay-tree. But
the mills of God were grinding even there, though I saw not,
neither did I hear them.

I could not see the fate which the future had in store for
Achmed.

# CHAPTER 36

# Back to Purgatory

That same afternoon I was leaning over the balcony, indolently smoking one of *Lewis Waller's* vile cigarettes, when I saw a little group approaching the camp. The leader detached himself, and came towards the officers' hut, his air being dejected and careworn in the extreme.

Arrived at the entrance, he squatted himself in the dust to await Achmed's pleasure. That individual was at the moment on the balcony with me, and something caused the newcomer to look up, so that I saw his face.

It was Selim, our commandant at Bir Hakkim! At once his air of dejection departed, for I, the cause of his sorrow, the pearl whom he had not properly appreciated until he had lost it, was restored to him. A look of joy and thanksgiving illuminated his dusky countenance, a look of relief. Poor man, he had come to report my escape, knowing well that he would himself have to pay the penalty for it, by degradation from the rank of captain to that of private. No wonder he looked pleased, and I could not grudge him his satisfaction, for I felt that the nature of my own conduct to him in escaping partook of unkindness. Not that I wouldn't have done it again, of course, if ever I had the chance.

Other guests arriving to the number of a dozen or so, the whole party spent a joyful evening sipping tea downstairs, but on this occasion I was not invited to be present.

That night I had the lower room to myself, being given a box of glowing embers to serve as a temporary night-light, and the door was locked on me. There was a great stir in the camp that evening, and I fancy most of the officers and troops left after dark, for I found that the sacks of provisions had all been removed from the room wherein I was quartered. This was a great disappointment to me, for I had entertained certain designs upon the bag of macaroni whereon my head had rested during the previous night, and had proposed to myself a glorious *blow-out* upon its contents. As it was, I lay down experiencing again some of the old familiar restless longings of hunger.

This sensation, however, did not endure a great while, for a diversion occurred which I shall not readily forget. As the last flickering flame from the box of embers expired, leaving me in the dark, I felt something drop on me. A moment later I could feel hundreds of descending objects. For a brief period I tried to hope that this was only some loose ceiling falling, but the maddening stings and irritation which accompanied the small objects soon rendered this optimistic belief futile. There could be no doubt about it. Fleas! Fleas in countless myriads, fleas who had hitherto banqueted on the entire Turkish army, but were now here assembled together to eat one person. They descended upon me literally in showers and shovelfuls!

In the dark I was helpless and defenceless, and I writhed and struggled frantically but vainly against them, as never did Laocoon against his pygmy python. It was truly a terrible time.

But my good friend, Lewis Waller, had not forgotten me. He visited me at a late hour with a light, which he left behind, and he filled my pockets once more with dates, and my heart with gratitude. The Arab nature is in many ways a strange and fickle one, its memory is short; but, in all the world, there is none more generous nor more truly hospitable. May my blessings go with you, Senussi Lewis Waller!

Thanks to the light which my friend had left behind him, I was enabled, after terrific slaughter, to sink into an exhausted sleep an hour or two later. At sunrise I left with Selim, escorted by guards who had come with him from the Wells of Bir Hakkim, a camel, and an ancient camel-woman. Selim greeted me with no reproaches, his manner being subdued and gentle; but the guards, and especially the old, woman, took no pains to conceal their feelings, and heaped imprecations and pious wishes for a painful death upon me; but, keeping close to Selim's side, I took no notice, and gradually their anger wore itself down.

Before starting, Selim and I had a bowl of camel's milk at the nearest tent, and then trudged steadily south at four miles an hour over a dead level country, until at about 11 a.m., after making a slight détour along a dry wadi we came upon an Arab camp. Here we obtained dates and milk and had a rest of about twenty minutes. Once again we moved off due south, the soil underfoot being still good going, a condition which was fortunate for me, for I was still raw and aching all over, and my feet resembled beef-steaks, the result of eight days of forced marches, sleepless nights, and uncertain food; it was a terrible gruelling, but I managed somehow to keep going, and, half stupefied, to place one foot in front of the other.

About 3 p.m. we passed across the Sollum road, which I measured, and found to be seven paces wide. Just to the south of it were what in the distance looked like mountains, but which I now found on ascent to be a mere incline thirty or forty feet high, and crowned by another desert plateau. On arrival near the crest we heard a great sound of rifle-firing, and I looked around in some alarm. Apparently it was caused by a party of four or five Turkish soldiers looting or hunting down Senussi in possession of modern rifles, Being unable to find the camp we were looking for, we presently stopped, and were shortly afterwards joined by the party we had seen firing. Their chief was a magnificent specimen of an Albanian, a fierce, proud-looking brigand, a scented exquisite, clad in all the barbaric splendour of brightly hued flowered silks. On his finger he wore an enormous silver ring a quarter of an inch thick, in which was set a large and mysterious stone—truly a formidable knuckle-duster! He was also adorned with a Turkish decoration on his breast of the size of a saucer, and was, in fact, a most imposing individual, of a type which I had hitherto only seen in comic opera.

Selim and he having engaged in conversation, and both parties being of about the same fighting strength, it was soon mutually agreed that there was no necessity for bloodshed; wherefore amity and knightly discourse reigned in its stead. The magnificent individual proffered me a cigarette, which I accepted, although, thanks to Selim's generosity in the matter of smokes since my recapture, I was no longer so grateful as a few days previously I should have been, and I had a much greater craving for something to eat. The *pow-wow* soon came to an end, and, having been redirected on our course, we retraced our steps across the Sollum road, and presently found the Arab camp we were looking for near by.

Here we were very hospitably received, and I found the sheikh in charge to be a dear old gentleman, a man truly worthy to be known by the honorific of *Holy*. Selim himself was by way of being religious, and whoever we met, he and the leader of the other party went through some Mohammedan rigmarole, a form of catechism and answer, an asseveration of the Unity of the Deity and of Mahomet being His prophet. It is rather a tedious proceeding when one is hungry, as it takes some five minutes to enact, and my thoughts at the time are apt to wander from religion to the flesh-pots of Egypt. But it is a formality rarely omitted by those who pose as religious.

In the old sheikh's tent I spent a very pleasant and comfortable night, being put in the place of honour, and feasting upon boiled mutton as well as on dates and milk. Selim and the old man spent the evening in religious discussion; the opinion of the former (who had been at one time a secretary to the Grand Senussi) being evidently looked up to on all controversial religious subjects.

That night will ever rest as a pleasant memory to me, for I slept snug and warm, with well-lined interior, in the good sheikh's tent. There were soft, luxuriant rugs upon which to lie, and others to cover me, and Selim made no attempt to guard me. I was thus spared the prolixity of rifles and hob-nailed, strong-odoured soldiers as bed-mates, a purgatory to which, through use, I had become almost resigned, but whose absence I none the less appreciated. I calculated that we had made good twenty-eight miles due south during the day.

The next morning was Leap Year's Day, Tuesday, February 29th, and although I received no proposals of marriage, still I experienced events of a nature not much less disconcerting. For once I was feeling thoroughly refreshed, which was well, for, as usual, we were out with the sun, and by 7 a.m. had crossed the Sollum road, this time heading to the east-south-east at four miles an hour. As we got further, it became very bad going over the pitiless stones—the red and black soapy flints, limestone rocks and coral reefs so familiar in the vicinity of Bir Hakkim. It was a great relief to me when we stopped about 11 a.m. in the vicinity of an Arab camp, to which the soldiers wore sent to procure food. My disappointment was all the greater when they returned empty-handed some twenty minutes later. There was no food to be got!

In this neighbourhood there were visible an extraordinary number of well-mounds of the ancient Roman bir; one which we visited had, by the bright yellow appearance of its mound, been recently cleaned out, and this, I fancy, was the place known as Grassa, a provision depôt a day's march from Bir Hakkim, of which as prisoners we had heard much, but never seen. There was at this time, however, no encampment there, and we wandered round for some time in a vain effort to find *other tents* of which Selim had evidently heard, and where he wished to obtain food. But our search was fruitless, and eventually we turned to the south-south-west, and continued thus at four miles an hour over ground, the stones of which became worse and worse. But despite the terrible aridity, there were numbers of butterflies, and my entomological instincts being aroused, I captured one, a beautiful little *copper* with iridescent green undersides and newly hatched. This I put between the leaves of my diary and have to this day.

By this time, having eaten nothing since the night before, I was becoming very hungry; but a soldier, finding a small tortoise, generously shared it with me. The method of cooking is simple; to fulfil the Mahomedan law, the animal's throat is first slit, then, still alive and kicking, it is placed upon its back on a fire. The heat soon shrivels and cracks the shell, whereupon it is pulled open and the oozing flesh extracted like caramel from its paper wrapper. Its flavour did not appeal to me, but I was too hungry to be particular.

But this was not the end of my food experiments. An hour or two later, a little crested lark got up at my feet in that flurried and unmistakable way which bespeaks a nest. Looking down, I saw three deep brown eggs under a tuft of grass. Pleasant recollections of past egg-flips flashed, across my mind, and without further thought I reached down a hand and thrust the eggs into my mouth. If I had only had the patience to wait a moment or two more I might have had young larks; for the eggs were hard set, ripe for hatching! I shall never forget my feelings as I felt the un-hatched fledglings struggle red hot in my mouth, or the way their bones gritted between my teeth. But necessity knows no squeamishness, and swallow them I did, although I was as nearly as possible sick during the process!

A few miles further on I tramped, then fell, utterly done. Selim was ahead on the camel, and the soldiers came back and prodded me with their rifle muzzles; but I refused to move until I had rested awhile. Then once more I stumbled forward again. Nothing seemed to tire the soldiers themselves, and one of them, who had brought a hawk with him, loosed it at a hare. They were soon running at top speed in ail directions, trying to recapture the bird, which was flying low and making no attempt to pounce on his quarry; eventually the hawk went off, and we saw neither him nor the hare again.

This neighbourhood appeared to be fairly swarming with ground game, and in a short time we espied another hare, squatting behind a bush. One of the soldiers tried to stalk it, rifle in hand, and got within six feet of the animal, which thereupon got up and lobbed leisurely out of sight, quite unheeding the furious fusilade of ill-aimed rifle shots which followed his flight.

Again I was done, and sank once more upon the stones, whereupon the soldiers were about to employ their usual brutal methods for revivifying me when Selim, observing my condition, came up on his camel and insisted that I should ride in his place. This humanity was all the remarkable, in that I was able to observe, at a short halt dining which Selim removed his shoes, that his own feet were one great blister from end to end. But ride I did, and that for nearly two hours, though the soldiers loudly protested at a malefactor such as myself being so pandered to, and the old woman frantically raved and swore, and cast her maledictions at me. That terrible journey across the stones appeared endless, and I believed that we had lost our way, for I had seen no landmarks, when, at about 4.30 p.m., I became cognisant of the stone beacon and water-walls of Bir Hakkim close at hand.

The soldiers at once signalled their approach by firing a *feu de joie* with their rifles in the air. Those were answered by more shots from the camp, and in a moment I saw the whole garrison of men, women and children advancing in a crowd to meet us. At the head of the mob was Holy Joe, elephant whip in hand, his yellow-red eyes flaming with rage and fanaticism, his Negro nostrils dilated.

As he came up to me he struck me a blow with his whip, and then followed me, slashing me liberally about the head and shoulders. Strange to say I hardly felt the thong, and holding up my hand, I invoked the name of Allah. I was walking alone, and I suppose Holy Joe's actions roused the passions of the others, which had until then been held in abeyance by Selim's presence. But now they all came at me with a rush, and I felt someone smack my face, and I received a blow or two from rifle butts. The women also spat and hurled stones, but their aim, like that of ladies in other lands, was fortunately bad, and I suffered little harm. Altogether I think I got off very lightly, and the actual hurt received was in no way commensurate with the intentions of the givers. Selim, I am sure, had no wish that such a thing should happen; but, for the moment, he was overpowered by the sentiment of the community, and mob-law ruled in Bir Hakkim. Besides, Holy Joe, in virtue of his status as priest, was a power in the land, not to be lightly thwarted, and Selim himself, though kind-hearted, was ever weak of will.

In this manner I was driven forward some two hundred yards or so to the block-house, on arrival at which place my clothes,

233

shoes, and all my possessions were stripped from me, and I was turned into the sheep-pen practically naked, to spend the night. Two soldiers were put over me to guard me, and, having made a special show of loading their rifles, forbade anyone to approach, or the other prisoners to have any communication with me.

Thus on the evening of Leap Year's Day, Tuesday, February 29th, 1916, did my last hope of liberty, aye of life itself, appear to have been taken away from me. Yet Providence was watching over me, over us, all that time. In the words of the Bible, "Now is our salvation nearer than when we believed."

# CHAPTER 37

# Things are Not Always
# What They Seem

There, in the sheep-pen, I remained for the night, an object lesson to my fellow-prisoners of what they might expect, should they, in their turn, attempt to escape. Perhaps I could not do better now than state how deplorable my condition *appeared* to them. I quote from the *Black Hole of the Desert*, a book published by Messrs. Hodder and Stoughton, and written from the diary of Allen, my Yeoman of Signals. I will begin from the beginning, as it gives a good idea of what had occurred at Bir Hakkim during my absence:

At about 6.30 p.m., on Saturday night, February 20th, just before the moon came up, our Captain made his escape. He got clear away without being detected. Some few of us knew that he was going and fully understood the perils he would have to encounter. We prayed earnestly to our Heavenly Father to protect and guide his footsteps. The distance, we believed, was by the quickest route seventy-five miles. The next day our captors were unaware what had happened, and we had hopes that our Captain would not fail. Unfortunately, the following day our interpreter became ill with an ulcer on the back, which caused him to keep his tent. The man in charge of the wells (Holy Joe), wishing to speak to him, entered the officers' tent at 8.30 a.m., and, on looking round, missed the face of the *Captain*. He at once told Salem Affendi (Selim), who visited each tent on the pretext of seeing the sick. It was the first time any of our captors had troubled their heads about them. All of us were fallen in and counted, and soldiers were sent off in all directions to search for the Captain. There was great excitement, and extra sentries were put on, even some of the women strutting about with rifles in their hands. At midnight on the 23rd, Salem Affendi hurried away *(Note:* He did not arrive at Gweider until the afternoon of the 27th, so probably he did some searching of his own on the way), and we were told by the Sergeant left in charge that he had gone to bring our Captain back, as he had been captured near the Italian frontier. *(Note:* An obvious lie, but the Senussi probably thought that I had made for Tobruk, which was nearer than Sollum.) We did not believe it, and anxiously watched the sky for the signal of the searchlights. . . .

On February 26th, four days after his escape, there was still no news of him. Meanwhile our food was reduced to four ounces of rice per man, and three days later there was no rice at all. In desperation we all fell in to see the Sergeant in charge, and ask for more food. The movement was made too suddenly for the guard. The whole lot of them took alarm, and, rushing out of their tents, opened fire on us with their rifles. Fortunately their aim was very bad, and no one was hit.

We appealed to the Sergeant, who promised us that on Monday, two days later, he would march us to a place where there was some food. Monday arrived, but there was no march, no food, and no news from the Captain. . . .

The next day all our slender hopes came crashing down. At three o'clock in the afternoon we heard a series of rifle shots to the north. The guard were fallen in and marched off in that direction. A few minutes later there appeared over the brow of a small hill some men and camels, and there, walking apart from the rest, was our brave Captain. We were now witnesses of one of the most degrading spectacles it has been my lot to see. When the guard of the Senussi reached our Captain they punched with their fists until his face was streaming with blood. He was struck with their rifles until he was nearly unconscious. The man in charge of the well lashed him with an elephant-thong whip. Soon afterwards up came the black women with large stones. They ran close up to him and hurled them in his face. Of course, we were powerless to interfere. They made him sleep in the sheep-pen that night, with a guard standing over him. . . .

This, no doubt, to the reader, will all sound terrible enough, and the spectacle no doubt succeeded for the time being in effecting the purpose it was intended to have, namely, to discount future rash attempts to escape. But, as a matter of hard fact, my public punishment did not *really* amount to much. After my two hundred mile walk, and the days of agony from blistered and bleeding feet, one hardly noticed a little thing like a whip. The blood seen streaming from my face was, I fancy, mostly sweat, and the black ladies' stones were as ill-aimed as they were ill-intentioned; and after the tragedy, as always, came the comedy!

For all that the other prisoners' eyes could see, I passed that night in the sheep-pen, bruised, hungry, and half naked; but as soon as it was fully dark, so that prying eyes could no longer observe what happened, my clothes and burnous were restored to me, two mats were placed at my disposal, one to lie upon and the other with which to form a roof, and, what was more important still, I was given water and a liberal supply of dates!

With a thankful heart, and a mouth still full of date-stones, I was fast asleep in a few minutes.

In an hour or so's time I was wakened by Mahmoud, the black-faced, bright-eyed, merry little nine-year-old body-servant of Selim. The sentry had kindled a bright fire to warm me, and I saw by its light that in his hand Mahmoud held out a huge bowl of rice. He was, for the time being, my black fairy god-mother, and he watched delightedly while I ate, obviously taking as much interest in the proceedings as I myself did. This rice was, in fact, Selim's own supper, and so liberal was my helping, that, for the first and last time as a prisoner, I was unable to consume it all. Such affluence amazed me, and, like a fool, I left some of the rice in the bottom of the bowl, instead of putting it in my pocket, an omission of which I was often to think regretfully in still hungrier days.

Before I finally closed my eyes, the sentry who had so ostentatiously loaded his rifle, gave me one of his own rare cigarettes to smoke. Such is the Arab character!

The next day, March 1st, I was kept still in durance vile in the sheep-pen, but as a matter of fact it was a rest cure which I thoroughly enjoyed, as I was given an unusual amount of food, the weather was mild and pleasant, and I felt none too strenuous or keen for exercise after my nine days of roving. From time to time, during my pleasant snatches of slumber, I became semi-conscious of the threatening figure of Holy Joe standing over me with uplifted whip. But I took no notice and the blow never fell. But towards evening, when it was already getting dark, Selim yielded to the representations of Captain Tanner and the other officers, and I was restored to their tent, a consummation of which, in my comfortable reserved quarters in the sheep-pen, with generous and well served cuisine, I was not nearly so solicitous as they themselves were in their misinformed and misdirected kindness. The ragged old tent was as crowded and the ground seemed harder than ever; but what I missed in other directions was more than made up by the kindliness of my reception. The prisoners had apparently been little worse off in their treatment for my escape, but their liberty had been slightly restricted, and they had been more closely guarded. They had successfully shelved the responsibility for my escape off their own shoulders, by hinting that I had lately gone a little bit mad, and had probably wandered off into the desert. They also told Selim that I had been talking about Tobruk, a fact true in itself, but one that was intended to put him on a false trail, and this apparently it did. At one time they had been very anxious about me, for a report came in that I had been recaptured seriously wounded in the head.

In the course of a few days, nearly all my possessions, including my diary, were returned to me. But the shoes I had been wearing, and the part of the burnous which I had left behind, were retained, and were made to fit the little Mahmoud, who proudly strutted about in them.

Naturally, for a while I was *persona non grata* with Selim, and I was not allowed to go out collecting firewood and snails with the other prisoners. But, after a week or so, on Captain Tanner taking responsibility for my future good conduct, my liberty was restored to me, though I was always suspect. My zeal for collecting fossils and other curios often led me into trouble, for I would unconsciously wander some distance from the guards and other prisoners, a fault which brought me swift and sharp punishment from the first Senussi to observe it, who discouraged these wandering habits by jabbing me in the ribs mercilessly with his rifle muzzle.

One of my first inquiries on my return had been about the sick, and I had gazed anxiously at the grave-mounds down to the southward, to see if there had been any addition to them. But there had been no more deaths, and the sick had apparently benefited from the change of diet from rice to rations of dates and barley-flour. Even Quartermaster Abbitt, whom I had left apparently *in extremis,* and who had been prostrate from dysentery ever since we landed, although now nothing but skin and bones, seemed to be making steady progress; but this was, in the main, due entirely to his own unfaltering and undaunted courage and resolution.

Our rations at this time were about half a pound of barley-flour and some fifty dates per head per day. It was decidedly pleasant food, but it left us eternally hungry. The barley-flour itself was whole-meal, ground with the husks on, and had much sand in it. Of the dates, some twenty per cent, were bad, but we ate them all just the same—caterpillars, dirt and rotten fruit; not one grain of anything was ever wasted. In addition to this, we got one lean and stringy goat between the hundred and three of us every day; the natives took the head, liver and offal, and an occasional limb; we, the major part of the carcase, which, after all was said and done, contained little more meat than that of a large rabbit.

The barley made three very small biscuits. For breakfast (I speak of the officers), we generally ate some twenty dates. For lunch, we had goat soup made from the day's ration (about two ounces per head with bones), and one of the biscuits. For supper, we had the remaining two biscuits, eaten with the remaining dates.

We also had date wine and date coffee, two beverages which we invented. Date wine was made by pouring hot water on a date, and stirring it up well at the bottom of the tumbler; if you felt very reckless and extravagant, and wanted it very strong, you sometimes used two, or, in almost unheard of cases, three dates. All our date-stones were collected, none of them were ever thrown away, for from these we made our date coffee. At first they had been a waste product, but some of the stones getting into the fire, an aroma which faintly suggested roasting coffee was detected coming from them. We were quick to make experiments, and we now roasted hundreds of these date-stones daily, on a small piece of tin which had somehow come into our possession. It was a process needing care, for, if the stones were roasted too little, you were unable to pulverise them afterwards; whereas, if you roasted them too much, all the oil would come out of them and they would become pure charcoal and probably catch fire as well. While one party roasted the date-stones, another party pulverised the *beans* by hammering them with a stone in the hollow of a rock; the coffee was then ready for making. After boiling this powder for twenty minutes or so we had a black fluid which *looked* like coffee, and sometimes *smelt* something like coffee, and which we tried to imagine *tasted* like coffee. We used to sit round the fire at night and quaff this charcoal water with the enjoyment of connoisseurs; and, in the end, from thinking about it so much, we began seriously to discuss its commercial possibilities as a paying concern *after the war*.

Even the Senussi became impressed with our faith in this concoction, and the sergeant visiting our tent one night was, upon our pressing invitation, prevailed upon to accept a cup. His exit, after a taste, was more rapid than his advent had been; it was also too reminiscent of *mal de mer* and seaside voyages for any further description of his condition on my part to be necessary!

We never succeeded in persuading anyone else to try it, and our hopes of being the future *Coffee Kings* of Europe began to wane from that day.

Another culinary novelty was, I think, mainly due to myself; it was the use of roots and herbs as food. Snails by this time had almost ceased to exist within a radius of five miles from Bir Hakkim, owing to the profligate way in which we had eaten them up. Moreover, for those which still remained, it was now close season, for they had taken to laying eggs and burrowing in the sand, and had become quite uneatable in consequence. The Snail King and his satellites had become as pelicans in the wilderness, with nothing to hunt for and nothing to eat. But the herbs, which, since the rains, had sprung up everywhere in unexpected places, helped to fill the gap. I am blessed with a digestion which nothing seems to impair, and when I could not persuade anyone else to be first to try a new dish, I was always willing to experiment myself. I remember, as a small boy, we used to dare each other to eat every imaginable kind of toad-stool, and none of us ever came to any harm by it. In later years, I had a steward whom my soul abhorred; whenever I caught a new kind of fish, I always gave him some of it to eat, and if he was not dead by breakfast time the next morning, I came to the conclusion that it was safe enough for me. Here in the desert, I had been experimenting for over two months on every green thing; all were wholesome, but some were nicer and less rope-like than others, and from my Arab and Turkish guards I had learned to know the more choice species. At first my companions, believing that my interior economy was a special dispensation of Providence, would not follow me in these vegetarian researches, indignantly denied them inclusion in the soup, and roundly asserted that, whatever I myself might be, they, at any rate, *were not goats.* But, after awhile, observing that I still continued to live and breathe, and that I also appeared to enjoy my green stew, the more daring of them also experimented and were instantly converted. From them the custom spread throughout the whole camp.

The amount of vegetable food we were thus able to collect

probably did not amount to an ounce per head a day; but even so, it gave occupation, and I think was a valuable food when, as later on, we had to subsist entirely on meat.

The best of all these herbs was what we called the *octopus plant*, and it was the only one I have been able to identify scientifically, as *Scorzonera, Alexandrina*. It had a central flower bud like a tulip, resembling also the beak of an octopus. From this radiated grey-green leaves flat on the ground, but writhing in all directions, and the edges being crinkled, they looked exactly like the extended arms of a small octopus covered with suckers. It flowered in March, and had a very pretty mauve bloom, in size and in general appearance like that of a china aster. It had a- long fibrous root, and some way down this was a bulb which, in the better specimens, was of the size and shape of a daffodil bulb. This bulb was excellent and like a nut; the leaves and flower were also good to eat, either boiled or raw.

The *pineapple potato,* another name of our invention, was a plant about eighteen inches high, and in March ablaze with lovely mauve blossoms shaped like the wild rose. The older plants had a small potato a foot or so below the surface, *if* you could find it, of an excellent pineapple flavour; but you would generally dig up a dozen plants before you found one potato, and, as the soil was mostly rock, and we had no digging implements, the strength and energy expended in getting these potatoes was generally more than their food value equivalent.

Besides these, there were a dwarf mallow, a climbing dandelion and an edible thistle, of little value as nourishment, but whose green leaves were excellent in the soup. There was also the camel-grass, which the men called celery, and some half-dozen other herbs. But they were too scarce to be other than rare and special additions to the soup.

Now that the weather was warming up, Papilio Machaon, the lovely swallow-tail butterfly, at one time numerous in our fen counties, was a frequent visitor. I used to think that this and the snail were moisture loving insects, but in that opinion I was evidently mistaken.

# CHAPTER 38

# The Last Rat Leaves

Our food situation was evidently getting daily more and more precarious, and there were now only a sack or two of dates and barley left in the block-house. A day or two of delay in the arrival of the promised supplies, and in the weakened state in which we now were, and the incoming caravan, when it eventually arrived, might well find, instead of our hungry selves but an empty desert littered with shrivelled corpses.

Ever since early December, when Achmed, the first rat, departed, we had been promised this caravan with supplies. It had never come—we had waited and hoped for it for four months—and now the original small stock of food had dwindled and almost vanished.

Captain Tanner and I now cornered Selim, and, refusing to be put off with further lying promises, we solemnly warned him that the British Government would hold him responsible for our lives if we died of starvation. Selim winced at this, as he had himself obviously been very nervous for some time about the food question; the desperation of our plight had gradually been reversing our relative positions. We were now beginning to dictate to our ruler what he should do; and he, the ruler, felt himself at fault, and shuffled and attempted to make excuses. The threat held out in the interview evidently impressed Selim, for the worm at last turned, or at least tried to wriggle back into its hole—we could not decide which. But on Wednesday, March 8th, Selim departed in the evening, leaving the camp in charge of the sergeant.

This was the sergeant who had already forsworn himself and had also fired on the prisoners in Selim's absence, a few days after I had made my escape.

We watched Selim go with some misgivings; *he* told us he was going to El Zebla, the well two days' march to the north, but that he would return in a couple of days with food. We hoped for the best, there was nothing else to do.

Selim was the third rat to go, and, if we had known it, he was also the last. He knew well that the ship was doomed; the possibility of any of the crew being saved must have appeared very slight to him. If he had been a stronger character we should have had some faith in his mission. But he was weak, unstable as water, and we took his departure as no good omen, although we were aware both of the kindliness and the generosity of his disposition.

During the time he was promising us most, and when his assurances were most vehement as to our immediate release, a straw showed me that the true wind was blowing in the opposite direction. Selim had caused the ground near his tent to be dug and manured with sheep droppings, and in this ground lie planted tomato, melon and other seeds, which he watered with diligence daily. If he and we were in in reality going to part so soon, why should he take so much trouble about plants whose fruit he could never gather?

Two days passed, and still no news of Selim. Three days, and on March 11th, the last of our barley-flour and dates were gone, and we became entirely dependent upon the small flock of goats and sheep which remained for our daily food. Rice had long ago disappeared, snails were now uneatable, and the very small number of herbs and roots within walking distance of the camp had been pulled up and eaten. Even the Arabs were now beginning to get weak, their women no longer tramped daily long distances for firewood, but the men did it for them. They assured us they had no more food than we ourselves. Probably they had very little, but the lie was given to the statement nightly by the unmistakable sound of grinding which reached our ears; the Arab women were grinding some kind of grain in their hand mills, under cover of night.

Our food now was entirely meat—the leanest and stringiest of goats, without one ounce of fat upon their bodies. Daily we counted the number remaining with increasing anxiety, for daily three were killed for our subsistence. These three carcases had to be shared by the prisoners, the guards, and their wives and families, some hundred and forty souls in all, and it probably worked out at five ounces of meat per head per day. Our hunger was no greater on this small meat diet than it was on far larger quantities of rice, or of flour and dates. But a purely meat diet, especially to us who had been so long practically vegetarians, acted as an irritant poison, and we got weaker and weaker at an accelerated pace.

We had to march longer distances every day to obtain firewood and roots, for everything within a mile or two of the camp had now disappeared. These long tramps, barefooted under the hot sun, smitten by a gale of sand-laden wind, were terribly exhausting, especially when we came labouring back under our loads of brush-wood. Day by day our bundles became smaller, until we had only strength to carry a pitiful handful of sticks. The shirkers, the sore-footed and those whom we assumed were only pretending to be sick, had a bad time of it; excuses no longer availed them, and they were driven forth by the rest to do their turn, for where all were sick with weakness and hunger, particular complaints had no further meaning. Home truths and hard words were hurled at the reluctant, and the only sign accepted as genuine proof of serious illness was inability to eat food. "If a man worketh not, neither shall he eat" was the universal motto, for we were fighting for our lives as we never had before, and with our utmost united efforts we could barely obtain enough fuel to keep a fire smouldering, and if it went out we had nothing with which to rekindle it, and should have to eat our goat's flesh raw.

Besides the date-stones, there was another waste product which we had recently made use of—the blood of the slaughtered sheep and goats. The Moslem is not allowed to eat this, so our probationer surgeon attended the animals' *execution* each morning and held a basin under their throats while they expired.

I made a pleasing little addition to my own food supply for a day or two—the gullets and wind-pipes of defunct sheep. This, after it had been well boiled in the soup, used to be thrown away, as it appeared to be all bone and sinew and quite uneatable; nobody wanted it. But I found that by holding it in a hot flame for a few minutes, it became like the crackling of pork, a savoury morsel. But when my discovery became generally known, I had to render this delicacy up to the general stock.

A kind of resigned sadness was gradually stealing over us; sorrow and despair had worn themselves out, and had given place to a cheerful resignation akin to that of consumptives. We felt the end to be very near, yet were always filled with a gentle hope. Life was still sweet, but we no longer feared death, and our minds still kept twisting and turning, looking for a way out.

The swallows had been passing on their way north ever since the beginning of March, and we looked at them regretfully. They, at any rate, had full freedom and were not tied by hateful shackles to the desert— the living grave which it seemed we were destined never to leave. Some of them would be going to England, some perhaps would even build their nests in our own loved homes so far away. If they could but take a message for us, but tell those whom we love, that we are thinking of them? The idea seemed to be quite practicable, and, if we could but catch a few and attach messages, perhaps some of these would fall into the hands of those who would act, and, hearing for the first time of our dire extremity, bring aid to us. But alas, we had no means of catching these birds of freedom, and they went on their way northward across the Mediterranean all unhampered by messages from us.

In March especially the sunsets became of extreme beauty, with wisps of diaphanous cloud streaming across the sky, having a colouring reminiscent of the rose and gold of an old Chinese fan. I found myself crooning the words of some verses I had composed long before, up in the old North Channel; they appeared to apply to our present straits so directly, and I invented a little tune to which the wailing notes of the sunset bugle fitted:—

*Gleaming orb of golden sunshine, gently sink;*
*Light the tired soldier's vision o'er the brink.*
*Sailing ever to the Islands of the Blest,*
*Little suns of life are setting, going West.*

*To the Westward, day is breaking, light is born:*
*There the Gates of Pearl are opening at the dawn.*
*To the Westward life is rising at his best:*
*There we'll meet and have no parting, going West.*

Wishing to be at peace with all the world, at this time I made several visits to the tent of Holy Joe, and reasoned with him as to his uncivilised conduct in flogging me after my recapture. The adage says that one "cannot make a silk purse out of a sow's ear," but I always held that if not a silk purse, at least some use could be made of that auricular organ, a receptacle of some kind—perhaps even a tobacco pouch! But Holy Joe, honest Negro that he was, was a hard man to convince. His manner was again sufficiently friendly, but anent the flogging all that I could elicit from him was that, although such a punishment might not be usual in Europe, it certainly *was* so out here. And with that I had to be content.

Sunday, March 12th, was our last Sunday; we all felt the end was very near. The spectre of death by starvation stared us in the face, and I think we looked back unafraid. We still had our hymn-singing services in the officers' tent every Sunday evening, and had recently got into the habit of having a kind of debate on certain controversial religious subjects; about which opinion was sharply divided. For we were of all sects—Church of England, Nonconformist, Unitarian, Christian Scientist, Roman Catholic, Greek Church, Agnostic, Fatalist, and I know not what other variety of opinion.

The subject this Sunday was, "Is prayer answered?" I do not think I said much myself, though I never had a doubt on it. I did not believe things happened because you asked for them, nor did I believe we were in a position to tell the Deity what He ought to do. But I did, and do, believe, that *the best always happens,* and that, with a lively faith and hope in Providence, Providence itself will direct our ends, even though the outer man perish.

To the human eye, our position seemed hopeless. With the best of intentions our gaolers could not now release us; for, with the means at their disposal, we were now all far too weak to be moved. Some might have come through, but the majority would have fallen by the way, and,, in any case, the weak and dilatory Selim was sure to procrastinate until it was too late.

I could see no way out. But still, deep inside me I had hope, and I could say with understanding the prayer I "Give us this day our daily bread, and forgive us our debts, as we forgive our debtors." I think we had all forgiven our debtors by then. We were ripe for the sequel.

CHAPTER 39

# The Grey Spectre
# Fights With Hope

On March 12th, our food allowance was still further reduced, our meat daily becoming something under four ounces, instead of the five ounces we had received until then; and there was nothing else, not even salt.

We prisoners, weak though we were, were every moment becoming more dangerous and defiant in our attitude, and I sent for the sergeant, and told him that we would take matters into our own hands, whatever the consequences, if food were not forthcoming. This I explained to him through Basil, and the sergeant, somewhat cowed by our threatening looks, placed his hand upon his own beard, and swore by the beard of Mahomet, that, if food did not come within twenty-four hours, he would march us to El Zebla. At that time there were only six goats left, and this oath, taken in the presence of all the assembled prisoners, raised from them a great shout, trailing off into a snarling yell. It was a dramatic moment, as the men all understood that the sergeant, by placing his hand upon his beard, had sworn an inviolable oath, and we all hoped that for once the promise would be kept.

That evening the officers seriously discussed the question of overpowering the guards, holding them as hostages and marching for the sea. Opinions were fairly evenly divided as to its practicability, but I personally strongly opposed it. About thirty of us were always on the sick list, and many of these would have had to be carried. All of us were barefooted and excessively weak. Even if we left the sick behind; which was unthinkable, I do not believe the remainder could have covered ten miles a day, even if we had food and water, which we had not, for the few water skins at the camp leaked badly. Tobruk, the nearest place to which we could look for succour, was seventy miles off as the crow flies, and its position, within twenty miles or so, was quite unknown to us. Even if we were unhindered, our first day's march would have been our last; we should have died of hunger and thirst in the wilderness, or prolonged life a few days more at best by the most terrible form of cannibalism, only, in the end, to perish in our tracks. Besides, I will frankly confess that I had no desire to throw away my life on so rash an enterprise by being the first to attack our guards; and, even if we secured them as hostages, there were their women and children also. It would be a horrible thing if, as hostages, we had to sacrifice them in self-defence.

The cruel truth was but too plain to me. Either Selim would keep his promise, and somehow get food to us—a very unlikely contingency, or else Providence would do some inconceivable thing, work some miracle we could not even guess at, and so get us out of this hell. And, if there were no Providence, as some asserted, then we must turn our faces to the ground, and die like men. However, on the morning of the 14th March, we having got to our last ration, the problem was temporarily solved for us all by the arrival of twenty-two more sheep, which meant another week's food at our present minimum scale—which barely sufficed to keep life in the body. With the sheep came a vague verbal message from Selim that he would be returning in the course of a few days, and that he was only awaiting the arrival of a ship. This mystery ship was one of which we were always hearing, but never got any visible proof of. It is just possible that the Senussi were expecting the arrival of some vessel with which they were attempting to run the blockade, either a surface craft or a submarine; but the ship, whatever it was, never materialised, and was as elusive as the phantom *Flying Dutchman*. Or possibly it may have been the same old muddle between the words ship and sheep, a mistake which Basil was incorrigibly fond of making. So we bided our time, and went on, hoping for the best.

But the next morning, March 15th, we were aroused by the sergeant before dawn, and told that a message had arrived over night. The message had come from Selim, and it was to the effect that Basil and Mr. Dudgeon (he was the officer next senior after Captain Tanner), were to go at once to El Zebla, taking with him lists of food, boots, etc., which would be required for a journey. Our hopes were at once raised to frantic heat, though the orders were unusually vague, and we had no idea whether the projected journey was to lead to our release, to our going further into the interior, or to a camp merely more convenient for supplies. But wherever the journey led to, we felt convinced that our condition in a new home could not possibly be worse than it was at Bir Hakkim, and we began freely to exchange bets.

A camel was waiting by the old Priest's tent, and, having dug a few roots as a farewell present for them, I saw Mr. Dudgeon and Basil proceed for the northward at about 10 a.m., my bosom filled with the most mixed feelings of hope and incredulity. But, in any case, we felt that this time it was not merely another rat deserting the ship; for this time it was two true and tried companions who were leaving us, individuals who we felt sure would do everything humanly possible to help us, and get food through, and we had in them advocates who would never tire in our cause.

They failed, as did every other human hope in which we had trusted, though not through any fault of their own. But I will give Mr. Dudgeon's own story in another chapter, and, for the present, will confine myself to narrating our own desperate plight at Bir Hakkim.

I do not consider myself superstitious, but it is a curious thing that, at about this time, I found my Arab horse-shoe again, and I connected it with this journey of Basil and Mr. Dudgeon's. I had carried it for two hundred miles with me at the time of my escape, but it brought me no special luck then, unless I may describe getting through with my life as luck. But this lack of luck

I attributed to not having found the horse-shoe myself; it had been given to me by someone else! And when I was put into the sheep-pen, it had been taken from me with all my other possessions, and thrown away.

But just about, this time, I think on this very morning, while wandering round looking for roots, I found it again, and put in it my pocket. And this time, it was I myself who had found the horse-shoe, so it was bound to bring me luck! And, what is more, it had a loose nail still in it, and this (so my lady friends inform me) is a wish. I certainly wished, though I did not then know the potency of the charm.

We all kept ourselves very busy, some way or another, so far as our physical weakness allowed us. We never seemed to have had a dull minute since we had been at Bir Hakkim, in spite of no scrap of news from the outside world. I myself, having an inveterate passion for any old *ology*, had been making a prodigious collection of marine fossils. Here there were fossil rock-boring shells exactly like date-stones, sea-urchins innumerable (I got a hitherto unrecorded variety for the British Museum), scallops, cockles, and whelks of a prehistoric age. The look of them made me hungry. If only they could have lived in our time, how much I should have preferred them to our celebrated Libyan lily-white snails! I actually talked zoology to Selim at one period, and told him that at one time Bir Hakkim had been a sea beach, washed by the waves. But he laughed me to scorn, for even the oldest Bedouin in those parts, he said, had never heard of such a thing. Which was quite likely, as I was talking of some two hundred thousand years ago!

The petty officers' chief industry seemed to be the making of camel-bone brooches; there were several of these, with the legend "a present from the Libyan Desert" inscribed cameo-wise upon them. The men seemed to have rather been out of occupation, but, with what strength they had left, they killed the numerous large snakes which appeared in the neighbourhood. With a view to further husbanding our food supplies I issued a request that anyone killing a snake in future would bring it to me to eat, as no one else seemed inclined to make the experiment.

But with this excitement of March 15th, we all at once prepared to gird ourselves up for a journey, and looked up our belongings. We busied ourselves in cutting up the camel-hair tent-flaps and sewing them together to form slippers for the march; at one time our captors would have strongly resented our doing this, but now they looked on smiling. The old centenarian grand-dame attached to Osman came round to seize the tent-flap, but we unblushingly sat on and hid it, and denied its existence, whereat she departed discomfited. The soldiers had lately taken a very great interest in our belongings, an interest which at one time we should have considered very ominous, but which, in view of the news, we now believed to be the happiest of augurs; we promised gleefully all and everything, when once we get to Sollum! I had an ancient blue-webbing cricket-belt, clasped by a metal snake, an object of special avarice to the Senussi, who fondly imagined the reptile to be silver. I had come in eleven inches in waist measurement, and lost four stone in weight since I landed; in fact, I scaled the same as I did when I was a boy of fifteen, so I was very proud of that belt. But now I was prepared to sacrifice even that, and allowed the guards to handle and gloat over it. Hungry we certainly were, and weak too; even I, one of the soundest, found myself spinning round and becoming dizzy every time I bent down to collect firewood. We all found it necessary to do this on our knees, and to rest every few minutes. Holy Joe went off on the evening of March 15th for some reason which we could not fathom, and we never saw him again; his wife came back for the remains of his belongings the next evening, so he evidently had not gone far. Had a bird whispered to him? I wonder. Perhaps it was only that he was afraid that his private store of food would be seized by us, and that he therefore determined to take time by the forelock.

And so we came to St. Patrick's Day, Friday, March 17th, 1916, the most memorable day of the lives of five score white men, and the last in that of a score of black ones. How unconscious we all were about it! We calculated that we had some five more days to live, and I have little doubt in my mind that our guards were even then preparing to decamp with the remaining food, leaving us to perish.

It was a grey, quiet day, with a lot of mirage. The men celebrated it in a feeble sort of way by killing what snakes were about, but I think none of us had much faith in St. Patrick or any other Saint at the time, and were thinking more about our approaching end. We were very hungry and very faint, and those who occupied themselves at all, were mostly doing the usual daily hunt in their clothing for lodgers. Any fine afternoon would always find ninety per cent. of our camp complement so employed.

For once I was allowed to be cook, and was sitting down by the fire with Apcar, having just put on some of the evening goat for soup. Then, time hanging heavy, I got out my little red diary which, nothing of importance having happened, I had not written up for two days, and began to write. I had actually written the following words:

*Wednesday, March 15th.*—Mr. Dudgeon and Basil left 10 a.m. to join Selim at Zebla and arrange provisions and shoes for march. No food except meat; all men very weak and fainting on any exertion and hardly able to get firewood.

*Friday, March 11th,*—Still on meat diet only and everyo—

Then something happened; my diary broke off short there! Somebody sang out that the guards had got very excited, had run up the well-mound and looked round, and then run down to their tents and got their rifles. I satisfied myself that this was so, and imagined that some caravan, possibly our long-expected one, or food from Selim, had been sighted from the look-out on the mound.

I was just about to resume my writing, when there was a new alarm. This time it was one of those lodger hunting to the eastward of the camp, who shouted in a weak voice, tremulous with emotion, "My God! There's a motor-car coming!"

Shrill voices were raised all over the camp; all was at once excitement. Those who had been on their backs for weeks sat up, the apparently dying came out of their tents. I am not certain what I said, but I think it was, "You—fool!" I was angry at such a pitiful practical joke!

But, looking to the eastward at that moment, I realised that

*I* was the fool, for *there was* a motor-car in sight! Its dull khaki body was clearly silhouetted against the horizon.

For a moment I gave it up.

Before proceeding any further with this narrative, it is necessary that I should now give Mr. Dudgeon's own story, and also the events which led up to the surprising apparition which came to us at 8 p.m. on the afternoon of St. Patrick's Day, March 17th, 1916.

# CHAPTER 40

# Mr. Dudgeon's Narrative

When Mr. Dudgeon and Basil set off on the morning of March 15th, they had but the vaguest of notions as to where they were going. El Zebla was their nominal destination, and they expected to see Selim, and to be employed in some kind of negotiations, either with the Italians for food, or, perhaps, to arrange the exchange or release of the prisoners at Bir Hakkim.

That things had taken a turn for the better from the prisoners' outlook they had no doubt; for on this occasion it was Mr. Dudgeon and Basil who rode, and the two escorting soldiers and the guide Hassan who walked, a truly topsy-turvy reversal of the hitherto universal procedure; but, as neither Mr. Dudgeon nor Basil had any footwear but a few rags bound round their feet, this was a necessary procedure in any case, if progress was to be made. Seated on the camel, Mr. Dudgeon in front and Basil behind, with the weather at its best, it seemed at first one huge joke as they joggled along.

But presently they began to find that sunny clouds have another side besides that with the silver lining. They had no stirrups, and the saddle was a peaked wooden one of the usual mercantile pattern, designed for carrying packs. Seated upon this wooden rack, riding rapidly developed into an exquisite agony; as a matter of fact, it was many weeks before either of them got over the effects of that first joy ride on a camel. Profiting by their painful experience, that evening they improvised stirrups out of two rice sacks they had brought with them, and by this means managed to take some of their weight off the saddle.

Soon after, midday a short halt was called, and they ate some of the cooked goat which they had brought with them. They offered some of this meat to their guards, who, however, refused to accept it, and instead started a jerboa hunt, for they had found the occupied burrow of one of these little kangaroo-rats. The burrow they tackled had two exits, and having closed one of these, the Senussi poked at the other end with a long stick, until the jerboa bolted, whereupon it was at once clubbed. Cooking it was a simple matter; it was merely *grallocked*, then roasted in its skin at a hot fire, and in a few minutes it was ready. The Senussi insisted on sharing the *rat* round, a generous hospitality which appears to be universal among both them and the Turks, and it tasted *very good*.

At 4.30 p.m. they came upon an Arab camp of some forty or fifty tents, where they spent the night, and where the old Sheikh or priest in charge (for, as in the days of Abraham, the two posts appear to be still very closely related in this ancient land of Libya) set a bowl of dates and another of soured milk before them. But Basil, ever the Admirable Crichton, was not content with this meagre fare, and, with the remainder of the day's meat ration, two falcon's eggs which one of the Senussi had picked up on the journey, and some *fil fil* (native pepper), he contrived a most excellent soup. Then the five lay down and slept snugly, warm rugs above and below them. But whenever they woke, they heard the old Sheikh praying fervently outside the tent, but whether for their sins or for his own, did not transpire.

On the 16th they were out at sunrise, and the guards went from tent to tent endeavouring to beg some food, but without success. So at 7 a.m. they started once more for the north with empty stomachs, save for a drink of milk. Thus they proceeded until about 2 p.m., when their guide left them, and the soldiers turned to the west. An hour later they sighted a familiar object; it was the Commandant's old white horse, the one that had been with us throughout our wanderings, and which I had meditated stealing before I made my attempted escape. He was ever a beacon in the landscape! About 8.30 p.m. they came upon a small encampment, from which a figure emerged. It was Selim, who had come out to greet them!

Selim appeared to be delighted, and was hospitality incarnate. Mr. Dudgeon and Basil at once began to tell him about our wretched condition at Bir Hakkim, describing how we had arrived at the last stages of starvation. Selim, liar that he was, assured them that he had sent off a large caravan with food on the previous day, specifying even the number of bags of rice, etc., and he expressed surprise that they had not met it on the way. Selim, with all his good points, was the most unmitigated liar I have ever met, and he probably just invented this caravan to make his guests feel at their ease; for, if the caravan had ever really existed, it would certainly have got to Bir Hakkim before the afternoon of St. Patrick's Day. However, Selim appeared to be very comfortable and well supplied where he was, and he gave his guests as much mutton and rice as they could eat, following it up with cigarettes and tea. The Rat was evidently happier here than he could have been witnessing the sinking of the doomed ship. His kind heart would also suffer no pangs from being a witness of an unpleasant spectacle.

The night they passed in comfort in Selim's tent, and, after a good breakfast, they started off at 10.30 a.m., each with a camel to himself. Selim came with them, but elected to go on foot, and all day he was as happy as a little cock-sparrow, digging up roots, which he presented to them. He had also brought a bag of dates with him, so they were not badly off for food. This day they caught a distant glimpse of the sea—their first for over four months—but their exact position I cannot locate; it was somewhere to the westward of Gweider, and they were heading in an easterly direction. This was March 17th, the ever memorable St. Patrick's Day, and, all unknown to them and Selim, the prisoners at Bir Hakkim were even then delivered, and speeding rejoicing on their homeward way, not many miles from them. It is possible the parties might have even sighted each other, or at least viewed a miraged reflection, had not a cold wind with rain showers set in from the north, and thus somewhat blurred the landscape. Just after dark they came to some shepherds' tents. They spent the night well sheltered from the rain.

The next day, the 18th, having gone a little further east-ward, they were left in a ravine for the day, while Selim betook himself elsewhere. He did not return until 5 p.m. He then unexpectedly announced to them that he was going back to the camp at Bir Hakkim, and, whilst in the act of bidding them an affectionate farewell, he deftly relieved poor Basil of a watch and chain, property which the latter had borrowed from Mr. Morris, the Chief Steward, before leaving. Basil had no other course open to him but to submit, and Selim performed the deed in such a suave and gentlemanly manner that they both found it difficult to realise for the moment that they were victims of the most bare-faced robbery !

Although I have no proof, I think there is no reasonable doubt that, during his absence that day, Selim had ascertained the events, or some of them, which had transpired on St. Patrick's Day. He was only an hour and a half's march from Gweider, which was on the telephone; and Gweider itself was less than twenty miles from the scene of the incident of the escaping horseman, an episode which the reader will find fully set forth later. Selim must have known definitely by then that the Turks had suffered a final and crushing defeat at Azais, that the British were even then upon him, and that in all probability the prisoners at Bir Hakkim were free. His action in taking Basil's watch and chain, and his haste to depart, are therefore easily explainable.

This little transfer complete, Selim departed, and with his departure he disappears from the pages of this book. Strange blend of liar, thief, diplomat; and hospitable humanitarian that he proved himself to be, he was seen by none of us again.

Basil and Mr. Dudgeon then went off in charge of two new guards, and at about 6.30 p.m. they came to the old telephone hut at the Turkish headquarters at Gweider. It was the hut that I personally knew so well, that to which I had been led by the Turkish soldiers that evening just three weeks before, to learn my fate from the lips of Achmed the Egyptian.

Here they found assembled about a dozen Turkish and Senussi officers, among whom was the black Sudanese, Tarrick Bey, late Commandant at Sollum. I wonder if the latter ever knew the fact that the letter which I had written to him on February 1st, and which he had so carelessly left in the abandoned car near Bir Waer on March 14th, was the cause of our release? Tarrick Bey himself expressed his regret at the short commons on which the prisoners at Bir Hakkim were living; but he also said that there was no food in the country, which was quite true; but, nevertheless, the Turkish army had never lacked the necessities of life as we had. Neither Basil nor Mr. Dudgeon knew at this time, nor did they hear until five days afterwards (March 23rd), the news of our rescue from Bir Hakkim; the only information which the Turks gave them led them to believe that things were going worse than ever for the British!

While at Gweider they encountered two old acquaintances from; Bir Hakkim; one was Mohammed, the cook, and the other the sergeant who used to spend all his time whacking the somnolent sentries. They also encountered a good-looking officer named Gassing whom I have no doubt was my old friend, Senussi Lewis Waller. In fact, their experiences at Gweider were much what mine had been, and they slept in the same lower room in which I had been attacked by those hopping hosts of Lilliput—the fleas.

The next day, March 19th, they were taken over by a Turkish officer, Abdi Bey by name, who supplied them with boots and socks, and later on with horses. Three days more they were destined to spend in this locality in uncertainty, worried both about their own fate and that of their shipmates at Bir Hakkim. All they could hope for was that Selim had in reality sent the caravan with food which he had said he had done; if they had known the real truth, that Selim had sent nothing, their anxiety would have been ten-fold. On the evening of March 19th they had a visit from a Turk, Galip Bey by name, who had a long talk with their then guardian Abdi Bey; after the former had left, the latter told them that they would be liberated. There can be little doubt that by then the Turks either knew or guessed that the *Tara's* had been liberated; but Abdi kept this information from his prisoners, and even asked leading questions as to whether he personally was likely to receive any reward for restoring them to their friends.

On the 19th, 20th, and 21st there were many journeyings backwards and forwards towards the Italian lines at Tobruk, while their captors attempted to enter into futile negotiations; but at 4 a.m. on the 22nd, Mr. Dudgeon and Basil were aroused for the last time, and marched the remaining twelve miles to Tobruk. There, at the old fort of the outer Italian lines, they were met by Italian officers; their feelings as they walked up the *glacis* can be imagined; tears were streaming down Basil's face, and they were both too moved to be able to speak. At the fort they were royally entertained, and thence, after a feast, they were driven in an automobile, amid cheering crowds, to the town itself. The next day their cup of joy wag filled to overflowing by hearing by wireless of the safety of their shipmates.

The reason for this strange journeying of Mr, Dudgeon and Basil has never been fully explained, but I think there is no doubt that they were brought forward to negotiate for food; the *Tara's* were to be the *poor relations* for whom doles were sought, and there was no intention of releasing us. The Turkish army was at that time subsisting almost entirely on meat, which it commandeered from the unfortunate shepherds, but the supply was precarious, as the shepherds were moving away. A second reason was that the Turks wanted a certain Hadji Cosain in exchange. Not until after their arrival at Tobruk did Mr. Dudgeon find out who Hadji Cosain really was. He was the villain of this book, Achmed Mansoor, the Egyptian traitor! Fortune thus gave them a chance to divulge the real identity of this worthy to the Italians, an opportunity which they did not fail to make use of. They also improved the shining hour by telling him a few of their own personal opinions about him. Needless to say, Achmed was *not* exchanged.

After a very happy stay at Tobruk, Basil and Mr. Dudgeon sailed for Alexandria, where they were once more re-united with the rest of the *Tara's*.

# CHAPTER 41

# The Battles of Agadir and Azais

Between the battle of January 23rd and their next advance, the British were fully occupied in collecting and organising transport; and, to facilitate their next step forward, they formed an advanced depôt at Unjeila.

It was on Sunday, February 20th (the day on which I myself escaped from Bir Hakkim), that the British, their preparations completed, and now augmented by the veteran South African Brigade, began their advance westward. Mile upon mile of camel-trains, of ambulances, wagons, horse, foot and artillery wound along the old Khedivial sea-girt road leading to Sollum. The weather was now clear and bright, and the hot sun tempered by sea-breezes, made open-air life a delight. The desert no longer presented a featureless brown surface, for it was carpeted with beautiful flowers; in places asphodel grew waist-high, and there were golden ranunculus, scarlet anemones, purple iris, and many another gallant bloom.

By the evening of February 25th, the British had arrived at Wadi Maktil, within striking distance of the enemy, and intended making an attack on the latter at dawn. But on this occasion they were forestalled, for, just at dusk, the enemy unexpectedly opened fire on the British camp with a mountain gun, causing a few casualties. Our artillery soon silenced the gun, but our General now considered it too hazardous to make a night advance with an enemy so much on the *qui vive*. At earliest light the British cavalry were out, and reported that the enemy had once more retired to his main position on a sandy ridge, about three miles inland from the Khedivial Road.

Here, on the morning of Saturday, February 26th, the decisive battle of Agadir commenced. It was fought on the day that, an escaped prisoner then recaptured, I was brought into the presence of Achmed for judgment. Achmed was at that very moment engaged in telephonic conversation with the battle area a hundred and fifty miles away, and the leniency and consideration with which he then, for the first time, treated me, I can only attribute to the moral effect of the battle on his nerves; it probably saved my life.

The battle began by the eager South African Brigade, under General Lukin, marching up in a south-westerly direction from the sea and crossing the Khedivial Road, where they found a force of armoured cars and motor ambulance convoy awaiting them. From a mound, whence they could observe the whole battle, the British General and his staff watched our troops advance line upon line, as if executing a parade movement. From the Senussi lines came occasional white puffs, showing that some of them, at any rate, were firing black powder, and this gave an excellent mark for our artillery to fire at. The enemy first made an attack on our left flank, but this was frustrated by our cavalry, and at 1 p.m., in face of a hot fire from machine-guns and rifles, our infantry made a magnificent attack with the bayonet across the open plain. As usual, the Senussi, not being themselves armed with or accustomed to use bayonets, did not wait to come into contact with ours. Trusting to their remarkable pedestrian powers, they made off as hard as they could; but our cavalry were not to be denied such an opportunity. After some hard riding the Dorset Yeomanry overtook the enemy's main body, with his artillery and machine-guns, and still forming an orderly and compact force. Without an instant's hesitation the yeomanry charged home, and went right through the enemy in spite of a withering machine-gun fire; then, disregarding their already heavy casualties, the yeomanry reformed and charged back again, sabring and shooting many hundreds of the enemy in their impetuous course. By this brilliant piece of work they captured two machine-guns and made prisoner the Turkish Commander-in-Chief, Jaffir Pacha himself.

This capture of Jaffir Pacha was a most dramatic affair, and came about thus wise. Colonel Soutar, who was leading the charge of the yeomanry, had his horse shot, under him, and got a nasty tumble. When he came to, his men had already galloped a long way ahead, and he found himself alone in the midst of a group of the enemy. Drawing his revolver, he rushed at the nearest Turkish officer and held it to his head, telling him at the same time to surrender and to order his men to cease fire. Some of the latter hesitating, he shot them down without further ado, and the Turkish officer, who by now had had about enough, and observed the cavalry to be returning, thereupon surrendered. He was Jaffir Pacha, and he, his officers, and men, had given in to the single-handed Colonel Soutar. The gallant South Africans, fine, seasoned soldiers, completed the work, and captured another Maxim. Jaffir himself, who was suffering from a sword-thrust in the arm, was quite philosophic as to his capture, remarking that it was the fortune of war. I have been told, but this was never corroborated, that the photograph which he took of the *Tara* prisoners at the Caves was found on him. For a long time afterwards, it was believed that Nouri Bey (Enver's brother) had been killed in this action; but, unfortunately, the report was found to be *much exaggerated*. *Brer Fox* was only shamming dead, and slipped away unharmed, to be for many a year yet a thorn in the side of Britain.

In this Battle of Agadir, the British had about two hundred and fifty casualties. They would unquestionably have been very much heavier had it not been for the presence of two armoured cars personally commanded by the Duke of Westminster, who advanced with the South African Brigade in its frontal attack, and by their traversing fire much reduced that of the enemy. The infantry who had to advance in the open for fifteen hundred yards in a dead flat country, were thus saved from much heavier losses; but the enemy's losses were very heavy, and it was a severe blow to them. It led to our occupying Barrani, hitherto the Turkish forward base, two days later without opposition; and from there, we were almost in sight of our old frontier port of Sollum. Barrani itself had been in enemy occupation since November 23rd, and besides having been burnt by the enemy, had suffered even more heavily by bombardment from the sea. Its occupation by the British made naval work even more arduous, for practically all transport was done by sea from Alexandria, even the water supply being dependent on this, the long stretch of road from the railhead at El Dabaa rendering land conveyance impracticable. There is no harbour at Barrani, only a wind-swept, storm-tossed cove; these winter months of campaign were no picnic for the Navy, nor for the trawlers, who did most of the work.

By March 8th, 1916, our preparations for a further advance were once more complete, our stores and transport collected. Bidding good-bye with relief to this inhospitable spot, on March 9th the infantry, and on the 11th the cavalry, marched with Sollum, then thirty-eight miles distant, for their objective. Our forces consisted of the South African Brigade under General Lukin, two regiments of yeomanry, a battery of artillery, an Australian camel corps, and the Duke of Westminster's Brigade of light armoured cars, some five thousand men in all.

At this time the Senussi camp was at Bir Waer, upon the heights which looked down on Sollum six hundred feet beneath. Bir Waer was, moreover, a munition factory, biscuit factory, and a depot of great importance to the enemy. It was situated two and a half miles across the Libyan plateau south-west from the old Turkish fort above Sollum, Where the Libyan plateau rises on the shore side, it is known as the Taref Mountains.

To occupy Sollum, without first driving the enemy from the heights which commanded it, was obviously not feasible; some method had to be devised for getting at, and if possible, turning, the enemy's position on the plateau at Bir Waer.

After a night march on March 11th and 12th, our troops bivouacked at Bag Bag on the plain, halfway between Barrani and Sollum, and two battalions of South Africans occupied the summit of the Medean Pass of the Taref Mountains. This latter move on their part would most probably have been very strongly opposed by the enemy, had not an unexpected move by the armoured cars rendered opposition to them futile. For, when the South Africans started to climb the steep and tortuous ascent, they found that the armoured cars were already at the top awaiting them; an apparently miraculous feat. Its accomplishment was brought about hi the following manner. The escarpment of the Libyan plateau is opposite Sollum a precipitous height of six hundred feet, but as it goes eastward it gradually diminishes, until opposite Matruh, a hundred and eighty miles distant, it is only a slope. But if the cars had gone back as far as Matruh, and from thence along the top, owing to the distance there would have been great, almost insurmountable, difficulties in the supply of petrol and water. With a view to finding some better way, the Duke caused the escarpment to be carefully reconnoitred on the previous day, and he eventually discovered a possible but extremely difficult ascent due south of Bag Bag, the plateau there being about six hundred feet high. By dint of superhuman exertions, the men of the Armoured Car Brigade, by moving rocks and filling in chasms, eventually succeeded in getting all their machines to the summit unknown to the enemy. And it was thus that, when the South Africans entered the Medean Pass, they were able to do so unopposed. I mention this matter at some length, for the armoured cars have not always been given the full credit they deserve for this magnificent achievement. In general, it was lost sight of in the thrill caused by the more spectacular and dramatic events which followed.

The Medean Pass was now safely occupied, but; owing to the shortage of water, the main body of our troops was still compelled to remain in the plain at Bir Augrin, and still eighteen miles from Sollum. At the top of the pass, and all along the crest of the Taref Mountains, there was no water, the bir or rock cisterns having been pumped dry by the wily Senussi before leaving. Our forces at the summit had to subsist on a limited supply brought up by camel train from the plain. All being now ready, the South Africans advanced at 5 p.m. on the evening of March 18th along the crest, supported by a mountain battery, a company of Australian camel corps, and the armoured cars scouting some miles ahead. They had been on the move barely half an hour, when an enormous cloud of smoke was observed to ascend above Sollum. It was the enemy, who, observing our advance, had blown up his magazines and was destroying his stores at Bir Waer, and was now in full retreat to the westward.

Hence it was that, thanks to the armoured cars, and the small body of troops backing them up on the plateau top, the British main army was able to advance concurrently with them upon Sollum quite unopposed at daybreak on March 14th, and to take possession of that little frontier seaport without a single casualty or a shot being fired. Thence, during the day, the yeomanry were able to mount from sea-level up the seven hundred feet of precipitous ascent through Halfaia Pass (aptly termed *Hell Fire Pass* by our men) and to regain the old Turkish fort of Sollum at its summit and the smouldering remnants of Bir Waer at the back of it.

After a period of sixteen weeks Sollum was once more in British hands, the Senussi invasion broken, and driven back across the Italian border whence it had come, and all the Egyptian territory bordering on the sea restored to its rightful owners. On the surface this seemed satisfactory, but the outstanding fact remained that the enemy forces were still intact and unbroken, a probable and potential source of trouble in the future. The tireless and predatory Senussi, still unpunished and defiant, were once more retiring to their unmapped desert wastes, there to watch an opportunity for further mischief. This was very undesirable, but could British troops ever overtake so nimble a foe? The sequel will show what the answer to this question was.

On this morning of March 14th, the Duke of Westminster's Light Armoured Cars, arriving at dawn at the head of Halfaia Pass, had surprised two Senussi who had not yet made good their escape. From these two prisoners the Duke had learned news of importance as to the enemy's movements.

With his unfailing faculty for quickly grasping the essentials of a military situation, thought and action usually came simultaneously. Without waiting for orders, or even for permission from his superior officer, like Hotspur of old, he clashed off with his cars in sharp pursuit of the retreating enemy, contenting himself with leaving behind one car to helio to General Peyton, the British Commander-in-Chief, news of what he was doing and to bring on his reply. The reply came long after the armoured cars had disappeared over the horizon, and it was in effect to tell the Duke to do what he was already doing, viz., "to pursue the enemy with vigour."

This pursuing force consisted in all of one Ford car with machine-gun, nine armoured cars, and one light touring car, a 1914 Rolls-Royce which the Duke always used and drove himself—a truly remarkable machine, which after many months of warfare is still as efficient as ever, and is now in daily use in London. Each car mounted a machine-gun, and the total complement of the ten vehicles consisted of thirty-two officers and men all told. With this force, un-backed by any other, they commenced the pursuit of the unbroken Turco-Senussi army of several thousands, equipped as it was with artillery and machine-guns! After covering two or three miles marked by innumerable intersecting tracks, which made very bad going, they picked up the road running westward from the old Fort of Sollum, and overtook many fugitives, who fired at them as they passed. Following this road they were able to go at a speed of nearly twenty miles an hour, and after about an hour's run at this pace, shortly before midday they sighted the enemy's camp. Immediately, enemy shells fired at them showed them its exact position, one which he had hurriedly taken up. It was on flat ground on the open plain, but between them and it stretched a belt of hummocky ground, the hummocks having been formed by sand gathered round the roots of the tough and heather-like desert shrubs. This surface was about as bad as it could be for breaking the springs of cars; but the drivers, who had now attained to an extraordinary degree of efficiency in such work, safely negotiated it. Once through, the cars formed in line abreast, and charged straight home at the enemy.

Never was surprise attack more effective; the enemy were caught just as they were about to march. Their camels were already loaded, some of the infantry were even then on the move, and many of the guns had just been limbered up. But the remainder at once opened a very hot fire on the advancing cars from everything available, machine-guns, mountain-guns, and rifles. As the cars dashed forward the shells whizzed just over the top of them, to burst harmlessly in the open desert a mile or two behind; but by a miracle, not a single car was directly hit, although the gunners stuck to their guns until the cars were right among them. The British Maxims, for their part, did deadly work at close quarters; the enemy artillerymen and officers were shot down or captured almost to a man.

In a very short time the enemy were in a state of panic and rout, and, casting away their arms, they fled helter-skelter in every direction, in a vain effort to find some avenue of escape from the death-spitting monsters who pursued them so relentlessly.

The cars continued this work of rounding up the demoralised bands of the enemy until late in the afternoon, shooting down the loaded camels, and scattering his forces to the four winds, until from physical exhaustion and repulsion to more killing, they could do no more. As night fell, they returned to the place where they had first surprised the enemy, Bir Azais, or Bir Aziza, as it is sometimes called.

At the commencement of this fight, a Turkish officer had been observed escaping on horseback. He was evidently of importance, but the cars were then too busily engaged with the main body of the enemy to trouble about individuals, and after a short chase he made good his escape, followed by a storm of machine-gun bullets. It was only afterwards that they learnt that this was Nouri Pacha, and that once more the old fox had eluded them. If ever man bore a charmed life Nouri was his name!

Another strange incident of the Battle of Azais was an extraordinary phenomenon displayed by some enemy camels. A train of twenty of these animals was already loaded up and moving off when the cars first came on the scene; to prevent their escape machine-gun fire was opened on them, with the surprising result that the poor animals at once burst into flames and then blew to pieces! An investigation disclosed the fact that the unfortunate beasts had been loaded with bombs and petrol.

The final result of this dashing action by the armoured cars was that on the British side one officer was slightly wounded. Against this, on the other side of the scale, was the Turco-Senussi army entirely smashed up and dispersed with very heavy losses, which included one German and ten Turkish officers killed or wounded, eighty prisoners, and the capture by the British of two mountain-guns, nine machine-guns, and a very large quantity of ammunition, food, and stores of all kinds. This by the unaided efforts of a British force of thirty-two: thus were the *Petrol Hussars* justified!

Content, they returned to their camp near the old fort at Sollum for the night, leaving three cars to guard the field of battle.

Now, at long last, had the Senussi discovered that there was something in the world more mobile than they were, a something which could mete out a swift and terrible punishment to the ruthless breakers of peace with Britain. This something, moreover, was a weapon of which they had never dreamed, one which the scheming school of submarine enthusiasts who had inveigled them into the war had never hinted at. Too late now, they saw that the submarine, that hitherto wonderful universal provider, which, with magician's cloak, could pass unharmed and unseen among its enemies on the sea, and deal to Britain her death-blow as it went, was now powerless to aid them.

Disillusioned, once and for all time, starving, perishing with thirst, the unhappy Senussi found themselves hunted out like rats, driven from corner to hole, in the vast and hitherto safe fastnesses of their own deserts.

# CHAPTER 42

# Providence Goes Nap

It was on March 14th, at the time that the armoured cars were making their way to the Battle of Azais, that an incident, big with fate for the men of the *Tara*, occurred. At a spot about midway between Bir Waer and Azais, one of the tyres punctured, and a temporary halt was called to collect forces and make good the damage. At this exact spot, a broken-down Ford car, abandoned by the enemy, lay by the roadside. Major Amphlett, an officer in one of the armoured cars which happened to be nearest to it, took the opportunity to overhaul the derelict. On first search, it appeared to contain nothing but some empty petrol-tins and a heap of rubbish, and he was just turning away, when his eye caught sight of a folded sheet of paper among the rubbish. The paper was a sheet of foolscap, addressed on one side to Tarrick Bey (late Turkish Commandant at Sollum), and on the other side was a pencilled letter written in French, dated Bir Hakkim Abbyat, February 1st, 1916, and signed by *myself*. It was the only letter in the abandoned Ford, and, as at that moment the armoured cars moved on, Major Amphlett thrust it hurriedly into his pocket; it was not until the next day, the 15th, that he had an opportunity of turning it over to the Adjutant, who sent it on to the Military Intelligence at Sollum.

*Providence had played her first card!*

This letter, so miraculously discovered in the abandoned car, was one of several written by me on February 1st. It was a letter imploring that food, clothes, boots, and medicine be sent at once to us unhappy prisoners. It described our number and pitiful condition, and it begged him to get into touch with the British General commanding with a view to the supply of these necessities. *It was the only letter ever written in which Bir Hakkim was named.* At the time when I wrote that letter, I remember clearly that a something, which I call Providence, prompted me to write the name Bir Hakkim across the top of the sheet, although my common-sense argued that to do so was foolishness, for the name of our place of internment was already well known to Tarrick Bey. But write it I did. On no other letters was it mentioned, for the good reason that, on the censoring of the letters, the discovery of such a notation would almost certainly involve their destruction and non-delivery.

Thus the first authentic news of the pitiable plight of the *Tara's*, and also the name of the place of their internment, came into the hands of the British. Subsequently this information was corroborated by the discovery, in a burning tent at Bir Waer, of letters written by other of the prisoners. But, in this instance, none of the letters told either the place of our internment, or any other news than such as would readily pass the Censor.

But even with this information, things were not really much better than before from the captives' point of view. Bir Hakkim Abbyat was an unknown place. It was marked on no map. It had been visited by no white man, since way back of the long centuries, when the Roman power which had built the wells had been driven out of Libya. No one in the British camp had ever heard of Bir Hakkim. The Turkish officer prisoners, ashamed of our treatment, would have been only too happy to help, but with the best of intentions they were unable to do so. They were nearly all wounded, and none of them had ever been to Bir Hakkim. They remembered that the British prisoners *had* been sent to a place of that name, but their impression was that it had been intended to remove them; that, in fact, this had already been done, And my letter was six weeks old!

The case seemed more hopeless than ever, and then *Providence played her second card!*

There was found in the camp a one-eyed Senussi, whose

name was Achmed. I am not clear whether this Achmed was a prisoner or whether he voluntarily came in, but I think the latter. However that may be, Achmed offered his services as a guide. He stated that thirty years before, when he was a youth, his father used to graze his flocks in the vicinity of Bir Hakkim, and that he himself often visited that well for water. He *thought* he could still find his way there, but he was not sure of it. With Achmed, there was another Senussi who volunteered to assist, and who professed to an intimate knowledge of the Red Desert, as that part of Libya is called; but it is doubtful whether he had actually been to Bir Hakkim itself, as it was an out-of-the-way, infertile spot, seldom visited by shepherds or caravans. Here then were two guides professing themselves willing to help, but they were subjects of a race at war with Britain, and they were, moreover, men who, by their own confession, were very doubtful of their own ability to find the way.

Was it likely that any man could be found so foolhardy as to trust his fate into these alien hands, to wander off the map into the waterless interior, to journey an unknown distance in an unknown direction in the enemy's country, on what appeared to be a fool's errand? It did not seem likely. *Then Providence played her third card!* On the morning of February 16th, the armoured cars having made good some of the damage incurred at the Battle of Azais, the Duke of Westminster happened to hear of the strange discovery of my letter. He at once went to General Peyton and volunteered his services to make an effort to discover and liberate the *Tara* prisoners. The General at once acquiesced, and realising the need for immediate action, not a moment was lost.

The armoured cars themselves were already on the top of the plateau, but if the prisoners were to be brought back, practically every serviceable motor vehicle with the army would have to be employed; they were all at sea level in the old town of Sollum, and had to be got up the seven hundred feet to the top. The troops were at once turned to, and, working with a will, up that steep mountain track with its hair-pin loops, and its rocky steps, in places eighteen inches high, they bundled ambulances and touring cars, until they mustered forty-three vehicles in all.

Whenever an engine struck work, a dozen eager hands practically lifted the car past the difficulty. Others, equally willing and enthusiastic, filled in the holes and toned down the worst corners. Petrol, water, and stores were dragged to the top, and working continuously, the last can of petrol was embarked at midnight on St. Patrick's Eve, March 16th, 1916. The motor ambulances were loaded with food, clothes, water, and spare petrol; nothing was forgotten, and the petrol carried was sufficient to carry the whole convoy an estimated distance of two hundred and fifty miles. At the time this amount was considered ample, for the distance to Bir Hakkim, carefully calculated from all available data, had been worked out at sixty-five, or at the most at seventy miles.

It was at 3 a.m. on St. Patrick's Day, March 17th, that forty-three cars left the old Turkish Fort above Sollum, and proceeded some eighteen miles to the scene of the Battle of Azais; here they waited for daylight. With the first pale streaks of dawn, the whole convoy were once more under way, speeding along that unknown road going westward, a road supposed to lead to Tobruk. Their average speed that day, allowing for stoppages for burst tyres, was about twelve miles per hour.

The *fool* journey, the knight-errant adventure on the hundred to one chance, had begun!

The adventure itself, for the first fifty miles of road, was featureless; they saw only the same dead, level, red-brown monotony of the desert, whose rim was broken only occasionally by the saddle-backed mounds of the ancient bir or the rare remains of a ruined building. But from mile fifty on, a low range of hills ran parallel with the road a couple of miles to the southward of them, it appeared to be about a hundred feet high.

Mile sixty-five, the supposed distance of Bir Hakkim, was passed, and they were still upon the road. The guides were vague, and could give them no idea how far they still were from their destination. For some time they had noticed the tracks of a motor-car, apparently ahead of them, on the road; but at mile sixty-five it was a small camel caravan which they overtook, and with it were two Turkish officers and the Turkish Surgeon-General.

The two officers, who were on white horses, galloped off at their approach, and succeeded in escaping among the hills; one, at the last moment, had his horse shot under him, and turning round as he sprang clear, he shook his fists at them, then, running, disappeared out of sight over the ridge. The Turkish Surgeon-General himself, thus abandoned by his companions, was apparently nervous as to what treatment he might receive, and fell on his knees in the dust to supplicate mercy. No one asked him his name, but his herculean figure and black whiskers render the description I have of this officer infallible—it was our old friend Dr. Béchie Fouad of the Caves in the life once more. There are no two Béchie Fouads in the world. The caravan having been destroyed, the trembling doctor was released: the cars desired no prisoners that day.

Seven miles further along, they came upon an abandoned car. It was the British Naval Wireless Telegraphy Wolseley car which had fallen into the enemy's hands four months previously. It was still in excellent condition, except for a buckled wheel, and the local made tyres. The latter had been made from sheet-rubber tightly rolled, and bound round with camel-hide, wire, and grass ropes, and this home-made affair was apparently quite a success; the sheet-rubber no doubt was the flotsam washed up on the coast from some torpedoed ship.

Leaving this derelict as it was, they once more resumed their journey, and at mile seventy they passed a line of telegraph poles without wire, running north and south across the road. These poles were probably the same that I had myself observed on two occasions in my journeyings.

But still there were no signs that they were nearing their destination. The guides were arguing vigorously with each other, and appeared more uncertain than ever as to their whereabouts. At mile eighty-two they took the cars off the road and headed across the open desert, at first south-west, and then south-south-west and south. Looking round at mile eighty-seven they saw that they had passed round the western edge of the low hills which had been to the southward of them since mile fifty.

The desert surface here was very stony, but, fortunately, on the whole it was hard going. Ninety miles went by, a hundred miles passed, and still there was no sign. There was a particularly bad mirage that day, and from time to time they would observe what appeared to be villages, horsemen, herds of cattle. But of these the guides took no notice—and, as they gazed, these phantoms vanished into thin air.

All this time they had been looking for a lone fig-tree which the guide had told them about; this fig-tree was the landmark by which he would know his position, and it was close to their destination. But neither of this tree, nor of any other fixed mark, could they see any trace; nothing but the deceptive oft-changing shimmer of the mirage.

A hundred and ten miles passed. No one any longer spoke. They were nearly halfway through their petrol, and they had the return journey to make. Everyone now believed that to go further was useless, everyone except one man. The Duke of Westminster that day was in a mood which is designated in the vulgar seaman's vocabulary as "bloody-minded," that is to say, obstinate, determined, brooking no opposition to his will, impatient of futile argument against his set purpose. To the arguments of the faint-hearted as to the danger of running out of petrol, he only replied that in that case they could stop where they were and send back some of the ears for more. So long as the guides held out the least hope of being able to find the way, so long as they did not acknowledge themselves utterly lost, he refused even to consider the possibility of failure.

They went on. A hundred and fifteen miles went by, and anxious looks were cast in the Duke's direction. To go further seemed madness!

Achmed the guide had been peering intently into the brown sea of desert on the left. Suddenly he shouted excitedly and threw himself off the automobile, which was then moving at twenty miles an hour.

*He had sighted the fig-tree, and Providence's fourth card was on the table!*

With his one eye Achmed had been the first to note what all those other eyes could not see; but now they all saw it clearly, standing alone and solitary, blasted and gnarled by a hundred years of drought and desert winds.

Achmed went up to the tree, fell on his knees, and having given thanks to Allah, the giver of all good things, he scraped away the sand with his hands, exposing as he did so the coping of an ancient bir. It was, he explained, the *Well of Sweet Waters*, a well at which he had often watered his father's flocks in his boyhood's days, but now it was choked with sand and useless. Only the ancient fig-tree remained to show where the well had been.

The way to Bir Hakkim was now clear and open; they were no longer lost. But what could they hope to find when they got there? The chances were still ten to one that the prisoners would have been moved elsewhere long before now. Or even at that moment, when the cars appeared, the guards might set on them and kill them, if they *were* still there. They knew not what forces they might have opposed to them, and Bir Hakkim was, for all they knew, a strongly-defended place. Were they, at long last, to find that this hare-brained quixotic venture against the Unknown, after giving some promise of success, was doomed to disappointment? It seemed more than probable.

With pent-up emotion, their cars raced forward once more. Ten or twelve miles further on they sighted a huge mound, and just to the right of it a small heap of stones on a low ridge; the guide informed them that it was their destination. A few seconds more and what looked in the mirage like a large encampment, with white-clad figures, came into view: it was the five tents of the prisoners at Bir Hakkim. But to those in the cars, owing to the mirage, it looked like a good-sized village, where considerable resistance might be expected. The Duke sent forward a car to reconnoitre, another following.

A faint British cheer came to his ears.

*Providence had played her last card. She had gone nap and won!*

At that cheer the whole convoy rushed forward. The sight of them was the spectacle that greeted my unbelieving eyes at, Bir Hakkim at 3 p.m. in the afternoon of St. Patrick's Day, 1916.

# CHAPTER 43

# Salvation

"In the Multitudes of Dreams and Many Words There are Also Divers Vanities: but Fear Thou God."—*Ecclesiastes* v. 7

The things which I actually said or did, or how others at the time behaved, is a vague and misty memory to my mind. But my mental state, my dominant emotions of incredulous joy, of inability to believe the unbelievable, these are indelibly, ineffaceably fixed there.

The light was bad for photography that day, but I am fortunate in being the possessor of a most happy snapshot of myself, taken within a minute or two of our rescue. This picture is remarkably like the advertisement for a well-known chocolate, which depicts a small boy who is supposed just to have eaten some of the advertised delicacy and he has the smile which *won't come off!* So it was with me, as barefooted, shirtless, a canvas rag about my head and my tattered uniform hanging loose from my emaciated body, I stood proudly up beside Brigadier-General (then Colonel) Laycock, in that supreme moment. Looking at this photo now, I can recall much of what I then felt!

When we prisoners saw the first car come round the corner to reconnoitre us, we felt excited; but never for a second even then did we guess that it could be any other than a Turkish car. But even a Turkish car we hoped meant good news for us; possibly it meant that we were going to be exchanged. More probably it conveyed someone of importance who had come to visit us, and we felt that such a visit would portend an improvement in our deplorable condition. We were like the inmates of a workhouse, pleasurably expecting a visit from the Squire's lady or some other local big wig, hopeful of gifts to come, anticipating a fruitful topic of conversation and tittle-tattle.

When we saw the second car, we began to wonder; but we had been told that the Turks had two cars somewhere in the country, and we still had little doubt as to these being enemy property.

But when we saw first, ten, then twenty, then thirty, forty and finally forty-three cars come rushing up, we began to get a glimmering of the truth, a half-fearful hope that the impossible *had* happened. It was then that our little world turned itself inside out, that we saw the heavens opening, and gazed terrified lest they should close again. We had to ask our saviours "Are we free?" and when we were told "Yes," we did not believe them!

I cannot remember even the cars coming up to us. I have a vague recollection of the whirr of motor engines, of the presence of a crowd of vehicles, and suddenly they were there! Near by was a Red Cross ambulance to which the men pushed, and presently some came away from it, and it dawned on me that they had open tins of food in their hands. This was too much. Forgetting my dignity, I also rushed to the car and snatched what I could get, and then came running back to the officers' tent, a tin of chicken in one hand, a tin of condensed milk in the other; these two I ladled indiscriminately with a piece of stick on to a hunk of bread and gorged!

While I was thus congenially and energetically engaged, I remember that X——, one of the officer prisoners, came up to me, and commented disparagingly upon my undignified and what *he* considered indecent haste to eat; in his opinion, as our food was now assured, it didn't matter whether we had to wait another hour or two or not, before satisfying our hunger. We had borne it so long, why not a little longer? He himself was apparently not the least moved by the arrival of the cars, nor by his manner would it appear to you that he was in the least bit hungry, and though I won't go so far as to say that he looked bored, he was not very far from it, and his expression bespoke strong disapproval of my then table manners. He was ever an epicure himself, even when it came to snails and the *innards* of goats! On this occasion his dignity was supreme, his self-control superb, but to the ravenous beast that I then was, they appeared to me superfluous, and with an oath I turned my back on him, and gorged harder than ever.

A minute or two later, one of the rescue party approached me, and asked: "Was Captain Williams there?" I replied with my mouth full, that I was that individual, and immediately afterwards I found that I was shaking hands with the Duke of Westminster, but at the same time keeping a very wary eye on the tin of bully-beef which I was consuming, lest his Grace should display a disposition to pinch it!

The Duke then asked me where our guards were. My mouth still being too full to speak, I waved my disengaging arm in the direction of the bushy plain to the westward, to which I knew our guards had run. A moment later and he gave an order, of which I took no note, for I had discovered a piece of cheese, and was dipping it into condensed milk. Suddenly my senses were aroused; there was a sharp crackling sound; it was the machine-guns of the armoured cars. What could this mean? Why were they firing? Time and again our gaolers had assured us that they were at peace with England—and now?

"Save them!" I cried, "they have been kind to us!" and together the Duke and I dashed up the old well mound, whence we could behold what was happening below.

But it was too late! Ere we gained the top, the Maxims had already completed their work. There, with their faces to the sky, or lying crumpled in a heap as they fell, was the whole toll of our guards, dead, like the brave and fearless outlaws they were, with arms in their hands. If they had only told us the truth sometimes instead of *always* lying, we would have known that the bitterest of wars still raged between Briton and Senussi, a war in which neither side gave quarter in the heat of action. But they had said there was peace where no peace was, and the lie was their undoing. For if we had but known the real facts, we could have interceded for them in time to avert their end. There they lay, for ever sleeping on the open plain, the plain on which we first slept, swept by the bitter winds during our first tent-less week at Bir Hakkim. Thither we had been brought by Achmed the Egyptian, and now, by a second Achmed, were we being delivered thence.

But that no Senussi is safe until he is a dead Senussi was amply demonstrated to us, and even a dead Senussi is generally alive! During the melee of the action, an Arab woman fleeing with the soldiers was unfortunately wounded. One of the cars observing this, at once sent a doctor to attend on her; near by lay a Senussi, apparently as dead as a door-nail. The car went on, leaving the surgeon attending to the woman; but its officer, happening to look round a moment later, observed to his surprise that the erstwhile corpse was crawling towards the group. Then, to his horror and before he could intervene, he saw the Senussi raise his rifle and fire at the surgeon at close range. By a miracle the bullet missed its mark, though it passed between the surgeon's legs. The car sprinted up, and with a burst of machine-gun fire, made certain, once for all, that, no more *dead* Senussi should again come to life. It was a good object lesson to those who saw it, as to the habits of these untameable nomads.

A quarter of an hour having now passed, the men were told to pack up their belongings ready to move off. As their belongings mostly consisted of only a piece of sacking, a verminous mat, a potted-meat tin and a bone needle, this process did not take long. Meanwhile the naked had been clothed in blue hospital suits, and the sick and those too infirm to walk had been tenderly carried and placed in the motor ambulances: we were soon ready to start.

Meanwhile the doctor, having attended to the more urgent cases, began to get nervous at our prodigious appetites; he feared we should do ourselves an injury by over-eating, and he tried to check it. As well might he have tried to take a bone away from a hungry tiger. We knew there *was* plenty of food, and we knew *where* it was, and we were quite prepared to fight with tooth and nail for the possession of it. The doctor gave up his attempt. As a matter of fact, nothing could hurt digestions such as we then had; India-rubber and concrete mixed would not have disagreed with us. We all continued eating for twelve or fourteen hours on a stretch, some for thirty-six hours, and, medical opinion to the contrary, I don't believe one of us was one atom the worse for it! For people who have only starved for a comparatively short time, I have no doubt it would have been injurious. But we had starved continuously for five months, our stomachs had become like those of wild beasts, and we could gorge to repletion as they do, and be none the worse for it.

So we packed up our little belongings, and still stuffing down food, and in many instances smoking two cigarettes at once, we stowed ourselves away in the various vehicles of the convoy. I have seen it stated that ere leaving many of us fell on our knees and thanked God. This may have been so, but if it, was, I did not observe it. But there *were* tears of gratitude and happiness welling down many a grimy bearded face; from every heart was ascending a prayer of silent thanksgiving to Heaven from captives set free; to this silent prayer, so sincere and heartfelt, words to most of us appeared superfluous.

They were a *nubbley* lot, the *Tara's* men! No one would ever have picked them out as a crew to be specially proud of. Some, of course, were what the prayer-books call livers of "godly, righteous and sober lives," The majority were the average Britisher, none too good, but all the same not a bad lot. And at the other end, we had some of the riff-raff of the sea— foul-mouthed, unclean in their personal habits, loose-livers in every respect. Men change the habits of a life-time with difficulty, and even after seeing the work which Providence wrought for them in the wilderness, I doubt if many of these are very different now. But at that moment, our hearts were very full and softened towards God; we had seen His work, and we believed. One of the last remarks which I heard before we sped away was that of an erstwhile Atheistic dweller in Whitechapel. It was this: "An' to think I went in *there* sayin' there was no Gawd!" Ensconcing myself in an armoured car, I was one of the first to start on the return journey. What a journey it was, as with an enormous piece of bread in my hand, reinforced with butter, marmalade and cheese, we bumped and thumped over a hundred and ten miles of happiness to Azais, the camp where we were to spend the night! Unlike many of the others, I remembered to bring back all my curios with me.

But even now, in the armoured car, I did not feel safe. That we should actually be free men, never to return to starvation and squalor, appeared too miraculous; it was a ridiculous absurdity, and I feared to wake up and hear the wind soughing through the ragged tent once more and see the stars glimmering through the hole in its roof. Anxiously I scanned the desert horizon, and assured myself that there was nothing in sight; then I examined the machine-gun, to make certain that it was in good order. The yellow dust rose in choking clouds as we sped along, but I fancied I could smell the salt of the free sea come with it, and once more I found the tears flowing down my face. And to think that X— had wanted me to look dignified about it all! The thought still rankled in my mind!

Soon after turning on to the road, we noticed the Wolseley naval car which had been left derelict on the outward journey. It was now burnt out; evidently Béchie Fouad's friend, the one who had his horse shot under him, had succeeded in getting some of his own back.

It was nearly 11 p.m. by the time we got to Azais. Some cars were already there before us, others continued to filter in, until by 3 a.m. the last had arrived. Thus, in twenty-four hours, all the cars had covered two hundred and fifty miles; not one of them was broken down or lost on the way, but all the forty-three got back. But the petrol which had been worked out for this distance was nearly gone.

I remember that night how I smelled a delicious smell, and how I tracked it to its source like a hound. Perhaps my readers may not consider that perfume to be balm of Araby, but, to my fat-starved interior, it was more appealing than attar of roses! It was a *kipper!* One of the drivers had extracted two kippers from a tin, and was cooking them over a petrol stove. How hungrily I watched him and drank in those delicious odours. He never offered me one; he probably thought I would despise such humble fare. But, if he could have read my thoughts, he would have known that I considered a five-pound note a payment far too small to offer for either of the two. But it was not to be; having watched him dispose of the last oleaginous morsel, I reluctantly departed.

CHAPTER 44

# " . . . . Happily Ever After!"

The reader who has so patiently followed me through the whole of this true history of the adventures which befell the men of the *Tara,* will now, I suspect, wish to be assured that, in this modern fairy-story, as in its ancient counterparts, we all at its conclusion "lived happily ever after."

In my last chapter I brought our story as far as that first joyful night of freedom, where, on the battlefield of Azais, we, like Jacob, saw the ladder leading up to heaven; where also I smelled that delicious smell—a kipper!

Dawn on the following day found us all still very much alive, and eating, if anything, rather harder than before; and at 8 a.m. we started on the final eighteen-mile stage of our journey to the sea, bumping our way in a varied collection of motor-cars to Sollum. An almost impenetrable sandstorm obscured both land and sky; through it we saw dimly the skeletons of the burned out buildings of the Turkish magazine at Bir Waer, also the abandoned motor-car in which my letter had been found, and then, a mile or two further along, we came at last to the old fort crowning the heights above Sollum. Waving from its ramparts floated the grand old Union Jack of Britain; it was the first sight we had had of it during five long months of pain and weariness, and, seeing it, we praised God anew for our deliverance.

Nothing could exceed the kindness and heartiness of our welcome from General and private soldier alike, and from thence we climbed down the last steep descent of seven hundred feet through Hell Fire Pass, mounted on camels, until we were at the border of the sea. In the bay, the one-time Egyptian gunboat *Rasheed,* now a hospital ship, was awaiting us, and a roar of cheering burst from all our throats as we got into the waiting boats, and felt again the first, lilt of the free sea-waves beneath our keel. Never had the world looked so beautiful before as it did on that perfect morning; a fresh north-west breeze was blowing in from seaward, causing the ships to dance and curvet at their anchors, and the turquoise Mediterranean to be capped with white-tipped wavelets which sparkled in the sunshine. As the oars dipped they shone like silver mirrors, and the clouds of sand blowing from the Libyan plateau, became gleaming, golden streamers, drifting across the face of the mountain.

Two days later we arrived safely at Alexandria, already very different individuals to the human wrecks who had lingered so hopelessly on St. Patrick's Day at Bir Hakkim but three sunrises before. There, at Alexandria, we remained awhile to recover our strength, our happiness being made complete by hearing, on March 26th, of the arrival of Basil and Mr. Dudgeon at Tobruk. At various dates, and by various ships, we all returned safely to our homes; Basil alone, being a Greek by birth, remaining in the East, and, for the remaining years of the war, he was attached as interpreter to the British Army in Egypt, where he still lives in happiness and contentment.

Paddy, the faithful fox-terrier-pug, who had so light-heartedly endured our captivity, and had so narrowly escaped being eaten by us, became the mascot of the Armoured Car Brigade. For four happy months he lived with them, when a sad accident befell. A sentry of another unit, a man who had received orders to shoot stray dogs in view of possible hydrophobia, not recognising the poor animal, fired at and killed him. His death was instantaneous and he suffered no pain, and grief was great at his loss. He was given a military funeral, and a handsome cross was put above his grave, which looks out on the Mediterranean near the British lines at Matruh. Poor doggie, you deserved a better fate than this; but such faithfulness does not go unrewarded, either here or in the hereafter. It is well with thee!

Port Bardia, the submarine nest where we had been landed by the U 85, was, on May 6th, 1916, occupied by the Italians, and for the last two years of the war it could no longer be used by U-boats, Said Hillal, the uncle of the Grand Senussi, the individual I believe who visited us at the Caves, himself came with the Italians and assisted. One complete wireless set was found there and two more in the desert south of Sollum, and they were of much use to the British, being sufficiently powerful to communicate with Alexandria. Maressa (the Dry Dock) was occupied on the preceding day.

Basil himself was able to visit the Caves, which he found just as we had left them, and with the grave of the heroic Quarter-Master William Thomas undisturbed. He was able to make arrangements with the Italian authorities for the remains to be re-interred in consecrated ground.

Even that nebulous place on the map, Bir Hakkim, has subsequently been visited by a British staff officer. Up to the present, unfortunately, I have been unable to get any account of this call, but I hope some day myself to revisit the spot and revive old associations. Of others, the Grand Senussi is, according to latest reports, still a fugitive in the depths of the Sahara, shorn of all temporal power and authority, adhered to by but a small band of faithful followers, fugitives like himself. In his place reign puppet Grand Senussi, set up in the British, Italian and French spheres of influence.

Nouri Pacha, the old fox, who so cleverly again and again eluded the British forces, was, according to reports in the Press, captured in the Caucasus in the autumn of 1918.

Achmed Mansoor, the Egyptian traitor, in the end met the due reward of his cruelty and treachery. The reader will recollect that Mr. Dudgeon and Basil recognised him at Tobruk, where he had fallen into the hands of the Italians, and they were able to inform the latter of his real identity. By the Italians he was subsequently handed over to the British, and was by them brought to trial, and finally executed as a deserter and traitor. Fevzi and Husni, the two Turkish officers who were so kind to me when we were first landed, were made prisoners by the British early in the war, and were at Cairo when we arrived at Alexandria. Doubtless, by now, they are enjoying the liberty they so longed for and deserved.

Jaffir Pacha, the Turkish General, who was captured at the Battle of Agadir, soon resigned himself to the *fortune of war*, and, recognising the futility of the pro-German policy pursued by the *Young Turks*, joined in on the side of the Allies. He did yeoman service on behalf of the King of the Hedjaz, and was of great service to the British at the occupation of Damascus; services which have now been recognised, for he has had a C.M.G. conferred upon him.

The Promised Land, of which the *Tara's* heard so much, but never saw, was undoubtedly Siva, that ancient outwork of Egypt, two hundred miles to the south of Sollum, one of the oases known to Pharaoh's ancient civilisation, and noted for its famous temple of Amnion, now buried in the sands. This oasis lies low on the south side of the Libyan plateau, and is abundant in springs of water, both hot and cold, in close proximity to one another. It is one of the strangest places in the world, and was the last hiding place of Sayed Ahmed, the Grand Senussi, on Egyptian territory. It was captured by a wonderful dash of armoured cars across the two hundred miles of waterless and trackless desert on February 5th, 1917, nearly a year after our rescue at Bir Hakkim.

On March 17th, 1916, the London and North Western Railway Company, to which the *Tara* had originally belonged, entertained the survivors at Euston. At a performance at the Coliseum subsequently, which we attended, I took a cloak-room ticket: the number of my ticket was the same as that of the submarine which sank us—U 85!

This may seem strange, but I encountered an even more curious coincidence. The streets of London were then darkened, and, proceeding one night along Bow Street, I ran into something soft and hairy—it was a camel! My friends frankly disbelieved the story, but, a week later, the identical phenomenon recurred in the same spot, and this time I determined not to be foiled, but stopped to investigate. It was then that I elicited from the small boy attendant on the animal, that the camel was destined to appear that evening in the performance of the *Bing Boys* at the Alhambra.

I left for the Arctic within a week of that event, a place where I was unlikely to encounter camels, and I remained there two years.

I am still *pulling faces for dates,* much in the manner in which I did in those memorable days when I escaped in the Red Desert of Libya. Thirty years at sea in the Navy, although it may collect some strips of medal ribbon, does not bring with it much financial affluence, and a retired naval man must needs cultivate all the *tricks* of which he .is capable.

If I have *pulled faces* successfully for you, reader, if I have made you see a little of the eternal desert, feel a little of the pains, the hopes, the anxieties and the joys which we felt, then I have done well. This book has been for me a labour of love; it has taken me nearly seven weeks of continuous writing to compile, and the going over of the notes and Press cuttings collected during the last three years, as well as the interviewing of many an actor who witnessed the events herein set forth.

If I have your approval, then I am content; my time has not been wasted. And if I have, beyond this, taken you out of yourself, and made you think of life without veneer, of the real rock-bottom facts which govern all, then I have more than succeeded; for I shall have achieved.

LEONAUR

# ALSO FROM LEONAUR
## AVAILABLE IN SOFTCOVER OR HARDCOVER WITH DUST JACKET

**DOING OUR 'BIT'** by *Ian Hay*—Two Classic Accounts of the Men of Kitchener's 'New Army' During the Great War including *The First 100,000 & All In It.*

**AN EYE IN THE STORM** by *Arthur Ruhl*—An American War Correspondent's Experiences of the First World War from the Western Front to Gallipoli and Beyond.

**STAND & FALL** by *Joe Cassells*—A Soldier's Recollections of the 'Contemptible Little Army' and the Retreat from Mons to the Marne, 1914.

**RIFLEMAN MACGILL'S WAR** by *Patrick MacGill*—A Soldier of the London Irish During the Great War in Europe including *The Amateur Army, The Red Horizon & The Great Push.*

**WITH THE GUNS** by *C. A. Rose & Hugh Dalton*—Two First Hand Accounts of British Gunners at War in Europe During World War 1- Three Years in France with the Guns and With the British Guns in Italy.

**EAGLES OVER THE TRENCHES** by *James R. McConnell & William B. Perry*—Two First Hand Accounts of the American Escadrille at War in the Air During World War 1-Flying For France: With the American Escadrille at Verdun and Our Pilots in the Air.

**THE BUSH WAR DOCTOR** by *Robert V. Dolbey*—The Experiences of a British Army Doctor During the East African Campaign of the First World War.

**THE 9TH—THE KING'S (LIVERPOOL REGIMENT) IN THE GREAT WAR 1914 - 1918** by *Enos H. G. Roberts*—Like many large cities, Liverpool raised a number of battalions in the Great War. Notable among them were the Pals, the Liverpool Irish and Scottish, but this book concerns the wartime history of the 9th Battalion – The Kings.

**THE GAMBARDIER** by *Mark Severn*—The experiences of a battery of Heavy artillery on the Western Front during the First World War.

**FROM MESSINES TO THIRD YPRES** by *Thomas Floyd*—A personal account of the First World War on the Western front by a 2/5th Lancashire Fusilier.

**THE IRISH GUARDS IN THE GREAT WAR - VOLUME 1** by *Rudyard Kipling*—Edited and Compiled from Their Diaries and Papers Volume 1 The First Battalion.

**THE IRISH GUARDS IN THE GREAT WAR - VOLUME 2** by *Rudyard Kipling*—Edited and Compiled from Their Diaries and Papers Volume 2 The Second Battalion.

**LEONAUR**

# ALSO FROM LEONAUR
### AVAILABLE IN SOFTCOVER OR HARDCOVER WITH DUST JACKET

**ARMOURED CARS IN EDEN** *by K. Roosevelt*—An American President's son serving in Rolls Royce armoured cars with the British in Mesopotamia & with the American Artillery in France during the First World War.

**CHASSEUR OF 1914** *by Marcel Dupont*—Experiences of the twilight of the French Light Cavalry by a young officer during the early battles of the great war in Europe.

**TROOP HORSE & TRENCH** *by R.A. Lloyd*—The experiences of a British Life-guardsman of the household cavalry fighting on the western front during the First World War 1914-18.

**THE LONG PATROL** *by George Berrie*—A Novel of Light Horsemen from Gallipoli to the Palestine campaign of the First World War.

**THE EAST AFRICAN MOUNTED RIFLES** *by C.J. Wilson*—Experiences of the campaign in the East African bush during the First World War

**THE FIGHTING CAMELIERS** *by Frank Reid*—The exploits of the Imperial Camel Corps in the desert and Palestine campaigns of the First World War.

**WITH THE IMPERIAL CAMEL CORPS IN THE GREAT WAR** *by Geoffrey Inchbald*—The story of a serving officer with the British 2nd battalion against the Senussi and during the Palestine campaign.

**STEEL CHARIOTS IN THE DESERT** *by S.C.Rolls*—The first world war experiences of a Rolls Royce armoured car driver with the Duke of Westminster in Libya and in Arabia with T.E. Lawrence.

**INFANTRY BRIGADE: 1914** *by Edward Gleichen*—The Diary of a Commander of the 15th Infantry Brigade, 5th Division, British Army, During the Retreat from Mons

**HEARTS & DRAGONS** *by Charles R. M. F. Crutwell*—The first world war experiences of a Rolls Royce armoured car driver with the DuThe 4th Royal Berkshire Regiment in France and Italy During the Great War, 1914-1918.

**TIGERS ALONG THE TIGRIS** *by E. J. Thompson*—The Leicestershire Regiment in Mesopotamia During the First World War.

**DESPATCH RIDER** *by W. H. L. Watson*—The Experiences of a British Army Motorcycle Despatch Rider During the Opening Battles of the Great War in Europe.

Lightning Source UK Ltd.
Milton Keynes UK
UKOW052223240613

212752UK00001B/137/P